A
GATHERING
OF BIRDS

DONALD CULROSS PEATTIE LIBRARY
PUBLISHED BY TRINITY UNIVERSITY PRESS

An Almanac for Moderns

A Book of Hours

Cargoes and Harvests

Diversions of the Field

Flowering Earth

A Gathering of Birds:
An Anthology of the Best Ornithological Prose

Green Laurels:
The Lives and Achievements of the Great Naturalists

A Natural History of North American Trees

The Road of a Naturalist

A GATHERING OF BIRDS

AN ANTHOLOGY OF THE BEST
ORNITHOLOGICAL PROSE

Edited, with Biographical Sketches, by
DONALD CULROSS PEATTIE

Illustrated by
EDWARD SHENTON

TRINITY UNIVERSITY PRESS
San Antonio, Texas

Published by Trinity University Press
San Antonio, Texas 78212

Copyright © 2013 by the Estate of Donald Culross Peattie

ISBN 978-1-59534-162-4 (paper)
ISBN 978-1-59534-163-1 (ebook)

Cover design by BookMatters, Berkeley
Cover illustration: barsik/istockphoto.com

All rights reserved. No part of this book may be reproduced in any form or by any electronic or mechanical means, including information storage and retrieval systems, without permission in writing from the publisher.

Trinity University Press strives to produce its books using methods and materials in an environmentally sensitive manner. We favor working with manufacturers that practice sustainable management of all natural resources, produce paper using recycled stock, and manage forests with the best possible practices for people, biodiversity, and sustainability. The press is a member of the Green Press Initiative, a nonprofit program dedicated to supporting publishers in their efforts to reduce their impacts on endangered forests, climate change, and forest-dependent communities.

The paper used in this publication meets the minimum requirements of the American National Standard for Information Sciences—Permanence of Paper for Printed Library Materials, ANSI 39.48-1992.

CIP data on file at the Library of Congress.

17   16   15   14   13 | 5   4   3   2   1

ACKNOWLEDGMENTS

THE editor wishes gratefully to acknowledge the assistance of Dr. Barbour of the Harvard Museum of Comparative Zoölogy who has read the entire manuscript in order to assist the work of editing material so highly miscellaneous, of such different eras in the science of ornithology, and such varying styles. At the same time the editor assumes entire liability for all errors or inadequacies which may remain.

Grateful acknowledgment for permission to reprint these selections is made to the following publishers:

D. Appleton-Century Company: *From* "Camps and Cruises of an Ornithologist," by Frank M. Chapman; *from* "The Mountains of California," by John Muir. By permission of D. Appleton-Century Company, publishers.

Curtis Brown Ltd.: *From* "The Island of Penguins," by Cherry Kearton.

Thomas Y. Crowell Company: *From* "Nature Near London" and "The Life of the Fields," by Richard Jefferies. By permission of the publishers.

E. P. Dutton Co., Inc.: *From* "A Hind in Richmond Park," by W. H. Hudson. By permission of the publishers.

Harper & Brothers: *From* "Canary," by Gustav Eckstein. By permission of the publishers.

Henry Holt and Company: *From* "Jungle Peace," by William Beebe. By permission of the publishers.

Houghton Mifflin Company: *From the Journals of Henry David Thoreau:* "Notes on New England Birds" and "Fresh Fields," published by Houghton Mifflin Company.

Alfred A. Knopf, Inc.: *From* "Birds and Man," by W. H.

Hudson. By permission of and special arrangement with Alfred A. Knopf, Inc., authorized publishers.

G. P. Putnam's Sons: *From* "Bird Islands of Peru," by Robert C. Murphy. By permission of the publishers.

A. P. Watt & Son: *From* "The Charm of Birds," by Viscount Edward Grey. By permission of the publishers and special arrangement with Sir Cecil Graves, Executor of the Estate of Viscount Grey.

TABLE OF CONTENTS

XIV

XV

XVI

XVII

XVIII

XIX

FOREWORD

CHIS anthology is offered only as a brief and selective collection gleaned from the works of those who have written admirably on birds. It is designed for the pleasure of people who enjoy birds, but it does not pretend to serve the professional ornithologist with facts he would not know. In the intention of this anthologist, these pieces, the most finished that he has found in the literature of ornithophily, were collected and set forth as if they were numbers upon a programme representing various composers of divers times and styles and some contrast of mood. So, for variety, are included the light or brief as well as the longer and more studied.

Biographical material which I have added is not, of course, biography at all in the serious sense. It is, rather, in the nature of programme notes.

The difficulty of selection has not been to find grist to my mill, but rather to omit. Instead of including short excerpts from a multitude of writers, as one might have done in preparing an anthology of poetry, I felt it more just to the prose writer to give each one enough space to get into his stride both in style and subject. This limited the number of my entries. So that if the reader should miss a favorite, he must remember that one book cannot contain everything of merit. Moreover, selection was made according to a dual standard, as science and as literature. It is surprising how some otherwise meritorious work is excluded by these two principles. A well-loved popularizer of the past generation proved, upon a re-reading of every word he ever wrote on birds, to have really very little to contribute about them. Again, some noted scientists do not appear here because a sympathetic and interested examination of their work discovered nothing of any length which they themselves, I believe, would have cared to lay down for comparison beside the accomplished style of Hudson or the rugged narratives of Coues. Admittedly the literary gifts of the authors here gathered are unequal, as are their scientific attainments. But every one of them is in some sense an ornithologist and every one is a good writer. Not a few are two-fold geniuses.

In the capacity of editor I have not disturbed the mannerisms of these diverse writers to attain consistency of punctuation, spelling, and capitalization. They wrote as they wrote, and I would not venture to begin changing them even to correct their grammar or to alter their scientific nomenclature with the current usage of taxonomy.

I have, however, been obliged by space limitations to condense their essays. In doing this I have seldom abbreviated by cutting out individual words or phrases. Rather, I have omitted entire passages that were digressive or technical.

The plan of the book has been to divide it somewhat equally between European birds, North American birds, and tropical or otherwise exotic species.

The order of arrangement is not chronological or geographical but, rather, stylistic, that the book may be read with a sense of modulated variety in the suite. In this I am aware that it would not be possible to satisfy all tastes.

D. C. P.

W. H. HUDSON

I

W. H. HUDSON

*I*N THE eighties of the last century a small discriminating group was discussing a novel, *The Purple Land*, of remarkable originality and charm. Its setting—Uruguay—was a fresh one for a novel in English, and the author even less well known, a tall, bent, wounded sort of a man, like a chained and gloomy heron, endlessly writing and puffing cigars at the back of his wife's London boarding-house.

Of this man, William Henry Hudson, British ornithologists were still largely unaware until in 1888-9 he produced his *Argentine Ornithology*. The systematics and anatomy were contributed by the well-known museum scientist, Prof. Sclater (with whom Hudson got on rather badly). But the remarkable field notes and life histories were the work of this same indigent and obscure novelist. Again, the subject and setting were unfamiliar to most readers, refreshing, and exciting—the avifauna of the south temperate zone in the western hemisphere. Here, it seemed, was indeed a New World, one about which most British and North American naturalists knew little and thought seldom.

When in 1892 Hudson published his *Naturalist in La Plata*, a remarkable piece of popularization, his fame spread beyond the technical ornithologists to Nature lovers generally. A new voice was heard, as startling as the call of some unknown bird. Other reminiscences of Argentina followed, and then lovely studies of the modest and endearing bird life of English countryside and village. And finally in 1904 Hudson returned, after lamentable failures in this line, to the novel form with *Green Mansions*, a book that slowly but surely made him

3

famous and is today still widening in popularity. Of what
other novels of that decade can as much be said?

Possessed of unique powers as a narrator and stylist, Hudson came to Nature with a magnificent equipment to write
of it. In the rôle of poet of Nature he has no rival save
Thoreau, and Hudson was distinctly the better naturalist,
though not so great and original a soul.

Hudson's life story has many obscurities and lacunæ. He
deplored any biography, enjoined against one in his will, and
carefully destroyed all documentary evidence he could find,
insisting that his books speak for him. His personality too was
an enigma. His brother said of him, "Of all the people I
know, you are the only one I do not know." This was precisely to Hudson's taste. He so far created a mystery or even
a deliberate legend about himself as to misrepresent his age
and his nationality.

William Henry Hudson was born an American. His mother
came from Maine, his father Daniel from Marblehead. Daniel
Hudson emigrated to Argentina to become a ranchero in the
state of Rio de Plata, and there, at Quilmes, in 1841, was
born the future naturalist.

On his father's hospitable and prodigal estancia, then on
the very frontier of the untamed pampas, young Hudson
grew up in a large and closely united family. What his life
was, among the gauchos and the steers, the pioneering Spanish and English settlers, is known now to everyone from that
fascinating book, *Far Away and Long Ago,* as well as in his
History of My Early Life and *A Little Boy Lost.* Of his romantic childhood Hudson continued to write all his life;
those are the only years of which he cared to speak. Even
so, he tells less about himself than about others and about
the birds of Argentina, the crested screamers and woodhew-
ers, mockingbirds, hummingbirds, rheas and Magellanic eagle
owls, and above all his favorite plovers. They filled the world

for him, the heavens and the plain and the marsh and the shore, with their cries and the beat of their wings. They were for him the birds of home, and thirty years later he could still remember the forms and the flight and the songs and calls of some two hundred and fifty New World species—a larger number than was to be found in all Britain.

Rheumatic fever fell early upon the boy, injuring his heart. A doctor informed his father that as the lad would only live a few years he might as well be allowed to do what he pleased. So Hudson never completed his education or sought a training in ornithology, but divided his time between devouring English literature and descriptions of rural life in Britain, and spurring across the Patagonian plains in pursuit of birds. He lived among the gauchos and as one of them. But he was a queer gaucho who was forever losing his rope or his knife or his horse; a gaucho who did not fight or wench; a gaucho with literary leanings and an obsessing desire for the England of Gilbert White and of Bloomfield the plowman poet, of Gray's *Elegy* and Gay's madrigals.

Before Hudson left for England in 1869 he had seen sweeping changes cross the pampas. Just as in North America the prairie wilderness long held back human invasion, and then suddenly gave way before the plow and the gun, the railroad and the barbed wire fence, so under Hudson's eyes began the pampas' end. The great prodigal estancias gave place to small landholdings, and the "bird hating Italian race" began to swarm and spawn there, supplanting the earlier settlers with a lower standard of living and another attitude toward the virginity of the continent.

Daniel Hudson's fortunes had dwindled before he died suddenly. Young Hudson seems to have taken his father's death as an irreparable calamity to his whole life. He left abruptly for England, never again to sit a horse, to know space, adventure, freedom from care. Yet, his life long, Argentina re-

membered, Argentina as it had been and could be again only
in his memories, infused his greatest books with nostalgia.

When he landed in England at Southampton, Hudson did
not proceed at once to London but set forth determined to
find the England of Jefferies and Constable. He took a carriage and, with a young lout of a coachman, drove out in the
country. The month was May and the glad bird chorus at
its height, but to Hudson every British songster was as unfamiliar and as much a foreign bird as to most Englishmen
are mynas and bulbuls. So he continually cried, "What bird
was that?" and, "I say, what song was that?" To all of this
he received but oafish answers.

It is a tribute to the power of poetry that the birds of
Europe have exercised such a sway over the minds of Americans and English colonials. The avifauna of Britain is really
small, both in variety of species and in respect to birds of
impressive dimensions. It is in many ways modest, too, in
plumage and utterance. Yet by the virtues of association,
English bird life exerts a powerful pull even upon ornithologists of other lands justly proud of their avifauna. John Burroughs, for instance, and Dr. Frank Chapman, have both
recorded their eagerness to hear and see English birds, and
journeyed across the seas for the sake of nightingales and
cuckoos, robins and skylarks. The sweet and domestic charm
of the European birds is something to which I can myself
attest, and to the praise that better ornithologists have uttered of the robin I would add my own, just as I share their
disappointment in the skylark.

The new-come Hudson viewed nothing in British bird life
with detachment. This was his adopted land, and he prepared
to love every note and pinion. So he brought to his writings
on European birds what no European can bring—a trained
and adult capacity to understand and describe bird actions,
coupled with an ear and eye fresh as that of a child. The

result of Hudson's unique approach was that, with his literary gift, he became the Englishman's favorite ornithological writer, and justly so.

It would be wrong to gather from these words that Hudson's life as a naturalist was one of carefree happiness in communing with the small and tender aspects of English Nature. Or that his career was a progress of triumphs, a ready acceptance and a swiftly widening circle of fame. On the contrary, his life, which began well and ended well, was in its core years one of obscurity, hunger for a fame which would not come, of disillusion and disappointment and a withering at the well-springs of many instincts whose gratification is essential to the whole soul. This period ate out the heart of his life from the age of twenty-eight until well into the fifties.

Hudson found no regular employment in England; he held some desultory positions with small pay. In consequence he suffered a poverty which so humiliated him that he could not speak of those times and obliterated the evidence of them. He had perhaps expected some literary employment and probably sought it in vain. His essays and stories were rejected for years, and many of his novels were failures both in popularity and in artistic construction. Doubtless he hoped, too, for acceptance among the ornithologists, and this did indeed come, but not before Hudson had awaited it so long that his anticipation had soured. Consequently he was inclined to quarrel with ornithologists like John Gould and Alfred Newton, and to dispute that they knew birds at all in the sense that he knew them. His taste was rather for bird lovers of the stamp of Grey of Fallodon, his friend.

In the meantime Hudson was still, apparently, in search of a somewhat anachronistic England. He can write pages lamenting that young country women no longer curtsey when they meet you. He longed for an English Nature that began to vanish when William Rufus rounded up the deer of the

New Forest. He can look backward as longingly as Jefferies, hate a steel bridge and admire a stone one as ardently as Ruskin. He loved a thatch, and what he knew was the chimney pots of London; he wanted lakes with wild swans, and could but feed bread to tame ones in the London parks. He had longed all his youth to breathe the air of Merrie England, and as he says, he had no sooner landed than he could *smell* it. That smell he later identified as the smell of the pub.

In this period of unhappiness he met and married Emily Wingrave, a woman with glorious hair, a warm heart, drab origins and a simple intelligence. By the time Hudson became famous she was a fat, sad, uninteresting woman so colorless that she seemed not to be in the room. Few could understand why such a great man had ever picked so null a wife. But it is doubtful if, in his eccentricity and poverty, he had a wide choice. And from her years of patient devotion to him, and of sufferance of his affectionate contempt, one might conclude that Emily married Hudson to take care of him, and kept a Bayswater boarding-house to support him. She did not understand his birds or his writings, his discontents or his genius. But she probably kept him alive in this world from which he would otherwise have departed earlier and with his great work undone.

The Hudsons had no children, and if they were ever lovers in the common experience of man and woman, that love was brief. So children haunt Hudson's writings, even his ornithological descriptions, especially little girls whom he loved with the worship and hunger of a man who has none of his own to love as they really are. Contrasted with his chilly and often crotchety relations with women, are the pictures of women in his stories. The immortal Rima of *Green Mansions*, clad in iridescent cobweb floss or hummingbird plumage, who takes flight in the forest and dies unpossessed, is of course no flesh and blood girl at all but a sort of bird-woman, an evanishing adolescent such as a boy pursues in his dreams but scarcely expects to see when awake. In consequence, *Green Mansions* is the favorite novel of men who rarely read novels. This idyll is less popular with women and realists, which is not to deny its hypnotic charm.

There is no need to speak much of Hudson's crowning years of triumph, still fresh in literary history, when fame and money came to him, and he had to flee from the attentions he had once hungered for pathetically. He died in 1922, at the age of eighty-one, and was buried near Richard Jefferies. Even before his death he had become a sort of saint among many bird lovers, and his name, like Audubon's and Francis of Assisi's, has been made to stand for the worship and protection of birds. A bird sanctuary in his name was established in Richmond Park, and a monument was there raised to him with funds given by his admirers, and executed, to the rage and grief of many of them, by Epstein.

From Hudson's writings I have chosen one Argentinian selection and one English, to represent the two disparate phases of his life. The selection on the daws has been compounded from two chapters in *Birds and Man* (1901) and was chosen because the jackdaw seems to me a bird peculiarly European, with its adaptation to the conditions of a dense civilization, and its traits, almost civilized, of audacity and intelligence. One may wish, after Hudson's account of the preference of daws for cathedral façades, to go back and read "The Jackdaw of Rheims" in Barham's *The Ingoldsby Legends*, and learn how a daw stole the bishop's ring.

The selection of the golden plover and other migratory birds of the pampas comes from the posthumous *A Hind in Richmond Park* (1922) and represents Hudson's most mature and beautiful style. To Americans this passage on the plovers is peculiarly moving, for Hudson's pampas birds are also North American birds. Only, in North America, they

pass the breeding season; Hudson knew them in that other
phase of their lives when they have departed from us and
gone to another temperate zone, an antipodean sort of prairie,
that most of us are as little likely ever to behold as the other
side of the moon.

MIGRATION ON THE PAMPAS

*I*T WOULD not be possible for me to convey to readers whose mental image of the visible world and its feathered inhabitants was formed here in England the impression made on my mind, in my early years in the land of my birth, of the spectacle of bird migration as witnessed by me. They have not seen it, nor anything resembling it, therefore cannot properly imagine or visualise it, however well described. I can almost say that when I first opened my eyes it was to the light of heaven and to the phenomenon of bird migration—the sight of it and the sound of it. For migration was then and there on a great, a tremendous scale, and forced itself on the attention of everyone. Nevertheless, it is necessary for me to say something about it before entering into a relation of certain facts concerning migration which other writers on the subject have failed to observe or else ignored.

Birds, it is granted, migrate north and south, but here in this northern island, cut off from Europe by a comparatively narrow sea, and again by a wider sea from the African continent, the winter home of the majority of our migratory species, it is plain that they could never get to their destination—from England to South Africa, let us say—without deviating a good deal from the north and south direction. America, North, South and Central, is land pretty well all the way north and south from pole to pole, seeing that the only break is a few hundred miles of deep sea between the Magellanic region and the Antarctic continent.

Migration as I witnessed it was not composed exclusively of South American species: many of the birds were from the northern hemisphere. The rock swallow (*Petrochelidon pyr-*

rhonota), for example, that breeds in Arizona and New Mexico, and migrates to southern Patagonia; also the numerous shore birds that breed as far north as the Arctic regions, then migrate south to the Argentine and to the extreme end of Patagonia—or as near as they can get to the Antarctic. The spectacle of the migration of these birds that come to us from another hemisphere—from another world, as it seemed, so many thousand of miles away—was as a rule the most arresting, owing to their extraordinary numbers and to their loquacity, their powerful, penetrative and musical voices—whimbrel, godwit, plover and sandpiper of many species.

My home was an inland one, a good many miles from the sea-like Plata river, the vast grassy level country of the pampas, the green floor of the world, as I have elsewhere called it. There were no mountains, forests or barren places in that region; it was all grass and herbage, the cardoon and giant thistles predominating; also there were marshes everywhere, with shallow water and endless beds of reeds, sedges and bulrushes—a paradise of all aquatic fowl. Thus, besides the numerous shore birds, the herons of seven species, the crested screamer, the courlan, the rails and coots and grebes, the jacana, the two giant ibises—the stork and wood ibis—and the glossy ibis in enormous flocks, we had two swans, upland geese in winter, and over twenty species of duck. Most of these birds were migratory.

South America can well be called the great bird continent, and I do not believe that any other large area on it so abounded with bird life as this very one where I was born and reared and saw, and heard, so much of birds from my childhood that they became to me the most interesting things in the world. Thus, the number of species known to me personally, even as a youth, exceeded that of all the species in the British Islands, including the sea or pelagic species that visit our coasts in summer, to breed and spend the rest of the year on the Mediterranean and Atlantic oceans.

It was not only the number of species known to me, but rather the incalculable, the incredible numbers in which some of the commonest kinds appeared, especially when migrating. For it was not then as, alas! it is now, when all that immense open and practically wild country has been enclosed in wire fences and is now peopled with immigrants from Europe, chiefly of the bird-destroying Italian race. In my time the inhabitants were mostly the natives, the gauchos, descendants of the early Spanish colonists, and they killed no birds excepting the rhea, which was hunted on horseback with the bolas; and the partridge, or tinamu, which was snared by the boys. There was practically no shooting.

The golden plover was then one of the abundant species. After its arrival in September, the plains in the neighbourhood of my home were peopled with immense flocks of this bird. Sometimes in hot summers the streams and marshes would mostly dry up, and the aquatic bird population, the plover included, would shift their quarters to other districts. During one of these droughty seasons, when my age was nine, there was a marshy ground two miles from my home where a few small pools of water still remained, and to this spot the golden plover would resort every day at noon. They would appear in flocks from all quarters, flying to it like starlings in England coming in to some great roosting centre on a winter evening. I would then mount my pony and gallop off joyfully to witness the spectacle. Long before coming in sight of them the noise of their voices would be audible, growing louder as I drew near. Coming to the ground, I would pull up my horse and sit gazing with astonishment and delight at the spectacle of that immense multitude of birds, covering an area of two or three acres, looking less like a vast flock than a floor of birds, in colour a rich deep brown, in strong contrast to the pale grey of the dried up ground all

round them. A living, moving floor and a sounding one as
well, and the sound too was amazing. It was like the sea, but
unlike it in character since it was not deep; it was more like
the wind blowing, let us say, on thousands of tight-drawn
wires of varying thicknesses, vibrating them to shrill sound,
a mass and tangle of ten thousand sounds. But it is indescribable and unimaginable.

Then I would put the birds up to enjoy the different sound
of their rushing wings mingled with that of their cries, also
the sight of them like a great cloud in the sky above me,
casting a deep shadow on the earth.

The golden plover was but one of many equally if not more
abundant species in its own as well as other orders, although
they did not congregate in such astonishing numbers. On
their arrival on the pampas they were invariably accompanied
by two other species, the Eskimo curlew and the buff-breasted
sandpiper. These all fed in company on the moist lands, but
by-and-by the curlews passed on to more southern districts,
leaving their companions behind, and the buff-breasted sandpipers were then seen to be much less numerous than the
plover, about one bird to ten.

Now one autumn, when most of the emigrants to the
Arctic breeding-grounds had already gone, I witnessed a great
migration of this very species—this beautiful sandpiper with
the habits of a plover. The birds appeared in flocks of about
one to two or three hundred, flying low and very swiftly due
north, flock succeeding flock at intervals of about ten or
twelve minutes; and this migration continued for three days,
or, at all events, three days from the first day I saw them,
at a spot about two miles from my home. I was amazed at
their numbers, and it was a puzzle to me then, and has been
one ever since, that a species thinly distributed over the immense area of the Argentine pampas and Patagonia could
keep to that one line of travel over that uniform green, sea-

like country. For, outside of that line, not one bird of the kind could anywhere be seen; yet they kept so strictly to it that I sat each day for hours on my horse watching them pass, each flock first appearing as a faint buff-coloured blur or cloud just above the southern horizon, rapidly approaching then passing me, about on a level with my horse's head, to fade out of sight in a couple of minutes in the north; soon to be succeeded by another and yet other flocks in endless succession, each appearing at the same point as the one before, following the same line, as if a line invisible to all eyes except their own had been traced across the green world for their guidance. It gave one the idea that all the birds of this species, thinly distributed over tens of thousands of square miles of country, had formed the habit of assembling, previous to migration, at one starting-point, from which they set out in successive flocks of a medium size, in a disciplined order, on that marvellous journey to their Arctic breeding-grounds.

Among the other species that swarmed in all the marshy places the glossy ibis was the most abundant, so that the whole air seemed laden with the strong musky smell of their plumage. In the autumn I have often watched their migration, usually in flocks of fifty to a hundred birds; and these would continue passing for hours, flying at a height of twenty or thirty feet, and invariably, on coming to water, dropping down and sweeping low over the surface as if wanting to alight and refresh themselves, but unable to overcome the impulse urging them to the north, they would rise again and travel on.

Then there were the species that had only a partial migration; birds that were residents all the year with us, but were migrants from the colder country to the south. One was our common dove (Zenaida), seen passing in flocks of many thousands; and, among the small birds, the common para-

sitical cow-bird. The entire plumage of this species is a deep
glossy purple which looks black at a little distance, and in
late autumn, when great flocks visited our plantation, the
large bare trees would sometimes look as if they had suddenly
put on an inky-black foliage. This bird too, when migrating
from the southern pampas and Patagonia, would appear and
pass in an endless series of flocks, travelling low and filling
the air with the musical murmur of their wings and the
musky smell which they too, like the ibis, give out from their
plumage.

But of the smaller birds with a limited or partial migration,
the military starling on his travels impressed and delighted
me the most. Like a starling in shape, but larger than that
bird, it has a dark plumage and scarlet breast. On the approach of winter it would appear all over the plains, not travelling in the manner of other migrants, speeding through the
air, but feeding on the ground, probing the turf as starlings
do, the whole flock drifting northwards at the same time.
The flock, often numbering many hundreds of birds, would
spread itself out, showing a long front line of scarlet breasts
all turned one way, while the birds furthest in the rear would
be continually flying on to drop down in advance of those
at the front, so that every two or three minutes a new front
line would be formed, and in this way the entire body, or
army, would be slowly but continuously progressing.

How pleasant it was in those vanished years of an abundant
bird life, when riding over the plain in winter, to encounter
those loose, far-spread flocks with their long lines of red
breasts showing so beautifully on the green sward! My memories of this bird alone would fill a chapter.

The autumnal migration, which was always a more impressive spectacle than that of the spring, began in February
when the weather was still hot, and continued for three long
months; for after the departure of all our own birds, the

south Patagonian species that wintered with us or passed on
their way to districts further north would begin to come in.
During all these three long months the sight and sound of
passage birds was a thing of every day, of every hour, so long
as the light lasted, and after dark from time to time the cries
of the night-travellers came to us from the sky—the weird
laughter-like cry of rails, the shrill confused whistling of a
great flock of whistling or tree duck; and, most frequent of
all, the beautiful wild trisyllabic alarm cry of the upland
plover.

Of this bird, the last on my list for this chapter, I must
write at greater length; in the first place, for the purely sentimental reason that it was the one I loved best, and secondly,
on account of the leading place it came to occupy in my
mind when I thought about the problem of migration. It
inhabits, or formerly inhabited, a great portion of the United
States of North America, its summer or breeding home, then
migrated south all the way to southern Argentina and Patagonia, and it was, I believe, most abundant on the great level
pampas where I had my home. In North America it is known
as the upland plover, and is also called the solitary plover
and Bartram's sandpiper—for a sandpiper it is, albeit with
the habits of a plover and a preference for dry lands. In the
Argentine its vernacular name is Batitu, from its trisyllabic
alarm note—one of the most frequently heard sounds on the
pampas. It is a charming bird, white and grey with brown
and yellow mottlings on its upper plumage, beautiful in its
slender graceful form, with a long tail and long swallow-like
pointed wings. All its motions are exceedingly graceful: it
runs rapidly as a corncrake before the rider's horse, then
springs up with its wild musical cry to fly but twenty or
thirty yards away and drop down again, to stand in a startled
attitude flirting its long tail up and down. At times it flies
up voluntarily, uttering a prolonged bubbling and inflected

cry, and alights on a post or some such elevated place to open and hold its wings up vertically and continue for some time in that attitude—the artist's conventional figure of an angel.

These birds never flocked with us, even before departing; they were solitary, sprinkled evenly over the entire country, so that when out for a day on horseback I would flush one from the grass every few minutes; and when travelling or driving cattle on the pampas I have spent whole weeks on horseback from dawn to dark without being for a day out of sight or sound of the bird. When migrating its cry was heard at all hours from morning to night, from February till April: and again at night, especially when there was a moon.

Lying awake in bed, I would listen by the hour to that sound coming to me from the sky, mellowed and made beautiful by distance and the profound silence of the moonlit world, until it acquired a fascination for me above all sounds on earth, so that it lived ever after in me; and the image of it is as vivid in my mind at this moment as that of any bird call or cry, or any other striking sound heard yesterday or but an hour ago. It was the sense of mystery it conveyed which so attracted and impressed me—the mystery of that delicate, frail, beautiful being, travelling in the sky, alone, day and night, crying aloud at intervals as if moved by some powerful emotion, beating the air with its wings, its beak pointing like the needle of the compass to the north, flying, speeding on its seven-thousand-mile flight to its nesting home in another hemisphere.

This sound lives in memory still, but is heard no more, or will shortly be heard no more, on earth, since this bird too is now on the list of the "next candidates for extinction." It seems incredible that in this short space of time, comprised in the years of one man's life, such a thing can be. But here on my writing-table is the book of the first authority in America on this subject: William T. Hornaday, in *Our Van-*

ishing Wild Life, gives a list of the eleven species which have become wholly extinct in North America since the middle of the last century, most of them in very recent years; also a partial or preliminary list of the species, numbering twenty-one, now on the verge of extinction. The first list includes that beautiful bird, the Eskimo curlew—the fellow-traveller and companion of the golden plover referred to in this chapter. The list of those now verging on extinction includes the golden plover, upland plover, buff-breasted and pectoral sandpiper. This last species is not mentioned above, but it was perhaps the commonest of all the small sandpipers in my time, and from August to March any year was to be met with by any stream or pool of water all over the pampas.

All this incalculable destruction of bird life has come about since the seventies of the last century, and is going on now despite the efforts of those who are striving, by promoting legislation and by all other possible means, to save "the remnant." But, alas! the forces of brutality, the Caliban in man, are proving too powerful; the lost species are lost for all time, and a thousand years of the strictest protection—a protection it would be impossible to impose on a free people, Calibans or not—would not restore the still existing bird life to the abundance of half a century ago.

The beautiful has vanished and returns not.

JACKDAWS

*D*AWS are more abundant in the west and southwest of England generally than in any other part of the kingdom. No county in England is richer in noble churches, and no kind of building seems more attractive to the "ecclesiastical daw" than the great Perpendicular tower of the Glastonbury type, which is so common here. Of the old towns which the bird loves and inhabits in numbers, Wells comes first.

The cathedral daws, on account of their numbers, are the most important of the feathered inhabitants of Wells. These city birds are familiarly called "Bishop's Jacks," to distinguish them from the "Ebor Jacks," the daws that in large numbers have their home and breeding-place in the neighbouring cliffs, called the Ebor Rocks.

The Ebor daws are but the first of a succession of colonies extending along the side of the Cheddar valley. A curious belief exists among the people of Wells and the district, that the Ebor Jacks make better pets than the Bishop's Jacks. If you want a young bird you have to pay more for one from the rocks than from the cathedral. I was assured that the cliff bird makes a livelier, more intelligent and amusing pet than the other. A similar notion exists, or existed, at Hastings, where there was a saying among the fisher folks and other natives that "a Grainger daa is worth a ha'penny more than a castle daa." The Grainger rock, once a favourite breeding-place of the daws at that point, has long since fallen into the sea, and the saying has perhaps died out.

At Wells most of the cathedral birds—a hundred couples at least—breed in the cavities behind the stone statues, standing, each in its niche, in rows, tier above tier, on the west front. In April, when the daws are busiest at their nest-building, I have amused myself early every morning watching them flying to the front in a constant procession, every bird bringing his stick. This work is all done in the early morning, and about half-past eight o'clock a man comes with a barrow to gather up the fallen sticks—there is always a big barrowful, heaped high, of them; and if not thus removed the accumulated material would in a few days form a rampart or zareba, which would prevent access to the cathedral on that side.

It has often been observed that the daw, albeit so clever a bird, shows a curious deficiency of judgment when building, in his persistent efforts to carry in sticks too big for the cavity. Here, for instance, each morning in turning over the litter of fallen material I picked up sticks measuring from four or five to seven feet in length. These very long sticks were so slender and dry that the bird was able to lift and to fly with them; therefore, to his corvine mind, they were suitable for his purpose. It comes to this: the daw knows a stick when he sees one, but the only way of testing its usefulness to him is to pick it up in his beak, then to try to fly with it. If the stick is six feet long and the cavity will only admit one of not more than eighteen inches, he discovers his mistake only on getting home. The question arises: Does he continue all his life long repeating this egregious blunder? One can hardly believe that an old, experienced bird can go on from day to day and year to year wasting his energies in gathering and carrying building materials that will have to be thrown away in the end—that he is, in fact, mentally on a level with the great mass of meaner beings who forget nothing and learn nothing. It is not to be doubted that the daw was once a builder in trees, like all his relations, with the exception of the cliff-breeding chough. He is even capable of reverting to the original habit, as I know from an instance which has quite recently come to my knowledge. In this case a small colony of daws have been noticed for several years past breeding in stick nests placed among the clustering foliage of a group of Scotch firs. This colony may have sprung from a bird hatched and reared in the nest of a carrion crow or magpie. Still, the habit of breeding in holes must be very ancient, and considering that the jackdaw is one of the most intelligent of our birds, one cannot but be astonished at the rude, primitive, blundering way in which the nest-building work is generally performed. The most we can see by carefully watching a number of birds at work is that there appears to be some difference with regard to intelligence between bird and bird. Some individuals blunder less than others; it is possible that these have learned something from experience; but if that be so, their better way is theirs only, and their young will not inherit it.

One morning at Wells as I stood on the cathedral green watching the birds at their work, I witnessed a rare and curious scene—one amazing to an ornithologist. A bird dropped a stick—an incident that occurred a dozen times or oftener any minute at that busy time; but in this instance the bird had no sooner let the stick fall than he rushed down after it to attempt its recovery, just as one may see a sparrow drop a feather or straw, and then dart down after it and often recover it before it touches the ground. The heavy stick fell straight and fast on to the pile of sticks already lying on the pavement, and instantly the daw was down and had it in his beak, and thereupon laboriously flew up to his nesting-place, which was forty or fifty feet high. At the moment that he rushed down after the falling stick two other daws that happened to be standing on ledges above dropped down after him, and copied his action by each picking up a stick and flying with it to their nests. Other daws followed suit, and in a few minutes there was a stream of descending and ascend-

ing daws at that spot, every ascending bird with a stick in
his beak. It was curious to see that although sticks were lying
in hundreds on the pavement along the entire breadth of the
west front, the daws continued coming down only at that
spot where the first bird had picked up the stick he had
dropped. By and by, to my regret, the birds suddenly took
alarm at something and rose up, and from that moment not
one descended.

Presently the man came round with his rake and broom
and barrow to tidy up the place. Before beginning his work
he solemnly made the following remark: "Is it not curious,
sir, considering the distance the birds go to get their sticks,
and the work of carrying them, that they never, by any
chance, think to come down and pick up what they have
dropped!" I replied that I had heard the same thing said
before, and that it was in all the books; and then I told him
of the scene I had just witnessed. He was very much surprised, and said that such a thing had never been witnessed
before at that place. It had a disturbing effect on him, and
he appeared to me to resent this departure from their old
ancient conservative ways on the part of the cathedral birds.

For many mornings after I continued to watch the daws
until the nest-building was finished, without witnessing any
fresh outbreak of intelligence in the colony: they had once
more shaken down into the old inconvenient traditional
groove, to the manifest relief of the man with the broom
and barrow.

Bath, like Wells, is a city that has a considerable amount
of nature in its composition, and is set down in a country
of hills, woods, rocks and streams, and is therefore, like the
other, a city loved by daws and by many other wild birds.

Daws are seen and heard all over the town, but are most
common about the Abbey, where they soar and gambol and
quarrel all day long, and when they think that nobody is

looking, drop down to the streets to snatch up and carry off any eatable-looking object that catches their eye.

Now the daw is capable at times of emitting both hoarse and harsh notes, and the same may perhaps be said of a majority of birds; but his usual note—the cry or caw varied and inflected a hundred ways, which we hear every day and all day long where daws abound—is neither harsh like the crow's, nor hoarse like the rook's. It is, in fact, as unlike the harsh, grating caw of the former species as the clarion call of the cock is unlike the grunting of swine. It may not be described as bell-like or metallic, but it is loud and clear, with an engaging wildness in it, and, like metallic sounds, far-reaching; and of so good a quality that very little more would make it ring musically.

Sometimes when I go into this ancient abbey church, or into some cathedral, and seating myself, and looking over a forest of bonnets, see a pale young curate with a black moustache, arrayed in white vestments, standing before the reading-desk, and hear him gabbling some part of the Service in a continuous buzz and rumble that roams like a gigantic blue-bottle through the vast dim interior, then I, not following him—for I do not know where he is, and cannot find out however much I should like to—am apt to remember the daws out of doors, and to think that it would be well if that young man would but climb up into the highest tower, or on to the roof, and dwell there for the space of a year listening to them; and that he would fill his mouth with polished pebbles, and medals, and coins and seals and seal-rings, and small porcelain cats and dogs, and little silver pigs, and other objects from the chatelaines of his lady admirers, and strive to imitate that clear, penetrating sound of the bird's voice, until he had mastered the rare and beautiful arts of voice production and distinct understandable speech.

Daws and starlings search the backs of cattle and sheep

for ticks and other parasites, and it is plain that their visits are welcome. Here a joint interest unites bird and beast; it is the nearest approach to symbiosis among the higher vertebrates of this country, but is far less advanced than the partnership which exists between the rhinoceros bird and the rhinoceros or buffalo, and between the spur-winged plover and crocodile in Africa.

One day I was walking by a meadow, adjoining the Bishop's palace at Wells, where several cows were grazing, and noticed a little beyond them a number of rooks and starlings scattered about. Presently a flock of about forty of the cathedral jackdaws flew over me and slanted down to join the other birds, when all at once two daws dropped out of the flock on to the back of the cow standing nearest to me. Immediately five more daws followed, and the crowd of seven birds began eagerly pecking at the animal's hide. But there was not room enough for them to move freely; they pushed and struggled for a footing, throwing their wings out to keep their balance, looking like a number of hungry vultures fighting for places on a carcass; and soon two of the seven were thrown off and flew away. The remaining five, although much straitened for room, continued for some time scrambling over the cow's back, busy with their beaks and apparently very much excited over the treasure they had discovered. It was amusing to see how the cow took their visit; sinking her body as if about to lie down and broadening her back, and dropping her head until her nose touched the ground, she stood perfectly motionless, her tail stuck out behind like a pump-handle. At length the daws finished their feeding and quarrelling and flew away; but for some minutes the cow remained immovable in the same attitude, as if the rare and delightful sensation of so many beaks prodding and so many sharp claws scratching her hide had not yet worn off.

Deer, too, like cows, are very grateful to the daw for its

services. In Savernake Forest I once witnessed a very pretty little scene. I noticed a hind lying down by herself in a grassy hollow, and as I passed her at a distance of about fifty yards it struck me as singular that she kept her head so low down that I could only see the top of it on a level with her back. Walking round to get a better sight, I saw a jackdaw standing on the turf before her, very busily pecking at her face. With my glass I was able to watch his movements very closely; he pecked round her eyes, then her nostrils, her throat, and in fact every part of her face; and just as a man when being shaved turns his face this way and that under the gentle guiding touch of the barber's fingers, and lifts up his chin to allow the razor to pass beneath it, so did the hind raise and lower and turn her face about to enable the bird to examine and reach every part with his bill. Finally the daw left the face, and, moving round, jumped on to the deer's shoulders and began a minute search in that part; having finished this he jumped on to the head and pecked at the forehead and round the bases of the ears. The pecking done, he remained for some seconds sitting perfectly still, looking very pretty with the graceful red head for a stand, the hind's long ears thrust out on either side of him. From his living perch he sprang into the air and flew away, going close to the surface; then slowly the deer raised her head and gazed after her black friend—gratefully, and regretting his departure, I could not but think.

John Muir

II

JOHN MUIR

SOME of the very earliest of John Muir's recollections were of birds. He remembers his rage and grief when as a very small child in Scotland he saw a soldier knock down a song bird's nest, and stuff the fledglings in his pocket, to sell them to a bird catcher. The lad would spend hours upon the moors watching and listening to the skylarks. The first call of the cuckoo in the spring, the first swallow that, for a child, makes summer, were indelible impressions of his boyhood. For he was born, in 1838, near Dunbar, on the Firth of Forth, and that is a country which belongs to the curlews, the murres and the gulls, and the gannets of the Bass Rock.

His schooling would today be considered criminal pedagogy. It consisted principally in memorizing Latin grammar and in weekly and daily encounters with the "tawse." At home his father, a Calvanistic fanatic, taught him, literally at the end of a strap, to repeat Bible verses, so that he could recite the New Testament from *Matthew* to *Revelation* without stopping.

But Muir thanks his lessons. He believed that his memory—an invaluable asset for a naturalist—was trained far beyond that of most men, and that by knowing with complete thoroughness a little literature but all of that great, the best was done toward the formation of his style.

When he was eleven years old his father removed to Wisconsin. He calls this a "sudden plash into pure wilderness." For the oak openings and prairies of Wisconsin in 1849 were still the America such as European boys delight to read of

29

in Fenimore Cooper. The red man's steps had not quite passed from the land; the sandhill cranes filled the heavens with their cries, the passenger pigeons darkened it in their passing, and from the wild prairie blooming with pasque flowers, beloved by the boy John, came the booming of the prairie chickens. He recalls his raptures over the beauty of redheaded woodpeckers, the ghostly sound of the whippoorwill in the lush twilights of earliest summer, the swirl of the nighthawks past his shoulder, the ringing jingling raptures of bobolinks and redwings and meadowlarks.

Life at home was, however, anything but idyllic. Tough prairie sod and tough hickory and burr oak woods had to be subdued, and his father's zeal was all for making a prim and thrifty farm like an Old World garden patch, out of a great tract of recalcitrant wilderness. The boy had to work at hard labor from before daylight till dark, even when sick with the measles. He was compelled to dig a deep well by hand, and to this exertion he attributed his lifelong shortness of stature; he dared not go to the spring for a drink for fear of being seen from the house, where his father was engaged in Bible study and picking out passages deriding the way of Martha.

From this atmosphere the boy broke away at the earliest possible moment, to attend the University of Wisconsin. Earning his own way, enduring great poverty while his father was sending ample sums for the distribution of the Bible to Igorots, young Muir early interested himself in geological studies and mechanics. A chance acquaintance showed him the family relationships of a locust blossom, and this seemed suddenly, as systematic botany has done for so many, to open a door into the antechamber of all Nature. He immediately rushed into the field and began collecting. His excursions took him farther and farther. Attendance at college was forgotten; he supported himself by teaching school, taking odd jobs in factories, and working as a harvest hand, and in this way he widened his scope until he was ready at last to set forth upon his walking trip from Kentucky to Florida. This famous excursion has been commemorated in A Thousand Mile Walk to the Gulf.

Without returning home, Muir set out for California. He arrived in San Francisco by boat in 1869 and at once inquired the quickest way of quitting the city. Tramping over the coastal ranges by the Pacheco Pass he beheld for the first time the Great Central Valley of California trooping with flowers and, etched far on the eastern horizon, the snowy summits of the Sierra. Thither he set out, always afoot (for it was his favorite mode of travel) and for the next decade he devoted himself almost entirely to Sierran Nature, studying flowers, trees, glaciers, streams, rocks, birds and mammals, sleeping in hollow Sequoia gigantea trees, sharing berries with bears, and brook water with ouzels. In this way, there is no doubt, he became conversant with mountain life and physiography, as few have ever done; there was not a canyon he did not explore, not an alpine meadow of whose flowers he did not gather; he visited every grove of the Big Trees, and discovered the presence, hitherto unknown, of "living" or moving glaciers in the Sierra. He was also the first to perceive that the strange and beautiful U-shape of the Yosemite valley was due to the carving by vanished and much greater glaciers of the ice age. This original contribution drew the admiration of Agassiz and Joseph Le Conte. The latter came to see for himself, and went away spreading the fame of a most original genius, part scientist, part poet, part man and part Nature itself in human form.

Muir, now the foremost guide of the Sierra, had the honor to show Emerson and Asa Gray and John Torrey, David Starr Jordan, Charles S. Sargent and Sir Joseph Dalton Hooker, Le Conte and Theodore Roosevelt, their first glimpses of that mountain life. It is said that when Roosevelt met Muir his first words were, "How can one tell the Hammond from the Wright flycatcher?" When asked what preparations he made for his trips, Muir said, "I put some bread and tea in an old sack and jump over the back fence."

Muir guided the first Coast and Geodetic Survey engineers to the top of Mt. Shasta. His explorations widened through the coast ranges and the "Redwood Empire," into Nevada and Utah, to Oregon and Puget Sound. He had begun to write; *Scribner's, Harper's, Century Magazine* and the *Atlantic* published his work which bubbled with fresh enthusiasm, the rapture of living, the very spirit of morning. In this period of his first flight upon literary wings he wrote the essay I have selected, on the water-ouzel. It appeared in *Scribner's* in 1878 under the title of "The Humming-bird of the California Waterfalls" and was reprinted as "The Water-Ouzel" in *The Mountains of California* (1894). More than anything else he ever wrote, this essay brought Muir fame. He was deluged with letters and praise, and was the literary lion of the Pacific States.

Just at this time Muir met and married Louie Wanda Strentzel, the daughter of an emigrated Polish patriot by a Tennessee woman. Muir rented his father-in-law's orchard near Martinez, on San Francisco Bay, and for ten years devoted himself to horticulture, for which he had a great talent, and to writing and family life. These did not prevent him from joining a cruise into the polar seas and Alaska, in the first year of his married life, nor from making other wide excursions. But it was on the whole a period of high literary production in which he drew upon his great fund of experience in the field.

Muir now took up his battle for the public ownership of the forests and beauty spots of the nation. He had seen the destruction of the timber around Shasta; he knew that both the coastal redwoods and the Sierra Big Trees were doomed to fall unless speedily saved, and that commercial exploitation was already threatening the glories of the West. With the aid of Robert Underwood Johnson, then a powerful editor, Muir began to agitate for the salvation of the forests. In this work there have been many courageous pioneers, but probably none who wielded such an immense popular sentiment. Even Congressmen read their Muir, and in the administration of President Cleveland, who paid Muir special tribute, the National Forests became a fact.

But more, the constant agitation of Muir to save Yosemite and other priceless playgrounds that were not primarily timberlands, and his friendship with Theodore Roosevelt, caused that President to enlarge the system of National Parks. So these too are monuments to the foresight of John Muir, to the power of his pen, and the infectious enthusiasm of his personality.

Muir's love of trees so struck Professor Sargent of the Arnold Arboretum that he took him on a tour of the world to see the greatest trees. They began with the Appalachian forests, travelled to Australia, Siberia, Russia, and other forested regions. Besides these trips, Muir enjoyed several arctic expeditions, where he does not fail to note the fascinations of far northern bird life, with its nesting ptarmigan and eiders, wild swans and plovers, emperor geese, snowy owls, auks, snow buntings and Lapland longspurs.

Muir died in Los Angeles in 1914. He lived as Thoreau would have had a man to live, but as he himself, chained by Concord and ill-health, could not do. Muir worshipped God through Nature as Wordsworth did without knowing as much about Nature as Muir knew. He was above all a botanist and glaciologist. "Some of my ancestors," he wrote, "must have been born on a Muirland, for there is heather in me, and tinctures of bog juices that send me to Cassiope,* and, oozing through all my veins, impel me unhaltingly through endless glacier meadows, seemingly the deeper and danker the better."

As an ornithologist Muir was, if not original, an observer with sensitive perceptions. So far as I know he never makes an ornithological mistake; when he refers to some bird it is never under such a general noun as "a gull"; he specifies unerringly "Burgomaster gull" or "Iceland gull." He had a flair for finding the nests of birds who are cryptic about their nidification, an ear for bird sounds; he was the sort of woodsman that birds instinctively trust and to whom they reveal themselves.

The water-ouzel or dipper of which he writes so feelingly is one of the glories of the western mountains of North America. Oddly enough, though related species are found in Eurasia, dippers do not occur in the Appalachian system which would seem, from its innumerable mountain torrents, to be adapted to them. Ouzels form a family having but a single genus and no close affinities unless perhaps to the wren-tits, another little family of Europe and western America, or to the true wrens. In form as in affinity, they are land birds. They do not swim and they cannot dive, and are yet able to carry on the business of their lives in deep and rushing waters. This they accomplish only through their ability to fly under the surface. As Coues has pointed out, it is as hard for the ouzels to keep *down* in this strange flight as it is for other birds to keep aloft.

Many writers—William Hudson and Bradford Torrey, Olive Thorne Miller, Robert Ridgway, Otto Herman and Elliott Coues, have paid homage to the ouzel. No one, I

* A genus of alpine flowers of Muir's favorite heath family. [Ed.]

think, has ever equalled Muir's description, and no one, surely, ever knew more about the bird. "Ouzel Basin" in the King's River valley of the Sierra, was named by David Starr Jordan in honor of this essay, for it is believed that it was there Muir wrote his first draft of the following pages.

THE WATER-OUZEL

THE waterfalls of the Sierra are frequented by only one bird—the Ouzel or Water Thrush (*Cinclus Mexicanus*, Sw.). He is a singularly joyous and lovable little fellow, about the size of a robin, clad in a plain waterproof suit of bluish gray, with a tinge of chocolate on the head and shoulders. In form he is about as smoothly plump and compact as a pebble that has been whirled in a pot-hole, the flowing contour of his body being interrupted only by his strong feet and bill, the crisp wing-tips, and the up-slanted wren-like tail.

Among all the countless waterfalls I have met in the course of ten years' exploration in the Sierra, whether among the icy peaks, or warm foot-hills, or in the profound yosemitic cañons of the middle region, not one was found without its Ouzel. No cañon is too cold for this little bird, none too lonely, provided it be rich in falling water. Find a fall, or cascade, or rushing rapid, anywhere upon a clear stream, and there you will surely find its complementary Ouzel, flitting about in the spray, diving in foaming eddies, whirling like a leaf among beaten foam-bells; ever vigorous and enthusiastic, yet self-contained, and neither seeking nor shunning your company.

If disturbed while dipping about in the margin shallows, he either sets off with a rapid whir to some other feeding-ground up or down the stream, or alights on some half-submerged rock or snag out in the current, and immediately begins to nod and courtesy like a wren, turning his head from side to side with many other odd dainty movements that never fail to fix the attention of the observer.

He is the mountain streams' own darling, the humming-bird of blooming waters, loving rocky ripple-slopes and sheets of foam as a bee loves flowers, as a lark loves sunshine and meadows. Among all the mountain birds, none has cheered me so much in my lonely wanderings,—none so unfailingly. For both in winter and summer he sings, sweetly, cheerily, independent alike of sunshine and of love, requiring no other inspiration than the stream on which he dwells. While water sings, so must he, in heat or cold, calm or storm, ever attuning his voice in sure accord; low in the drought of summer and the drought of winter, but never silent.

What may be regarded as the separate songs of the Ouzel are exceedingly difficult of description, because they are so variable and at the same time so confluent. Though I have been acquainted with my favorite ten years, and during most of this time have heard him sing nearly every day, I still detect notes and strains that seem new to me. Nearly all of his music is sweet and tender, lapsing from his round breast like water over the smooth lip of a pool, then breaking farther on into a sparkling foam of melodious notes, which glow with subdued enthusiasm, yet without expressing much of the strong, gushing ecstasy of the bobolink or skylark.

The more striking strains are perfect arabesques of melody, composed of a few full, round, mellow notes, embroidered with delicate trills which fade and melt in long slender cadences. In a general way his music is that of the streams refined and spiritualized. The deep booming notes of the falls are in it, the trills of rapids, the gurgling of margin eddies, the low whispering of level reaches, and the sweet tinkle of separate drops oozing from the ends of mosses and falling into tranquil pools.

The Ouzel never sings in chorus with other birds, nor with his kind, but only with the streams. And like flowers that bloom beneath the surface of the ground, some of our favorite's best song-blossoms never rise above the surface of the heavier music of the water. I have often observed him singing in the midst of beaten spray, his music completely buried beneath the water's roar; yet I knew he was surely singing by his gestures and the movements of his bill.

His food, as far as I have noticed, consists of all kinds of water insects, which in summer are chiefly procured along shallow margins. Here he wades about ducking his head under water and deftly turning over pebbles and fallen leaves with his bill, seldom choosing to go into deep water where he has to use his wings in diving.

He seems to be especially fond of the larvæ of mosquitoes, found in abundance attached to the bottom of smooth rock channels where the current is shallow. When feeding in such places he wades up-stream, and often while his head is under water the swift current is deflected upward along the glossy curves of his neck and shoulders, in the form of a clear, crystalline shell, which fairly incloses him like a bell-glass, the shell being broken and re-formed as he lifts and dips his head; while ever and anon he sidles out to where the too powerful current carries him off his feet; then he dexterously rises on the wing and goes gleaning again in shallower places.

The Ouzel is usually found singly; rarely in pairs, excepting during the breeding season, and very rarely in threes or fours. I once observed three thus spending a winter morning in company, upon a small glacier lake, on the Upper Merced, about 7,500 feet above the level of the sea. A storm had occurred during the night, but the morning sun shone unclouded, and the shadowy lake, gleaming darkly in its setting of fresh snow, lay smooth and motionless as a mirror. My camp chanced to be within a few feet of the water's edge, opposite a fallen pine, some of the branches of which leaned out over the lake. Here my three dearly welcome visitors took up their station, and at once began to embroider the frosty air with their delicious melody, doubly delightful to me that particular morning, as I had been somewhat apprehensive of danger in breaking my way down through the snow-choked cañons to the lowlands.

The portion of the lake bottom selected for a feeding-ground lies at a depth of fifteen or twenty feet below the surface, and is covered with a short growth of algæ and other aquatic plants—facts I had previously determined while sailing over it on a raft. After alighting on the glassy surface, they occasionally indulged in a little play, chasing one another round about in small circles; then all three would suddenly dive together, and then come ashore and sing.

The Ouzel seldom swims more than a few yards on the surface, for, not being web-footed, he makes rather slow progress, but by means of his strong, crisp wings he swims, or rather flies, with celerity under the surface, often to considerable distances. But it is in withstanding the force of heavy rapids that his strength of wing in this respect is most strikingly manifested. The following may be regarded as a fair illustration of his power of sub-aquatic flight. One stormy morning in winter when the Merced River was blue and green with unmelted snow, I observed one of my ouzels perched on a snag out in the midst of a swift-rushing rapid, singing cheerily, as if everything was just to his mind; and while I stood on the bank admiring him, he suddenly plunged into the sludgy current, leaving his song abruptly broken off. After feeding a minute or two at the bottom, and when one would suppose that he must inevitably be swept far downstream, he emerged just where he went down, alighted on the same snag, showered the water-beads from his feathers, and continued his unfinished song, seemingly in tranquil ease as if it had suffered no interruption.

The Ouzel alone of all birds dares to enter a white torrent. And though strictly terrestrial in structure, no other is so inseparably related to water, not even the duck, or the bold ocean albatross, or the stormy-petrel. For ducks go ashore as soon as they finish feeding in undisturbed places, and very often make long flights overland from lake to lake or field to field. The same is true of most other aquatic birds. But the Ouzel, born on the brink of a stream, or on a snag or boulder in the midst of it, seldom leaves it for a single moment. For, notwithstanding he is often on the wing, he never flies overland, but whirs with rapid, quail-like beat above the stream, tracing all its windings. Even when the stream is quite small, say from five to ten feet wide, he seldom shortens his flight by crossing a bend, however abrupt it may be; and even when disturbed by meeting some one on the bank, he prefers to fly over one's head, to dodging out over the ground. When, therefore, his flight along a crooked stream is viewed endwise, it appears most strikingly wavered—a description on the air of every curve with lightning-like rapidity.

The vertical curves and angles of the most precipitous torrents he traces with the same rigid fidelity, swooping down the inclines of cascades, dropping sheer over dizzy falls amid the spray, and ascending with the same fearlessness and ease, seldom seeking to lessen the steepness of the acclivity by beginning to ascend before reaching the base of the fall. No matter though it may be several hundred feet in height he holds straight on, as if about to dash headlong into the throng of booming rockets, then darts abruptly upward, and, after alighting at the top of the precipice to rest a moment, proceeds to feed and sing. His flight is solid and impetuous, without any intermission of wing-beats,—one homogeneous buzz like that of a laden bee on its way home. And while thus buzzing freely from fall to fall, he is frequently heard giving utterance to a long outdrawn train of unmodulated notes, in no way connected with his song, but corresponding closely with his flight in sustained vigor.

The Ouzel's nest is one of the most extraordinary pieces

of bird architecture I ever saw, odd and novel in design, perfectly fresh and beautiful, and in every way worthy of the genius of the little builder. It is about a foot in diameter, round and bossy in outline, with a neatly arched opening near the bottom, somewhat like an old-fashioned brick oven, or Hottentot's hut. It is built almost exclusively of green and yellow mosses, chiefly the beautiful fronded hypnum that covers the rocks and old drift-logs in the vicinity of waterfalls. These are deftly interwoven, and felted together into a charming little hut; and so situated that many of the outer mosses continue to flourish as if they had not been plucked. A few fine, silky-stemmed grasses are occasionally found interwoven with the mosses, but, with the exception of a thin layer lining the floor, their presence seems accidental, as they are of a species found growing with the mosses and are probably plucked with them. The site chosen for this curious mansion is usually some little rock-shelf within reach of the lighter particles of the spray of a waterfall, so that its walls are kept green and growing, at least during the time of high water.

In choosing a building-spot, concealment does not seem to be taken into consideration; yet notwithstanding the nest is large and guilelessly exposed to view, it is far from being easily detected, chiefly because it swells forward like any other bulging moss-cushion growing naturally in such situations. This is more especially the case where the nest is kept fresh by being well sprinkled. Sometimes these romantic little huts have their beauty enhanced by rock-ferns and grasses that spring up around the mossy walls, or in front of the door-sill, dripping with crystal beads.

Furthermore, at certain hours of the day, when the sunshine is poured down at the required angle, the whole mass of the spray enveloping the fairy establishment is brilliantly irised; and it is through so glorious a rainbow atmosphere as this that some of our blessed ouzels obtain their first peep at the world.

In these moss huts three or four eggs are laid, white like foam-bubbles; and well may the little birds hatched from them sing water songs, for they hear them all their lives, and even before they are born.

I have often observed the young just out of the nest making their odd gestures, and seeming in every way as much at home as their experienced parents, like young bees on their first excursions to the flower fields. No amount of familiarity with people and their ways seems to change them in the least. To all appearance their behavior is just the same on seeing a man for the first time, as when they have seen him frequently.

On the lower reaches of the rivers where mills are built, they sing on through the din of the machinery, and all the noisy confusion of dogs, cattle, and workmen. On one occasion, while a wood-chopper was at work on the river-bank, I observed one cheerily singing within reach of the flying chips. Nor does any kind of unwonted disturbance put him in bad humor, or frighten him out of calm self-possession. In passing through a narrow gorge, I once drove one ahead of me from rapid to rapid, disturbing him four times in quick succession where he could not very well fly past me on account of the narrowness of the channel. Most birds under similar circumstances fancy themselves pursued, and become suspiciously uneasy; but, instead of growing nervous about it, he made his usual dippings, and sang one of his most tranquil strains. When observed within a few yards their eyes are seen to express remarkable gentleness and intelligence; but they seldom allow so near a view unless one wears clothing of about the same color as the rocks and trees, and knows how to sit still. On one occasion, while rambling along the shore of a mountain lake, where the birds, at least those born that

season, had never seen a man, I sat down to rest on a large
stone close to the water's edge, upon which it seemed the
ouzels and sandpipers were in the habit of alighting when
they came to feed on that part of the shore, and some of the
other birds also, when they came down to wash or drink.
In a few minutes, along came a whirring Ouzel and alighted
on the stone beside me, within reach of my hand. Then suddenly observing me, he stooped nervously as if about to fly
on the instant, but as I remained as motionless as the stone,
he gained confidence, and looked me steadily in the face for
about a minute, then flew quietly to the outlet and began to
sing. Next came a sandpiper and gazed at me with much the
same guileless expression of eye as the Ouzel. Lastly, down
with a swoop came a Steller's jay out of a fir-tree, probably
with the intention of moistening his noisy throat. But instead
of sitting confidingly as my other visitors had done, he rushed
off at once, nearly tumbling heels over head into the lake
in his suspicious confusion, and with loud screams roused the
neighborhood.

Even so far north as icy Alaska, I have found my glad
singer. When I was exploring the glaciers between Mount
Fairweather and the Stikeen River, one cold day in November, after trying in vain to force a way through the innumerable icebergs of Sum Dum Bay to the great glaciers at the
head of it, I was weary and baffled and sat resting in my
canoe convinced at last that I would have to leave this part
of my work for another year. Then I began to plan my
escape to open water before the young ice which was beginning to form should shut me in. While I thus lingered drifting with the bergs, in the midst of these gloomy forebodings
and all the terrible glacial desolation and grandeur, I suddenly heard the well-known whir of an Ouzel's wings, and,
looking up, saw my little comforter coming straight across
the ice from the shore. In a second or two he was with me,

flying three times round my head with a happy salute, as if saying, "Cheer up, old friend; you see I'm here, and all's well." Then he flew back to the shore, alighted on the topmost jag of a stranded iceberg, and began to nod and bow as though he were on one of his favorite boulders in the midst of a sunny Sierra cascade.

Such, then, is our little cinclus, beloved of every one who is so fortunate as to know him. Tracing on strong wing every curve of the most precipitous torrents from one extremity of the Sierra to the other; not fearing to follow them through their darkest gorges and coldest snow-tunnels; acquainted with every waterfall, echoing their divine music; and throughout the whole of their beautiful lives interpreting all that we in our unbelief call terrible in the utterances of torrents and storms, as only varied expressions of God's eternal love.

GILBERT WHITE

III

GILBERT WHITE

THE facts in Gilbert White's life can be very briefly told. Indeed there is little possibility of expanding them much beyond the following, for his eventlessly happy career was so intensely private that he entered scarcely at all into public notice, was known even to his friends chiefly by correspondence, and died almost unremarked by the world. Yet, as Prof. Alfred Newton, the editor of the famous *Dictionary of Birds*, has said, "It is almost certain that more than half the zoölogists of the British Islands for many years past have been infected with their love of the study by Gilbert White; and it can hardly be supposed that his influence will cease."

Gilbert White was born in 1720 in Selborne vicarage in Hampshire, and died in that hamlet in 1793. This makes him the contemporary of Linnaeus, Buffon, Haller, Lamarck; his life extended through the reigns of the first three Georges.

His absences from Selborne were few. He went as a boy to school at Basingstoke, then to Oriel College at Oxford, where he remained for three post-graduate years, then became curate at Swarraton for a short time, returned to Oxford for three years as a junior proctor, and in 1755, being then thirty-five years of age, he settled down in Selborne again there to remain for thirty-three years.

White was not, I understand, the vicar of Selborne at all; it was his grandfather, of the same name, who held that modest post. White was more modest even than that. Though ordained, he never practised his calling in Selborne, unless perhaps to assist in the duties of the real curate during ab-

47

sences. So that even from ministering to the village folk and rustics he was aloof. With an assured income, with a modest but beautiful old-world home in the village, without wife or child (and having no apparent desire for them), his time was completely his own—or, rather, his time was the birds'.

To the modern temper this is well-nigh annoying. But he is to be judged by his times, and his class, and his training. We owe to his leisure, his tastes and his habits, a life work which has set many of us upon the road both to the art and science of bird watching, and to a love of Nature in its intimate aspects. We must not quarrel with the times, or the man, but try to understand both.

As for the man, Grant Allen has said that he seems perfectly to exemplify Austin Dobson's lines on an eighteenth century gentleman:

> He liked the well-wheel's creaking tongue—
> He liked the thrush that stopped and sung—
> He liked the drone of flies among
>   His netted peaches;
> He liked to watch the sunlight fall
> Athwart his ivied orchard wall;
> Or pause to catch the cuckoo's call
>   Beyond the beeches.

To this picture there is something in every contemplative soul that responds. We feel that Gilbert White lived for us the life of delicate appreciation of simple and beautiful things, that we may not have and would not, for our restlessness, be able to maintain for some seventy-odd years if we had the opportunity. Here was a man who picked up acorns and put them in his pocket so as to be able to press one into the ground where, it seemed to him, an oak should grow. Here was a man who saw English Nature as Constable saw it— firm-rooted, deep-breasted, velvet-lawned, high-hedged, who heard its rural sounds as they were when the tolling of a

bell was the loudest sound upon the air, or the bellowing of
an unmilked cow, the scream of a rabbit in the jaws of a
weasel. He knew nothing of trains, airplanes, motor cars,
factory whistles, wireless; his was the England to which Englishmen long sometimes to return.

True that in the world about him great events were afoot.
He lived in the days of Clive and Wolfe, of Pitt and Burke,
of Washington and Danton. But neither empire nor parliament, not revolt in America nor regicide in France, disturb
his tranquil pages. His science is serene above the clash of
arms and opinions, as science should be. But so good a paro-
chial was White that he probably did not care whether the
empire expanded or contracted, while Selborne's evening
blackbirds were not interrupted at vespers. He belonged to
an England that was perfectly sure of itself.

His scientific age was also more full of stir than he ever
recognizes. Even in his times he was a bit anachronistic. He
is slow to adopt the convenience of Linnaean binominal
nomenclature, though he admires its latinity. Deliberately he
seems to cultivate his amateurism; he stays with no subject
long, pursues none to the bottom, is nothing of a "grind,"
and yet, though he is enthusiastic or even poetic about nothing, is not quite ever a pedant, for the smell of fresh turned
loam is on every page of his book, and he seems to have
come in from listening to the first cuckoo's call only the
moment before.

For this very reason he has raised up admirers by the thousand and hundreds of thousands; he is just as popular today
as ever. For he is somehow wondrously accessible to all of us;
his is a book to dip in, and dip and dip; it is inexhaustible
in its light sweet charm. No art could have achieved this
effect, but only complete ingenuousness. The man must have
been precisely what the book is; the man, since nothing else
much is known of him, is the book, and this has gone through

some seventy-five editions.

The Natural History of Selborne first appeared in London in 1789, but some of the materials had appeared earlier in scientific journals. Such is the case with the selections I have made, which were printed in the *Philosophical Transactions* in 1774 and 1775, constituting a little monograph on the swallow family in England. More, the materials of the book were in great part a compilation of letters written to his two friends, the eminent ornithologist Thomas Pennant, and the fellow dilettante, Daines Barrington. He began writing to the Welsh ornithologist in 1767, and a little later to Barrington, who like White was an antiquarian, a lover of the Greek and Latin writers, and was, moreover, the author of a tract of observations upon singing birds, and another on the speech of birds. To Barrington, White could write a letter about lightning, another on gypsies, one on the strange predilection of an idiot boy for bees, and still another on the possibility that swallows hibernate under the water, without in any way violating Barrington's ideas of the business of natural science. Barrington was even more of a dabbler than White.

The book as White finally arranged it opens with nine fictitious letters; that is to say, they take the form of correspondence but are really introductory passages giving the reader the topography and natural history of the parish at a glance. It closes with more of the same sort. The real letters, living and strong in literary style, occupy the great central portion of the book, and from these I have made my selection.

I chose the swallows, martins and swift because they are the most famous and justly famous of White's pages. And for the curious fantastical theorizing of the times which they reveal. And because, as it seems to an American, these are such typically European birds, intimate with man, adapted to nesting about his dwellings, gentle and sweet. True that the swifts are no longer considered to belong to the swallow family which superficially they resemble in form, flight, and habit. But White thought of them so; his age accepted their classification together. So I leave them.

It was to antiquity, even classic naturalists, that White and Barrington owed the notion of the hibernation of these birds. Nobody now believes that swallows in autumn crowd on a twig over the river till, bending under the weight of the birds, it lowers them beneath the surface—they singing all the time a doleful dirge. Nobody believes that sand martins hole up in cliffs and sleep out the inclement season, or that swifts curl up like bats in belfries, in a state of torpor. But in White's day, naturalists could not bring themselves to accept the idea that the swallow family migrated, at least not wholly. Peter Kalm, and his countryman Wallerius, assert hibernation as something they actually witnessed. Be it noted that our Gilbert White, though longing for evidence to support hibernation, and searching for it everywhere, never once asserts that he witnessed any fact to prove his theory. He reports hearsay with all due skepticism and brings forth evidence for the migration of swallows frankly and completely. This should rank him with any modern scientist, and confirm our complete trust in what he has to say.

THE SWALLOW

To the Honorable Daines Barrington

Selborne, *Jan.* 29th, 1774.

DEAR SIR,—The house-swallow, or chimney-swallow, is undoubtedly the first comer of all the British hirundines.

It is worth remarking that these birds are seen first about lakes and mill-ponds; and it is also very particular, that if these early visitors happen to find frost and snow, they immediately withdraw for a time. A circumstance this much more in favour of hiding than migration; since it is much more probable that a bird should retire to its hybernaculum just at hand, then return for a week or two only to warmer latitudes.

The swallow, though called the chimney-swallow, by no means builds altogether in chimneys, but often within barns and outhouses against the rafters.

In Sweden she builds in barns, and is called *ladu swala,* the barn-swallow. Besides, in the warmer parts of Europe there are no chimneys to houses, except they are English-built: in these countries she constructs her nest in porches, and gateways, and galleries, and open halls.

Here and there a bird may affect some odd, peculiar place; as we have known a swallow build down the shaft of an old well, but in general with us this *hirundo* breeds in chimneys; and loves to haunt those stacks where there is a constant fire, no doubt for the sake of warmth. Not that it can subsist in the immediate shaft where there is a fire; but prefers one adjoining to that of the kitchen, and disregards the perpetual smoke of that funnel, as I have often observed with some degree of wonder.

Five or six or more feet down the chimney does this little bird begin to form her nest about the middle of May, which consists, like that of the house-martin, of a crust or shell composed of dirt or mud, mixed with short pieces of straw to render it tough and permanent; with this difference, that whereas the shell of the martin is nearly hemispheric, that of the swallow is open at the top, and like half a deep dish: this nest is lined with fine grasses, and feathers, which are often collected as they float in the air.

Wonderful is the address which this adroit bird shows all day long in ascending and descending with security through so narrow a pass. When hovering over the mouth of the funnel, the vibrations of her wings acting on the confined air occasion a rumbling like thunder. It is not improbable that the dam submits to this inconvenient situation so low in the shaft, in order to secure her broods from rapacious birds, and particularly from owls, which frequently fall down chimneys, perhaps in attempting to get at these nestlings.

The swallow lays from four to six white eggs, dotted with red specks; and brings out her first brood about the last week in June, or the first week in July. The progressive method by which the young are introduced into life is very amusing; first, they emerge from the shaft with difficulty enough, and often fall down into the rooms below: for a day or so they are fed on the chimney-top, and then are conducted to the dead leafless bough of some tree, where, sitting in a row, they are attended with great assiduity, and may then be called perchers. In a day or two more they become flyers, but are still unable to take their own food; therefore they play about near the place where the dams are hawking for flies; and, when a mouthful is collected, at a certain signal given, the dam and the nestling advance, rising towards each other, and meeting at an angle; the young one all the while uttering such a little quick note of gratitude and complacency, that a person must have paid very little regard to the wonders of Nature that has not often remarked this feat.

All the summer long is the swallow a most instructive pattern of unwearied industry and affection; for, from morning to night, while there is a family to be supported, she spends the whole day in skimming close to the ground, and exerting the most sudden turns and quick evolutions. Avenues, and long walks under hedges, and pasture-fields, and mown meadows where cattle graze, are her delight, especially if there are trees interspersed; because in such spots insects most abound. When a fly is taken a smart snap from her bill is heard, resembling the noise at the shutting of a watch-case; but the motion of the mandibles is too quick for the eye.

Each species of hirundo drinks as it flies along, sipping the surface of the water; but the swallow alone, in general, washes on the wing, by dropping into a pool for many times together: in very hot weather house-martins and bank-martins dip and wash a little.

The swallow is a delicate songster, and in soft sunny weather sings both perching and flying; on trees in a kind of concert, and on chimney-tops: is also a bold flyer, ranging to distant downs and commons even in windy weather, which the other species seem much to dislike; nay, even frequenting exposed sea-port towns, and making little excursions over the salt water. Horsemen on wide downs are often closely attended by a little party of swallows for miles together, which plays before and behind them, sweeping around them, and collecting all the skulking insects that are roused by the trampling of the horses' feet: when the wind blows hard, without this expedient, they are often forced to settle to pick up their lurking prey.

This species feeds much on little *Coleoptera*, as well as on gnats and flies; and often settles on dug ground, or paths, for gravels to grind and digest its food. Before they depart, for some weeks, to a bird, they forsake houses and chimneys, and roost in trees; and usually withdraw about the beginning of October, though some few stragglers may appear on at times till the first week in November.

Some few pairs haunt the new and open streets of London next the fields, but do not enter, like the house-martin, the close and crowded parts of the city.

Both male and female are distinguished from their congeners by the length and forkedness of their tails. They are undoubtedly the most nimble of all the species: and when the male pursues the female in amorous chase, they then go beyond their usual speed and exert a rapidity almost too quick for the eye to follow.

I am,

With all respect, &c. &c.

THE SAND-MARTIN

To the Honorable Daines Barrington

Selborne, *Feb.* 26th, 1774.

DEAR SIR,—The sand-martin, or bank-martin, is by much the least of any of the British hirundines, and, as far as we have ever seen, the smallest known hirundo, though Brisson asserts that there is one much smaller, and that is the *hirundo esculenta.*

It is curious to observe with what different degrees of architectonic skill Providence has endowed birds of the same genus, and so nearly correspondent in their general mode of life! for while the swallow and the house-martin discover the greatest address in raising and securely fixing crusts or shells of loam as cunabula for their young, the bank-martin terebrates a round and regular hole in the sand or earth, which is serpentine, horizontal, and about two feet deep. At the inner end of this burrow does this bird deposit, in a good degree of safety, her rude nest, consisting of fine grasses and feathers, usually goose-feathers, very inartificially laid together.

Perseverance will accomplish anything, though at first one would be disinclined to believe that this weak bird, with her soft and tender bill and claws, should ever be able to bore the stubborn sand-bank without entirely disabling herself; yet with these feeble instruments have I seen a pair of them make great despatch, and could remark how much they had scooped that day by the fresh sand which ran down the bank, and was of a different colour from that which lay loose and bleached in the sun.

One thing is remarkable—that, after some years, the old holes are forsaken and new ones bored; perhaps because the old habitations grow foul and fetid from long use, or because they may so abound with fleas as to become untenantable. This species of swallow, moreover, is strangely annoyed with fleas; and we have seen fleas, bed-fleas (pulex irritans),* swarming at the mouths of these holes, like bees on the stools of their hives.

The following circumstance should by no means be omitted —that these birds do not make use of their caverns by way of hybernacula, as might be expected; since banks so perforated have been dug out with care in the winter, when nothing was found but empty nests.

The sand-martin arrives much about the same time with the swallow, and lays, as she does, from four to six white eggs. But as this species is cryptogame, carrying on the business of nidification, incubation, and the support of its young in the dark, it would not be so easy to ascertain the time of breeding, were it not for the coming forth of the broods, which appear much about the time, or rather somewhat earlier than those of the swallow. The nestlings are supported in common like those of their congeners, with gnats and other small insects; and sometimes they are fed with *libellulæ* (dragon-flies) almost as long as themselves. In the last week in June we have seen a row of these sitting on a rail near a great pool as perchers, and so young and helpless, as easily to be taken by hand; but whether the dams ever feed them on the wing, as swallows and house-martins do, we have never yet been able to determine; nor do we know whether they pursue and attack birds of prey.

These hirundines are no songsters, but rather mute, making only a little harsh noise when a person approaches their nests. They seem not to be of a sociable turn, never with us congregating with their congeners in the autumn. Undoubtedly they breed a second time, like the house-martin and

* White is in error. The flea of the sand-martin is a special species. [Ed.]

swallow, and withdraw about Michaelmas.

These birds have a peculiar manner of flying; flitting about with odd jerks, and vacillations, not unlike the motions of a butterfly. Doubtless the flight of all hirundines is influenced by, and adapted to, the peculiar sort of insects which furnish their food. Hence it would be worth inquiry to examine what particular genus of insects affords the principal food of each respective species of swallow.

Notwithstanding what has been advanced above, some few sand-martins, I see, haunt the skirts of London, frequenting the dirty pools in Saint George's Fields, and about Whitechapel. The question is where these build, since there are no banks or bold shores in that neighbourhood; perhaps they nestle in the scaffold-holes of some old or new deserted building. They dip and wash as they fly sometimes, like the house-martin and swallow.

Sand-martins differ from their congeners in the diminutiveness of their size, and in their colour, which is what is usually called a mouse-colour. Near Valencia, in Spain, they are taken, says Willughby, and sold in the markets for the table; and are called by the country people, probably from their desultory jerking manner of flight, *Papilion de Montagna*.

I am,

With all respect, &c. &c.

THE SWIFT

To the Honorable Daines Barrington

Selborne, *Sept. 28th,* 1774.

DEAR SIR,—Swifts, like sand-martins, carry on the business of nidification quite in the dark, in crannies of castles, and towers, and steeples, and upon the tops of the walls of churches under the roof; and therefore cannot be so narrowly watched as those species that build more openly; but, from what I could ever observe, they begin nesting about the middle of May; and I have remarked, from eggs taken, that they have sat hard by the ninth of June. In general they haunt tall buildings, churches, and steeples, and breed only in such; yet in this village some pairs frequent the lowest and meanest cottages, and educate their young under those thatched roofs. We remember but one instance where they breed out of buildings, and that is in the sides of a deep chalk-pit near the town of Odiham, in this county, where we have seen many pairs entering the crevices, and skimming and squeaking round the precipices.

As I have regarded these amusive birds with no small attention, if I should advance something new and peculiar with respect to them, and different from all other birds, I might perhaps be credited, especially as my assertion is the result of many years' exact observation. The fact that I would advance is, that swifts tread, or copulate, on the wing; and I would wish any nice observer, that is startled at this supposition, to use his own eyes, and I think he will soon be convinced. In another class of animals, viz., the insect, nothing is so common as to see the different species of many genera in conjunction as they fly. The swift is almost continually on the wing; and as it never settles on the ground, on trees, or roofs, would seldom find opportunity for amorous rites, was it not enabled to indulge them in the air. If any person would watch these birds of a fine morning in May, as they are sailing round at a great height from the ground, he would see, every now and then, one drop on the back of another, and both of them sink down together for many fathoms with a loud piercing shriek. This I take to be the juncture when the business of generation is carrying on.

As the swift eats, drinks, collects materials for its nest, and, as it seems, propagates on the wing, it appears to live more in the air than any other bird, and to perform all functions there save those of sleeping and incubation.

It is a most alert bird, rising very early, and retiring to roost very late; and is on the wing in the height of summer at least sixteen hours. In the longest days it does not withdraw to rest till a quarter before nine in the evening, being the latest of all day-birds. Just before they retire whole groups of them assemble high in the air, and squeak, and shoot about with wonderful rapidity. But this bird is never so much alive as in sultry thundery weather, when it expresses great alacrity, and calls forth all its powers. In hot mornings, several, getting together in little parties, dash round the steeples and churches, squeaking as they go in a very clamorous manner; these, by nice observers, are supposed to be males serenading their sitting hens; and not without reason, since they seldom squeak till they come close to the walls or eaves, and since those within utter at the same time a little inward note of complacency.

Sometimes they pursue and strike at hawks that come in their way; but not with that vehemence and fury that swallows express on the same occasion. They are out all day long in wet days, feeding about, and disregarding still rain: from whence two things may be gathered; first, that many insects abide high in the air, even in rain; and next, that the feathers of these birds must be well preened to resist so much wet. Windy, and particularly windy weather with heavy showers, they dislike; and on such days withdraw, and are scarce ever seen.

There is a circumstance respecting the colour of swifts, which seems not to be unworthy of our attention. When they arrive in the spring, they are all over of a glossy, dark soot colour, except their chins, which are white; but, by being all day long in the sun and air, they become quite weather-beaten and bleached before they depart, and yet they return glossy again in the spring. Now, if they pursue the sun into lower latitudes, as some suppose, in order to enjoy a perpetual summer, why do they not return bleached? Do they not rather perhaps retire to rest for a season, and at that juncture moult and change their feathers, since all other birds are known to moult soon after the season of breeding?

Swifts are no songsters, and have only one harsh screaming note; yet there are ears to which it is not displeasing, from an agreeable association of ideas, since that note never occurs but in the most lovely summer weather.

They never can settle on the ground but through accident; and when down, can hardly rise, on account of the shortness of their legs and the length of their wings; neither can they walk, but only crawl; but they have a strong grasp with their feet, by which they cling to walls. Their bodies being flat they can enter a very narrow crevice; and where they cannot pass on their bellies they will turn up edgewise.

In London a party of swifts frequents the Tower, playing and feeding over the river just below the bridge; others haunt some of the churches of the Borough, next the fields, but do not venture, like the house-martin, into the close crowded part of the town.

Swifts feed on *coleoptera*, or small beetles with hard cases over their wings, as well as on the softer insects; but it does not appear how they can procure gravel to grind their food, as swallows do, since they never settle on the ground. Young ones, overrun with *hippoboscæ*, are sometimes found, under their nests, fallen to the ground, the number of vermin rendering their abode insupportable any longer. They frequent in this village several abject cottages; yet a succession still haunts the same unlikely roofs—a good proof this that the same birds return to the same spots. As they must stoop very low to get up under these humble eaves, cats lie in wait, and sometimes catch them on the wing.

On the 5th of July, 1775, I again untiled part of a roof over the nest of a swift. The dam sat in the nest; but so strongly was she affected by a natural στοργὴ for her brood, which she supposed to be in danger, that, regardless of her own safety, she would not stir, but lay sullenly by them, permitting herself to be taken in hand. The squab young we brought down and placed on the grass-plot, where they tumbled about, and were as helpless as a new-born child. While we contemplated their naked bodies, their unwieldy disproportioned abdomina, and their heads, too heavy for their necks to support, we could not but wonder when we reflected that these shiftless beings in a little more than a fortnight would be able to dash through the air almost with the inconceivable swiftness of a meteor; and perhaps in their emigration, must traverse vast continents and oceans as distant as the equator. So soon does Nature advance small birds to their ἡλικία or state of perfection; while the progressive growth of men and large quadrupeds is slow and tedious.

I am, &c.

CHERRY KEARTON

IV

CHERRY KEARTON

*O*NE of the pioneers of Nature photography has been Mr. Cherry Kearton, especially in the field of motion pictures. Many celebrated film sequences by Mr. Kearton have been shown in England and America, and his work of photographing wild animals has, as he says, carried him right "across the world." And not only across, but up and down, for he has made a great specialty of African Nature pictures, from the lion country of the Equator all the way to the oceanic islands off the Cape, where breed the black-footed penguins.

Mr. Kearton was born in 1871 in Thwaite Swaledale, Yorkshire, son of a yeoman farmer. Under the influence of his brother Richard, the celebrated explorer, writer, and photographer, Kearton early began his career with the lens, illustrating all of Richard Kearton's early books.

About 1911 Mr. Kearton accompanied Buffalo Jones as his motion picture photographer to East Africa. Buffalo Jones and a few cowboys lassoed rhino, giraffe, lion and other animals. Shortly after this, Mr. Kearton again carried his lens to East Africa, in company with James Barnes, an American explorer, returning by a journey across the Belgian Congo in the following year. In 1914 as captain of the Fifth Royal Fusiliers, Kearton returned to East Africa in the World War campaigns against the German colonies, and saw three years of service. He was reported killed but, happily for photography, survived. More natural history expeditions in Africa followed after the war, and in 1926 he was summoned to Windsor Castle to show his pictures at royal command. His Nature photography has taken him to the Far West of the United States and he is well known to the scientists of New York, who speak of his winning personality and outstanding ability.

Mr. Kearton lives at present at "The Jungle," Kenley, Surrey, where his diversions are rifle shooting, boxing, and billiards. His wife has accompanied him on many of his most daring trips and assisted in his work. He states that even when photographing African elephants, rhinoceros, crocodiles, lions and buffalo, he never goes armed. He considers that if he is quite unarmed he will be triply cautious and therefore actually in less danger, and that from the point of view of natural history more is learned if one is forced to rely entirely upon a camera record and cannot take the short-cut of securing specimens by killing them.

There was certainly no need of a gun on his island of penguins, for there are no birds less belligerent than the domestically inclined, peace-loving, and flightless *Sphenisciformes*. The island, off the coast of South Africa, is the breeding ground not only of the black-footed or Cape penguin (*Spheniscus demersus*) but is visited by sea gulls, terns and gannets, and is the permanent residence of cormorants, oyster-catchers, gulls, ibis, and sand-plovers.

The island which Mr. and Mrs. Kearton visited is little more than a rock four square miles in area and surrounded by some of the stormiest seas of the South Atlantic, northwest from the Cape of Good Hope; humanly it is inhabited only by the attendants of the lighthouse. Here the Keartons spent many months, and came to know individual birds and their individualistic behavior as well as the types of behavior that are determined by age and sex and the race as a whole. As Mr. Kearton says:

"I studied young penguins and old penguins in all conditions, in sickness and in health, in fair weather and foul. I met the proud and the meek, the bully, the mischief-maker, the comfortable old gentleman, the despised weakling and the social outcast."

The black-footed or jackass penguins, in Mr. Kearton's view of them, are not increasing or are positively losing ground. Gulls and ibises take the eggs. At sea, the octopus and shark lie in wait for the swimming birds. Men take penguins in nets and use them as bait for crayfish. Yet Mr. Kearton calculates the penguin population at the height of the breeding season as five millions, which would put its numbers up with those of any capital in the world except London and New York. Such a vast congregation in so crowded a space necessarily means that complex social adjustments would be set up among penguins, just as they would among ants, men or bees. The society of the hive is well understood, since the honey bee has been a highly accessible object of study to man for ages. But the haunts of penguins are the opposite of accessible. The twenty living species of this ancient and unique order of birds are scattered over the islands of the antarctic seas, save for a few outposts where islands technically tropical are swept by cold currents. So, scientists who have wished to study them have been compelled to undertake special expeditions and to dwell amongst them under conditions of great difficulty. Yet probably no social bird has attracted so much attention as the penguin. For though instinct, and not intelligence, may be the guiding principle of penguin society, intelligence of a sort is not wanting and the analogies of penguin life and human life are sufficiently striking (however little they may be true homologies in the scientific sense) to have attracted the satiric wit of many writers, notably Anatole France and his *L'Ile des Pengouins*.

Mr. Kearton has also played with this fantasy, not however as intended to expose human foibles through penguins, but rather to make penguin behavior more comprehensible to us.

This anthropomorphism is employed, I believe, entirely in a jocose spirit, and if it is so understood by the reader and not taken literally, it will be seen that, fundamentally, the author almost nowhere violates serious science but has, with a peculiarly light and charming gesture, done his bit to elucidate it.

PENGUINS' NESTS

*J*T IS a low-lying island, roughly in the shape of a tortoise, two and a half miles long and a mile and a half wide. It is a flat rock, and nothing but a rock, rising out of the water, although the rock surface is partly covered with shallow earth and sand.

Except for the few patches of bare rock, the whole surface of the island is pitted with holes a few feet or less apart—the nesting burrows of penguins. Every patch of earthy ground, every overhanging rock, every spot where tunnelling can be performed, is made use of.

They lie down and scrape at the earth with their feet and flippers until a little is loose enough to be removed; then they shift forward and start to kick out with their feet. In this way they gradually dig in a sloping direction a sort of tunnel to a depth of one, two or three feet, so that at last they have what is in effect an open front garden and a roofed house beyond.

This is hard work, of course. The two penguins that have mated take it in turns, one resting while the other toils, and they do most of the work in the morning, usually keeping at it for two or three hours at a stretch. Each day, at the end of the work, they go down to the sea, partly to fish and partly to wash. For the past three hours, earth has been flying to a height of two or three feet all round the burrow, and a good deal of it has fallen on the workers—you can imagine what a state they are in, with earth and sand matted into their black and white feathers. But a bath soon works wonders, and the toilers quickly return to an appearance of respectability.

Burrowing is by far the commonest method of constructing

a home on the Island of Penguins, but shelter is the first concern in the design of these homes, and from that point of view nothing could possibly equal a nest under a rock; therefore I imagine that the penguins who have been lucky enough to provide themselves with a stone roof are envied by the rest. Here and there you will see, as on all rocky coasts, great slabs of rock which by long action of the sea have been hollowed out underneath, so that there is a long, shallow, open cave. In any such place as that, you may be certain to find several penguin families.

Some birds only make shallow holes on the surface in open country, with no shelter above them at all. But I think these homes belong to inexperienced penguins and are not returned to: for the occupants clearly suffer a great deal from the sun, during the heat of a summer's day.

I have seen holes in rocks one above the other, just like flats; holes only half dug under protecting bushes; one nest that was so framed in a well-grown bush that no digging had been necessary at all; and a burrow which had the decided attraction of possessing a back entrance as well as a front door.

In fact, every method of construction that the ingenious mind of the penguin can devise is put to good use.

When once a nest has been completed, the next thing to be considered is the furniture. This is all made locally, and therefore the variety is not very great. But self-respecting birds naturally want some kind of flooring for their nests, and consequently any sort of stick is brought into use. As I have said, there is very little vegetation on the island—but I have also said that the penguin has an ingenious mind. If he can, he takes twigs or roots from the bushes. If he lives in a district where there are no bushes, he finds that seaweed can serve as a very good substitute. And as a last resort there are the dried, straw-like grasses which sprout thinly on the island during the wetter months.

It can be imagined what an effect this desire for furniture is having on the scanty vegetation of the island. Bushes are slowly being torn to pieces, and many of them are withering because their roots, if not always torn off, have been pulled free of earth and left exposed to the sun. Building operations, too, often bare the roots and cause bushes to die.

I once saw a penguin cast a longing eye at a partially exposed piece of root which clearly was exactly the thing he wanted. He went up to it, took hold of it with his beak, and pulled. But the root was firmly planted and there was no result. Yet he wasn't going to be beaten, so he pulled and twisted in a real effort to break it. So persistent was he that he came back again to that bush, working from every direction, though it was not until he had struggled with it for the greater part of three days that he succeeded in wrenching it away; and at the moment when that happened, he was pulling so hard that the sudden release toppled him right over on to his back. But he immediately got up, none the worse, and went off, carrying the root in his beak to show it to his wife, and looking quite the proudest and happiest little penguin that I have ever seen.

Similarly, I have seen penguins with long, trailing bits of seaweed, struggling up the slope from the sea—a matter, as often as not, of half a mile or more—the seaweed becoming entangled in their legs and nearly tripping them up.

Just a few penguins on the island—about a dozen in all—think that neither sticks nor straws nor seaweed are even to be compared, in this matter of furniture, with stones. This is very curious, for though stones are not the natural nest-covering of these Blackfooted Penguins, they are used almost exclusively in the nests of the penguins who inhabit the much more southerly regions. Stones are scarce on some parts of the Island of Penguins, but these particular birds will take any amount of trouble to secure them. I found one nest, for example, which was furnished with small stones about the size of a hen's egg and furnished so thoroughly that there must have been quite half a barrow-load in the one nest; and every one of these stones must have been carried for a distance of half a mile, although entirely suitable sticks lay close at hand on every side.

Now and again one bird will take a fancy to something which doesn't at all appeal to the others. One day I saw a penguin leave a nest to seek for furniture, apparently with quite definite instructions from his wife as to the kind of thing he was to get. He collected a number of sticks, carrying each back to the nest and then setting out for more. Suddenly he saw on the ground a beautiful smooth stone. There was something about it which clearly appealed to him, for he walked round it two or three times, viewing it from every angle; he reminded me rather forcibly of the young husband who sees in a shop window something which he longs to buy for his wife, though he knows he cannot afford it. In the case of the penguin the price was certainly a high one—the carrying of the stone for a hundred yards. But at last he made up his mind. He picked up the stone in his beak after some initial difficulty, and started off. Twice he had to stop and rest, setting the stone carefully down on the ground. But he stuck to his task and at last he came waddling proudly up to the nest and dropped the stone just in front of his wife.

She gave it one look—but that was enough. "Didn't I tell you," she seemed to say, "that we were going to furnish this nest with sticks?" And the wretched husband, with all his joy and pride suddenly turned to gall, picked up the stone and carried it away again.

I was curious to see how far he would take it; whether he would take it whence it came or whether he would drop it disgustedly at the first opportunity. As a matter of fact, he took it twenty yards—just far enough for him to be able to leave it where his wife was not likely to notice it again and remind him of that painful incident. But he didn't go on with his work. All his enthusiasm about the new home and its furnishing was gone and—like the punished child who went into the garden "to eat worms"—he picked up a straw of grass and carried it, not homewards, but down to the sea.

FAMILY MATTERS

*E*VEN when, as with the penguins, the husband and wife are so house-proud and so fearful of burglars that they cannot both leave home at once, there is, nevertheless, such delight in the house itself, and in life generally, that that hardly seems to matter. And even the short separations seem to add to happiness, because they must end some time and then there is the joy of being re-united. Mr. Penguin, for instance, goes down to the sea in search of his dinner, leaving his wife drowsily meditating on the perfect bliss of married life. Mr. Penguin is just as contented with, at the moment, the added joy of going into the sea and of catching succulent fish. He comes back, clambers on to the rock, and starts waddling up the slope, finding progress just a little bit difficult because he really is rather excessively, and almost uncomfortably, full of food. But though he goes slowly, he nevertheless goes steadily, eager to see his wife. And there she is, with her head at the edge of the nesting hole, watching for him! He tries to break into a run, nearly falls over in his eagerness, stops for a moment to think how beautiful she is, and then, coming nearer, he leans down to put his head affectionately against hers. Then he goes into the hole beside her, caresses her, and embraces her with his flippers. How good it is to be home again, feeling so comfortably well fed, and to have such an adorable wife awaiting him!

Of course I do not know, any more than anybody else does, to what extent penguins manage to convey ideas to each other, but if you watch Mr. and Mrs. Penguin together it seems perfectly certain that they do manage it somehow. At any rate, they do a great deal of love-making, becoming vastly sentimental in the process. A penguin's expression at these times is easily recognisable. The feathers round his throat seem to puff out and he lowers his head into them, so that his general attitude is rather in the shape of a question mark. His eyes, too, become a little more distinct, he sets his head slightly on one side, and every shade of his expression is that of a love-sick coon.

I have no doubt that he is very genuinely in love. He is certainly not an opportunist. He does not confine his love-making to the time of wooing, but continues it right through his married life, kissing and embracing his wife merely to show his constant joy in her. Almost every separation ends in an embrace, and often you will see Mr. and Mrs. Penguin in the middle of doing nothing in particular suddenly get up and start making love to one another.

The egg comes as a rule within the second week after the wedding, although it may be a little later than that or even earlier. Mrs. Penguin, of course, though she may be a little surprised, is not in the least disconcerted and she knows exactly what to do with the egg, gently lowering her body on to it, so that it will be warm under her feathers. But these things require practice; the egg does not easily get into the right position and she has constantly to move it with her beak. Meanwhile, Mr. Penguin has a great deal to say. He appears to chatter constantly, doubtless extolling his own cleverness and drawing the attention of all listeners to the fact that he has had quite a lot to do with the egg. Certainly he gives advice to his wife about the proper method of sitting and the best way of getting the egg into the right position. He waggles his head as he chatters, and Mrs. Penguin, not to be outdone, waggles hers.

But Mr. Penguin, though he may talk rather a lot and may overdo his very natural pride, is quite a model in fatherhood. He takes his turn in the hatching of the egg, sitting on it as long and as frequently as his wife does, and as time goes on he as well as his wife acquires the distinctive mark of penguin parenthood—a kind of crease down the centre of the lower half of the body, in which the eggs lie among the feathers. Each parent sits for about twelve hours, at the end of which there is a little ceremony.

Whoever has been off-guard comes back to the nesting-hole after a visit to the feeding grounds, hurrying for the last ten or fifteen yards in eagerness to see that all is well. He (or it may be she) puts his head down over the edge of the hole with a peculiar shivering movement which I take to be a sign of pride and joy, and then both father and mother make a noise which may or may not tell the story of all that has happened during the day. Sometimes that part of the ceremony is repeated several times, then the sitting penguin leaves the eggs, and on the lip of the nesting-hole both penguins stand to make a further demonstration of affection which frequently ends in a rapturous kiss. But the egg must not be deserted, so the new arrival goes down into the nest and seats himself (or it may be herself); while the relieved sentry having waited for a few minutes to see that all is well, waddles off towards the sea.

Two or three days after the arrival of the first egg, there comes another; there may be a third or even a fourth, but that is rather unusual.

It is an extremely anxious time for the parents, for the chances of hatching cannot exceed sixty in a hundred, the other forty eggs being taken by the gulls and the ibis.

And then, at last, comes the outward and visible sign of the miracle which neither Mr. Penguin nor Mrs. Penguin nor you nor I can ever fully understand. A new living being appears on the earth. One minute there is an egg, smooth and inactive, only the vehicle by which that being is to come into existence; in another a crack has begun across the thick shell, and a living thing is stirring within.

Soon the crack widens and perhaps a little hole is broken in the shell—the first earthly activity of the new-comer. And at last the shell falls apart and there appears a creature which no one would know for a penguin—dark-coloured, rather skinny and extremely ugly. It is rather more like a bird than penguins are when they are fully grown—but it also bears a striking resemblance to a teddy bear.

Its brother or sister follows it into the world from one to three days later, and in a remarkably short space of time the two little birds develop and begin to show their energy.

The back portion of the nesting-hole becomes the nursery, because it is farthest from danger, and still either the father or the mother has to mount guard in the doorway, for the dangers are by no means over yet. The ibis and the gull are always active among the nesting-holes, for they take not only eggs, but also young chicks, gobbling them up as a single meal.

The two parents take equal shares—one going to the fishing grounds while the other both acts as a guard and serves the meals (if I may so express it) made from the food last collected. The chicks at this age have to be fed every twenty minutes. The parent's digestive machinery turns into oil the food that she, or he, has collected, and this oil is brought back into the beak. Then, the children's dinner having thus been prepared, the young chicks insert their own small beaks into the parent's larger beak and so draw the nourishment which they badly need.

As they grow, the space between feeding times is lengthened, until meals take place only every hour; and eventually the menu is improved, the children being now strong enough to take—still from their mother or father—small fish from which they can extract the oil for themselves.

During the time in which the young penguins "grow up," they gradually change colour, losing the appearance of dark-brown teddy bears and becoming each day more like their parents. White feathers first appear on their chests at the end of four or five weeks: then slowly the whiteness spreads while the dark feathers come on the back of the birds until at last they have all the black-and-white beauty of full-grown penguins.

Quite early in life they begin to show the curiosity about their surroundings which is one of the chief traits of penguin character. As soon as they are strong enough to reach up and peer over the top they do so. But that kind of thing, of course, is not allowed with children at such an early age. How can they, unable to walk far, and even less able to defend themselves, go out to face the dangers of the world, the beaks of the ibis and the gull? So mother or father, whichever happens to be on duty at the moment, turns and gives the young adventurers a sharp peck, to remind them that they aren't to go out into the garden without parental permission.

But the time comes eventually when Mr. Penguin decides that it is time the children learnt to look after themselves, and Mrs. Penguin, nervously, no doubt, and knowing that it is going to cause her a great deal of anxiety, agrees. Then out come the youngsters, very much pleased about it all, walking to the edge of the nesting-hole, standing on its rim and taking their first look at the outside world. They stretch their flippers, thinking doubtless that they would go farther if mother were not watching.

Still, even that comes in time, and off the little penguins go to explore, wandering among the holes of their neighbours, interested in everything. Sometimes, curiously enough, they seem to imagine that their flippers are wings and that with a little practice they could fly—like the gull and the ibis, and even the cormorants. At any rate, I have often seen young birds deliberately flapping their wings as if they were quite certain that that was the way to do it. This attempt is so frequent that it cannot, I think, be only the easing of muscles.

Perhaps it is all a legacy of former ages, an instinct remembered through centuries from the days, if there were such days, when the penguins really did fly.

Once the children have reached that important age when they are allowed to wander more or less unrestricted, they have a great deal of fun on the island. They are extremely imitative, like all children, and anything that mother and father do they want to do likewise.

They also make friends with the other children in the neighbourhood, squabbling with them and making up parties to go exploring among the rocks. Climbing is one of the things that they have got to learn, and they soon start practising among the smaller boulders, learning to grip edges of rock with their beaks.

At last the day comes when the most important lesson of all has to be learnt, and it is usually mother's job to teach it: the art, that is, of swimming.

It is odd, of course, that young penguins, being birds of the sea, should so often at first be afraid of the water. Perhaps the answer lies in history: it may well be that the earliest penguins had wings instead of flippers, so that there is an instinct of sea-hatred as well as one of sea-love. But however that may be, the fact remains that this first introduction to the water is quite often a very troublesome business. The young penguins are led or driven to the nearest rippling waves, then some start back, ready to run to their mother's sides rather than wet their feet.

But as with children, it is all a matter of perseverance. A wave comes farther in than usual, the feet that were imagined to be safe are overtaken—and the terrible-looking water is discovered to be not so terrible after all.

I don't think there are actual lessons in swimming; but there is certainly instruction, or at least an example, in diving. The mother will lower her head, put out her flippers, and disappear beneath the water—and then she will pop up a moment later and turn to see that her children have followed suit.

When at last the lesson has been learnt, and the young penguins are about three months old, a day comes when childhood is considered definitely at an end. So the family swims from the island, away out to sea, to the region of the fishing grounds: and there their parents leave them, with a little anguish, perhaps, but with thoughts already beginning to be set on the next annual adventure of a penguin's life.

GUSTAV ECKSTEIN

V

GUSTAV ECKSTEIN

*W*HEN in 1936 I received for review Gustav Eckstein's Canary, from which this selection is made, I recall that I wholly disbelieved he could interest me in his subject. What we most love in birds, the wilderness and fugitive delight of them, must ever be lacking in these cheery little domesticated immigrants. And like many another who has known a canary merely as a childhood pet, or has too often yet too heedlessly heard its loud caged song, I had decided that canaries were banal.

Then I began to read this book of Dr. Eckstein's. Minute and literal, noted in a sort of stylistic shorthand—which, since it is the English of his personal correspondence, must be the natural style of the man—these observations piled up into an exciting discovery of canaries. They populated the pages with distinct and vivid individualities, and it became impossible to resist Dr. Eckstein's own ardor for them. This is not the ardor of a sentimental pet-keeper, nor yet the impersonal enthusiasm of a strictly theoretical scientist, for Dr. Eckstein neither started to keep canaries for pets nor did he introduce them into his laboratory as specimens. They seem simply to have "happened" to him. To his own surprise, one would say, for he writes to me thus:

"Oddly, even to me, I had little to do with animals when I was a child. We lived in a densely populated part of the city, brick or stone all around, and my mother was very clean, so that having a pet would have been difficult, and there wasn't even too many in the neighborhood. I never had a dog, nor a cat, and I think that there was some feeling of fright about the wings of birds.

"It is true that Hato, the pigeon, came, or rather was thrust into my laboratory, before there was any canary. She was not with me long, about two years, when she flew away. Then came the 'persons,' one after another, that were later to make my book *Lives*. It seems unlikely, and yet it is entirely true that each entered by chance, and that, except for an occasional canary, I had never sought an animal. There has been a sick one, and I have tried to cure it. There has been a lost one, and some one has brought it, and I have let it stay. Always something like that, but that can bring you a good deal."

What it has brought him, and us through his pages, is a vivid realization of individuality within the species. Possibly life in the wild does repress individuality to some extent; certainly, birds cannot be easily studied for their particular behavior, except under laboratory conditions. The beauty of Dr. Eckstein's canaries, however, was that though they happened to inhabit a laboratory of physiology in the University of Cincinnati, they were not in cages and were not put through rigid experiments. They were at liberty to fly, sing, mate, fight, nest and in general comport themselves as they pleased. Thus their observer came as near to knowing birds at home as it is possible in this airy world to do. Perhaps one reason birds so draw us is that we can never wholly know them. But at any rate, if there is anywhere a study of the individuality of wild birds that is comparable in detail with this one of a domestic species, I have never read it.

Gustav Eckstein was born in Cincinnati in 1890, and is a doctor of medicine and of dentistry; he is an assistant professor of physiology at the University of his native city. Thus it would seem that canaries were remote to his subject. But he has brought to his fondness for them the curiosity and power to learn of a trained man of science. Another letter tells me this:

"I am not happy this morning. You remember Billie, the lame one. She was ill only since yesterday, but died in the night. Maybe she had one fall too many, though I think more likely it was her heart, she twelve years old and the effort of ordinary things always so much greater with her. She learned more than any, and you will not think it strange when I say that I myself learned enormously from her."

It is this power to learn, uncorrupted yet warmed by love of his subject, that makes of Canary a valuable though informal contribution to the study of animal behavior. That Eckstein disciplines his interest to this end is made plain when he writes:

"Latterly my unprofessional interest has become somewhat more professional. I do in the late years think of the physiology and the psychology, to use rather rigid terms for what with me began casually and only in the course of things grew somewhat exact. My idea of the right way, for me, would have been about the same, I suspect."

So he reminds us that there are other ways than the hard and well-trodden ones to get to the heart of things. Working in his laboratory, he listened to his canaries and learned about bird behavior. Singing, of course, is in our human view of it, a canary's business. Dr. Eckstein made it his, and broadens the general view of bird song. For, if scientifically trained, we have come to believe that male birds sing primarily to "proclaim territory." A bob-white whistles over a certain area, and keeps on posting his land this way until he has won his mate and often until he has seen her well through incubation. If any other male whistles in his bailiwick, the birds advance upon each other, still calling, till they meet and come to blows.

In this conventional view whistling is not then an expression of a heart full of happiness, nor is it a concert intended to charm a mate with sweet nothings. This generality is a good if rough approximation of the facts. But I think that any one who reads Dr. Eckstein's account of the various situations under which canaries sing will admit that there is more to the story than that. Song is the language of song birds, a language without words, but not without meaning. Dr. Eckstein has listened for that meaning, and translated some of it for us to understand.

CANARY

The Music Lesson

WHERE Father got his unusual musical powers I never knew. I never heard a bird like Father, and have not since. At the bird store they said he was taught by a famous tutor owned by a famous German breeder, and of course Father was born unusual. When Father planted his feet on the edge of a music book on the Steinway rack and prepared to sing, I was always able to make anybody see how much he resembled that big-bodied Belgian violinist, Ysaye, who formerly conducted the orchestra here in Cincinnati, and who also planted his feet as if he were determined to draw the melodies up through his body out of the earth.

But Father was not only an extraordinary singer. He was an extraordinary teacher too.

I never knew that a bird lesson could be that formal, or a bird teacher have such patience. Ordinarily Father taught one or two sons at a time, but more if more drifted in. He would sing their notes with them till they got them clear, perhaps three notes, then lengthen the three, sing upwards from them, sing downwards from them, and only after that start the trills. I do not mean that the lessons began with a clock and ended with a clock, or that there was a professional silence in the laboratory, or that there were not temperamental irregularities as in any healthy teaching—but the lessons were lessons, unmistakably. I do not mean either that Father taught anything essentially different from what all his ancestors taught before him, but he did what he could to keep that teaching true.

87

In the course of a lesson Father might wander off on something that interested him more as artist than as teacher, and for that he liked quiet and if he did not get quiet might lean across and give someone near him a whack.

Father because of much hearing of the piano knew things the later canaries never had the chance to learn. I had less time to play when they came—especially during that year and a half after Hinge. Father had a range of two notes over three octaves. Hinge had almost that. All the sons could sing triads and liked to. The low notes were difficult at first and would come out husky and slip about. I never tried teaching our kind of tunes, but that also would have been possible up to a point. In the best periods the male voices all modulated as fast as the piano—did not follow the melody, but changed key as the piano changed key. I say best because many things made the quality go up and down.

Right in the middle of a lesson you would see a pupil bend over, reach between his feet, nibble a bit of paper out of the music page. Hundreds of pages were so autographed. Even Father reached. But Hinge never reached. This is one of the ways Hinge differed. I sometimes used to wonder whether Hinge liked this standing in a row to take your lesson. He so often kept away, or came late, sang a few notes, hopped off. He seemed lazy, yet even to my ear it was clear he was making progress—or finding what was in him. I used to fancy that he had been so near Father, whom he could never equal, that he thought: "My father does it—so what is the use?"

The Groom

The laboratory was black after the deaths, especially after Father's, the song so much reduced. Therefore when Christmas came round again I went to the bird store and bought the canaries another bird. A Christmas present—Christmas 1931. We shall see how my good intention worked out.

The bird was a male. I called him Striped Male. He now would be the only one not born in the laboratory.

They had packed him in an ice cream carton, and all the way up the hill to the Medical College I could hear his toes fighting to get a hold on the pasteboard bottom, and once in the laboratory it was a different story from that first bird five years before. Out of his prison in a flash! Gay yellow and brown, head bristling, back arched—drum major!

I think he had the longest legs I ever saw on a canary. In a minute I knew the legs were not so long, that it was the smart-aleck's way he stood on them, also the way the belly feathers form-fitted round the belly. He tramped to the front of the Steinway, estimated the distance to my table, gambled, made it. He had not had too easy a time keeping himself in the air, yet no sooner did he land and get a fresh footing, on he continued to the sectional bookcase.

The whole population was silent.

Several were below the bookcase on the zinc-top table, eating. They stopped. He looked down on them, joined them. His diet at the bird store had not been much besides water and seeds, but that did not prevent him recognizing higher food. However, he thought best first to make sure that all this was his—without warning gave the amazed bird next him a half dozen pecks, and the one next, so on, everybody scooting to the four corners. No one had ever treated them that way before. One female with a hurt foot took a head dive to the concrete.

The table thus cleared of vermin Striped Male began nonchalantly to eat.

And this continued. When Striped Male ate egg no one ate egg. When Striped Male ate banana no one ate banana. When Striped Male thought he liked one special perch whoever was on got off. The Community did not understand him, but it behaved.

Late that first evening, an hour or two after dark, having dined a good many times and having lubricated his wings with a good many flights, he mounted to the heights of the book-closet, stepped to the edge, crashed into song. And the song was like the rest of him—shrill, over-healthy, unmusical, resembled his legs. Who the song was for, if anyone, I could not see.

The Teaching of the Lesson

Through all this Striped Male's voice still had not changed. The worst was, from my point of view, it was affecting the other voices. Canary voices are affected by anything. In the parts of the year when I am using the typewriter most, all the voices go up.

And for his private concerts Striped Male continued to mount to the heights of the book-closet, as he did that first night. The book-closet stuck like a platform out over the laboratory, and I had noticed long before this that when a male was feeling particularly male he was apt to go up there to sing. Striped Male might give eight to ten to twenty performances a day.

This was a matinee.

The program was already part over when I noticed Hinge fly to the fishpole. That put Hinge higher than Striped Male because the fishpole was higher. After a while Striped Male came to a rest in the music. He stopped, as if to clear his throat. Then he began again—and instantly Hinge began. This in itself was not unusual except for how Hinge's trill came right on top of Striped Male's trill, and except—and this was the amazing—how Hinge's exactly reproduced Striped Male's own harsh high-pitched quality. And Hinge's kept up. It kept up for as long as Striped Male's kept up, and when Striped Male's couldn't any longer, still kept up. This Hinge could do because he had big lungs by nature, and because for all his laziness I suspect he had learned considerable from

Father. Then, with great skill, Hinge dropped from Striped Male's quality down to his own, lingered on that a while too. Thumbed his nose, it seemed.

This was only the sample. In fact, had it occurred but once I would not have believed it. Every time now that Striped Male began to sing Hinge began to sing. I think there can be no question what it meant. Whoever in those days visited the laboratory thought the scene farce. I too, and I was happy besides because I believed I could once more detect a change in the Community singing—as though Hinge's lessons were bringing back a courage for the singing of the old days. But even had it only been that I was wanting this to be true, and therefore made myself think I saw signs that it was, what clinched it for me was the effect on Striped Male. That anyone could see. He had lost his dominance. He was very changed. He was as quiet as the quietest. He worried me. I tried to think it was his time for moulting, but it was not. You could see the change in his walk. His head feathers scarce ever rose up now.

All this transpired less than a year after the birth of Junior, Penguin, and Candy. Junior began to look more drum-major than his father. From Striped Male the drum-major was faded out. He would even, like one of the duller birds, go up on the window-sash and stand long periods in the sun—a sick old man taking his constitutional. His long legs looked longer. Anybody could eat egg when he ate egg. Anybody could eat banana.

Toscanini's Concert

Sundays when the New York Philharmonic would begin to come over the radio the whole spirit of the place would change. Rossini, Beethoven, Wagner, would make a happy canary program, particularly if the Beethoven happened to be the Pastorale. And that would make a happy Toscanini program also.

The radio stands against the south wall between the windows, and after a while you always believed that the orchestra was literally down in that box. This gave to the laboratory out in front of the box the feeling of having grown much bigger —of being a great hall with the singing canary audience all around the edges of the balconies of it. Hinge would be high to the back on the fishpole. Hinge always occupied the same place. Sometimes he would sing uninterruptedly through an entire concert, which meant the full two hours, because Hinge sang also through most of the intermission. There would be Sundays when there were breaks in his concentration, when he could not get his mind off some female, or some annoyance at a male, anything, but on those Sundays when his being was calm he would surpass the others to a point that made him seem another species of bird. Father, you always would decide then, had not wasted his time on Hinge in spite of Hinge's lazy ways.

As the Toscanini program mounted to its glory Hinge would show an increasing freedom. He would not look like a canary anymore. It was inspiration. A splendor would come over us all. There was something of sky and ocean—in the face of the scientists.

Below Hinge on the book-closet would be Striped Male, in his old place, from which he sang that fatal concert five years before, but no thought of equaling Hinge now, just a modest pleasure in singing along with the others. To the right of the hall on the desk might be Chicken, usually to be joined after a while by Chicken-like—much less dramatic singers but listening very carefully to what the orchestra was playing, keeping very close to it, especially Chicken who had a finer and finer voice. On the other side of the hall, on the instrument case, many Sundays the striped ones all together —Junior, Penguin, Striped Male, with the striped females on and off joining them, Junior and Penguin facing partly toward each other and partly down toward Mr. Toscanini. A tier lower than they, on the chemical bench, would be Crusty's Son, born about nine months before, with a voice already so big that you would wonder whether he might not be the off-spring of some secret pledge with Hinge. The other males would be strewn wherever they happened to alight, and there would be a good deal of changing of places during the concert, but the singers on the whole would continue in a great semicircle low on the sides and rising high to Hinge at the back, the hundred-man New York orchestra down in the bowl in front of them.

Fabulous canary singing on those fabulous Sundays. All the males would sing, often a female. Once Striped Daughter sang through half a concert. It was that heavenly afternoon when great Toscanini played the Ninth Symphony—took Schola Cantorum, Metropolitan soloists, Philharmonic Society, wrenched them out of themselves, or back into themselves, I do not know which, but for that hour made them into something that you did not remember them to have been, something diabolic and mad that cracked the dark and let us who were listening see the outlines of Beethoven and, I feel, even the outlines of God.

And this canary singing was not speech, not love-making, not the inexorable path of sexual selection. No, these tiny birds with their tiny voices on those Sunday afternoons came very near to man's own high conception of art for art's sake, song for song's sake, the creation of impersonal beauty.

Lovely and young, out in front of everybody, on the jutting tip of the first tree, quietly, often keeping the same place through the two hours, never a thought of singing, in her brilliant yellow dress—Candy.

PETER KALM

VI

PETER KALM

$\mathcal{C}$HE Linnaean age, which began two hundred years ago, was an epoch in science when the naturalists of Europe were ready and eager to investigate the nature of the ends of the earth. Commerce had opened the road into Asia, there was light even from the Dark Continent, Australia yielded its first fruits to natural history. And, from pole to pole, across the tropics, stretched the two Americas, a great bestiary of unique treasures still largely unknown to science.

What Linnaeus did for plants, Ray and Latham were doing for the classification of birds. Buffon struggled with his ornithological life histories, and Brisson took up comparative anatomy where it had been dropped from the hand of murdered Belon two centuries before.

Corresponding to this golden age at home was the rise of purely scientific exploration, a new thing in the history of travel. In quest of birds Sonnerat was off to the Indies, Osbeck to China, Pallas over the vast dominions of the Tsar; Forster voyaged round the world with Captain Cook, Richardson to the arctic with Sir John Franklin, and Le Vaillant got into the antipodean world of South Africa.

Only one of the great scientific explorers of the time, Peter Kalm, turned his attention to temperate North America. To do so was Linnaeus's idea, obediently executed by his pupil with business-like precision.

Europe was not unaware of American bird life, but knew it only through dead specimens, or the domesticated turkey or caged songsters like the mockingbird and cardinal. Or it heard reports, which became garbled or grossly superstitious, through early travelers like Mark Catesby or John Lawson. It knew of the exquisite hummingbird, the smallest and most brilliant of all feathered creatures, and the torrential storms of the passenger pigeon. It had heard, but only at third hand, of the ghostly whippoorwill who cries out so strangely on the twilight. Species had been described from skins and feathers, by Forster and Latham. It remained for an honest and a trained scientist to set foot upon these shores and speak, as a modern speaks, of its great avifauna.

Pehr Kalm (to use his real name) was born in 1716 in Angermanland, Sweden, the son of a Finnish clergyman. He was destined for the church and deeply attracted by it; religion seems to have consumed all the emotional side of his nature; otherwise he was reasonable, logical, and precise to a fault, a young man with a very practical turn of mind. At the University of Åbo he fell under the influence of the naturalist Bishop Brovallius who taught him all he knew and then sent him to Linnaeus at Upsala.

Kalm's interests in natural history were catholic, though his specialty was economic botany. His conception of his mission in America was to collect plants and animals which could be naturalized for use in Europe. So in his passage on the grackle we note how he stressed its damage to crops. His writings gain an almost modern flavor from his attention to the food relations, life habits, and economic significance of birds.

Kalm arrived in Philadelphia in 1748 with an assistant, and for almost two years traveled extensively from Delaware to Quebec, and New York to Niagara (then in the wilderness). He was deeply interested in the vocal organs of the bull-frog, the pouch of the opossum, the light of the firefly, the constricting of the blacksnake, the venom of the Jersey mosquito, and the singular history of the seventeen-year cicada. His descriptions of American trees and flowers of the Appalachian zone were enthusiastic, and it is pleasant to record of one blossom, the mountain laurel, that Linnaeus named it *Kalmia* in his honor.

Kalm made the acquaintance of Benjamin Franklin and his learned friends. He was thus armed with a respectable body of opinion about New World Nature, and resists the hair-raising myths with which he was regaled by others. In a bewildering world of new forms he makes no real mistakes, hews to the important and in all ways does credit to his great teacher.

The pastor of the Swedish colony at Raccoon, New Jersey, having died, Kalm married his widow, so that his American journey in every way crowned his life.

Returned to Finland, Kalm labored diligently to grow his American plants and to prepare his notes and diary for the press. They were published in 1753 and appeared in English translation in 1760, edited by Forster, under the title *Travels into North America*. From this work, selections are here made. By all odds it is the most worthy account of American natural history up to that time. Kalm was a straightforward but not a poetic writer. His almost dry precision is undoubtedly part of his character, and it has a charm of its own that is quite eighteenth century. Romanticism, with all its color, we must not expect of him or his age. Yet, useless though grackle and hummingbird and whippoorwill must have seemed to his practical nature, we find that he cannot resist the magical spell of American birds. Despite his great sobriety, he finds himself describing sights and sounds because he cannot forget them.

Kalm, honored and highly placed at the University of Åbo, passed the rest of his life in scholarly tranquillity, and became at last an ordained Lutheran clergyman.

But probing history has unearthed a trace of a long-cherished project to return to the western world; Kalm seems to have proposed the plan to Linnaeus, but it never bore fruit.

Yet he longed, sometimes, it would seem, to see the sugar maples blaze in glory, to smell the honeyed azalea flowers again, to hear the cardinals and scarlet tanagers whistle, and the axes of the pioneers ringing at the trunks of hickory and balsam.

RUBY-THROATED HUMMINGBIRD

O F ALL the rare birds of North America, the humming-bird is the most admirable, or at least most worthy of peculiar attention. Several reasons induce me to believe that few parts of the world can produce its equal. Dr. Linnaeus calls it trochilus colubris. The Swedes, and some Englishmen, call it the king's bird; but the name of humming-bird is more common. Catesby, in his Natural History of Carolina, vol. i. page 65. tab. 65. has drawn it, in its natural size, with its proper colours, and added a description of it. In size it is not much bigger than a large bumble-bee,* and is therefore the smallest of all birds. It is doubtful if there is a lesser species in the world. Its plumage is most beautifully coloured, most of its feathers being green, some grey, and others forming a shining red ring round its neck; the tail glows with fine feathers, changing from green into a brass colour. These birds come here in spring, about the time when it begins to grow very warm, and make their nests in summer; but, towards autumn, they retreat again into the more southern countries of America. They subsist barely upon the nectar, or sweet juice of flowers, contained in that part which botanists call the nectarium, and which they suck up with their long bills. Of all the flowers, they like those most, which have a long tube; and I have observed that they have fluttered chiefly about the impatiens noli tangere, and the monarda with crimson flowers. An inhabitant of the country is sure to have a number of these beautiful and agreeable little birds before his windows all the summer long, if he takes care to plant a bed with all sorts of fine flowers under them. It is indeed a diverting spectacle to see these little

* Kalm underestimates its size. [Ed.]

active creatures flying about the flowers like bees, and sucking their juices with their long and narrow bills. The flowers
of the above-mentioned monarda grow verticillated, that is,
at different distances they surround the stalk, as the flowers
of our mint (mentha), bastard hemp (galeopsis), mother-
wort (leonurus), and dead nettle (lamium). It is therefore
diverting to see them putting their bills into every flower in
the circle. As soon as they have sucked the juice of one flower,
they flutter to the next. One that has not seen them would
hardly believe in how short a space of time they have had
their tongues in all the flowers of a plant, which when large,
and with a long tube, the little bird, by putting its head into
them, looks as if it crept with half its body into them.

During their sucking the juice out of the flowers they never
settle on it, but flutter continually like bees, bend their feet
backwards, and move their wings so quick that they are hardly
visible. During this fluttering they make a humming like bees,
or like that which is occasioned by the turning of a little
wheel. After they have thus, without resting, fluttered for a
while, they fly to a neighbouring tree or post, and resume
their vigour again. They then return to their humming and
sucking. They are not very shy; and I, in company with several other people, have not been full two yards from the place
where they fluttered about and sucked the flowers; and though
we spoke and moved, yet they were no ways disturbed; but,
on going towards them, they would fly off with the swiftness
of an arrow. When several of them were on the same bed
there was always a violent combat between them, in meeting
each other at the same flower (for envy was likewise predom-
inant amongst these little creatures), and they attacked with
such impetuosity that it would seem as if the strongest would
pierce its antagonist through and through with its long bill.
During the fight, they seem to stand in the air, keeping themselves up by the incredibly swift motion of their wings. When

the windows towards the garden are open, they pursue each
other into the rooms, fight a little, and flutter away again.
Sometimes they come to a flower which is withering, and
has no more juice in it; they then, in a fit of anger, pluck it
off, and throw it on the ground, that it may not mislead them
for the future. If a garden contains a great number of these
little birds, they are seen to pluck off the flowers in such
quantities that the ground is quite covered with them, and it
seems as if this proceeded from a motion of envy.

Commonly you hear no other sound than their humming;
but when they fly against each other in the air, they make a
chirping noise like a sparrow or chicken. I have sometimes
walked with several other people in small gardens, and these
birds have on all sides fluttered about us without appearing
very shy. They are so small that one would easily mistake
them for great humming-bees or butterflies, and their flight
resembles that of the former, and is incredibly swift. They
have never been observed to feed on insects or fruit; the
nectar of flowers seems therefore to be their only food. Several people have caught some humming-birds, on account of
their singular beauty, and have put them into cages, where
they died for want of proper food. However, Mr. Bartram
has kept a couple of them for several weeks together, by feeding them with water in which sugar had been dissolved; and
I am of opinion that it would not be difficult to keep them
all winter in a hot-house.

The humming-bird always builds its nest in the middle of
a branch of a tree, and it is so small that it cannot be seen
from the ground, but he who intends to see it must get up
to the branch. For this reason it is looked upon as a great
rarity if a nest is accidentally found, especially as the trees in
summer have so thick a foliage. The nest is likewise the least
of all; that which is in my possession is quite round, and
consists in the inside of a brownish and quite soft down,

which seems to have been collected from the leaves of the great mullein or verbascum thapsus, which are often found covered with a soft wool of this colour, and the plant is plentiful here. The outside of the nest has a coating of green moss, such as is common on old pales, or enclosures, and on trees; the inner diameter of the nest is hardly a geometrical inch at the top, and its depth half an inch. It is however known, that the humming-birds make their nests likewise of flax, hemp, moss, hair, and other such soft materials; they are said to lay two eggs, each of the size of a pea.

PURPLE GRACKLE

A SPECIES of birds, called by the Swedes maize-thieves, do the greatest mischief in this country. They have given them that name because they eat maize both publicly and secretly, just after it is sown and covered with the ground, and when it is ripe. The English call them black-birds. There are two species of them, both described and drawn by Catesby. Though they are very different in species, yet there is so great a friendship between them, that they frequently accompany each other in mixed flocks. However, in Pennsylvania, the first sort are more obvious, and often fly together, without any of the red-winged stares. The first sort, or the purple daws, bear, in many points, so great a likeness to the daw, the stare, and the thrush, that it is difficult to determine to which genus they are to be reckoned, but seem to come nearest to the stare; for the bill is exactly the same with that of the thrush, but the tongue, the flight, their sitting on the trees, their song, and shape, make it entirely a stare; at a distance they look almost black, but close by they have a very blue or purple cast. The iris of the eyes is pale: the forehead, the crown, the nucha, the upper part, and the sides of the neck, are of an obscure blue and green shining colour: the sides of the head under the eyes are obscurely blue; all the back and coverts of the wings are purple. The throat is blueish green, and shining; the breast is likewise black or shining green, according as you turn it to the light; the belly is blackish, and the vent feathers are obscurely purple-coloured; the parts of the breast and belly which are covered by the wings, are purple-coloured; the wings are black below, or rather sooty; and the thighs have blackish feathers. Dr. Linnaeus calls this bird gracula quiscula.

A few of these birds are said to winter in swamps, which are quite overgrown with thick woods; and they only appear in mild weather. But the greatest number go to the south at the approach of winter. To-day I saw them, for the first time this year. They flew in great flocks already. Their chief and most agreeable food is maize. They come in great swarms in spring, soon after the maize is put under ground. They scratch up the grains of maize, and eat them. As soon as the leaf comes out, they take hold of it with their bills, and pluck it up, together with the corn or grain; and thus they give a great deal of trouble to the country people, even so early in spring. To lessen their greediness of maize, some people dip the grains of that plant in a decoction of the root of the veratrum album, or white hellebore, and plant them afterwards. When the maize-thief eats a grain or two, which are so prepared, his head is disordered, and he falls down: this frightens his companions, and they dare not venture to the place again. But they repay themselves amply towards autumn, when the maize grows ripe; for at that time, they are continually feasting. They assemble by thousands in the maize-fields, and live at discretion. They are very bold; for when they are disturbed, they only go and settle in another part of the field. In that manner they always go from one end of the field to the other, and do not leave it till they are quite satisfied. They fly in incredible swarms in autumn; and it can hardly be conceived whence such immense numbers of them should come. When they rise in the air they darken the sky, and make it look quite black. They are then in such great numbers, and so close together, that it is surprising how they find room to move their wings. I have known a person shoot a great number of them on one side of a maize-field, which was far from frightening the rest; for they only just took flight and dropped at about the distance of a musket-shot in another part of the field, and always changed their

place when their enemy approached. They tired the sportsman before he could drive them from off the maize, though
he killed a great many of them at every shot. They likewise
eat the seeds of the aquatic tare-grass (zizania aquatica) commonly late in autumn, after the maize is got in. In spring
they sit in numbers on the trees, near the farms; and their
note is pretty agreeable. As they are so destructive to maize,
the odium of the inhabitants against them is carried so far,
that the laws of Pennsylvania and New Jersey have settled a
premium of threepence a dozen for dead maize-thieves. In
New England, the people are still greater enemies to them;
for Dr. Franklin told me, in the spring of the year 1750, that,
by means of the premiums, which have been settled for killing them in New England, they have been so extirpated, that
they are very rarely seen, and in a few places only. But as, in
the summer of the year 1749, an immense quantity of worms
appeared on the meadows, which devoured the grass, and did
great damage, the people have abated their enmity against
the maize-thieves; for they thought they had observed, that
those birds lived chiefly on these worms before the maize is
ripe, and consequently extirpated them, or at least prevented
their spreading too much. They seem therefore to be entitled, as it were, to a reward for their trouble. But after these
enemies and destroyers of the worms (the maize-thieves) were
extirpated, the worms were more at liberty to multiply; and
therefore they grew so numerous that they did more mischief
now than the birds did before. In the summer 1749, the
worms left so little hay in New England that the inhabitants
were forced to get hay from Pennsylvania and even from Old
England. The maize-thieves have enemies besides the human
species. A species of little hawks live upon them, and upon
other little birds. I saw some of these hawks driving up the
maize-thieves, which were in the greatest security, and catching them in the air. Nobody eats the flesh of the purple

maize-thieves or daws (gracula quiscula); but that of the red-winged maize-thieves, or stares (oriolus phoeniceus) is sometimes eaten. Some old people have told me that this part of America, formerly called New Sweden, still contained as many maize-thieves as it did formerly. The cause of this they derive from the maize, which is now sown in much greater quantity than formerly; and they think that the birds can get their food with more ease at present.

WHIPPOORWILL

April 22d. The Swedes give the name of whipperiwill, and the English that of whip-poor-will, to a kind of nocturnal bird, whose voice is heard in North America, almost throughout the whole night. Catesby and Edwards both have described and figured it. Dr. Linnaeus calls it a variety of the caprimulgus Europæus, or goat-sucker: its shape, colour, size, and other qualities make it difficult to distinguish them from each other; but the peculiar note of the American one distinguishes it from the European one, and from all other birds: it is not found here during winter, but returns with the beginning of summer. I heard it to-day, for the first time, and many other people said that they had not heard it before this summer; its English and Swedish name is taken from its note; but, accurately speaking, it does not call whipperiwill, nor whip-poor-will, but rather whipperiwip, so that the first and last syllables are accented, and the intermediate ones but slightly pronounced. The English change the call of this bird into whip-poor-will, that it may have some kind of signification: it is neither heard nor seen in day-time; but soon after sun-set, it begins to call, and continues for a good while, as the cuckoo does in Europe. After it has continued calling in a place for some time, it removes to another, and begins again: it usually comes several times in a night, and settles close to the house; I have seen it coming late in the evening, and settling on the steps of the house in order to sing its song; it is very shy, and when a person stood still, it would settle close by him, and begin to call. It came to the houses in order to get its food, which consists of insects; and those always abound near the houses at night; when it sat and called its whipperiwhip, and saw an insect passing, it flew up

and caught it, and settled again. Sometimes you hear four or
five, or more, near each other, calling as it were for a wager,
and raising a great noise in the woods. They were seldom
heard in towns, being either extirpated there, or frightened
away, by frequent shooting. They do not like to sit on trees,
but are commonly on the ground, or very low in bushes, or
on the lower poles of the enclosures; they always fly near the
ground; they continue their calling at night till it grows quite
dark; they are silent till the dawn of day comes on, and then
they call till the sun rises. The sun seems to stop their mouths,
or dazzle their eyes, so as to make them sit still. I have never
heard them call in the midst of night, though I have heark-
ened very attentively on purpose to hear it, and many others
have done the same. I am told they make no nest, but lay
two eggs in the open fields. My servant shot at one which
sat on a bush near the house, and though he did not hit it,
yet it fell down through fear, and lay for some time as if dead,
but recovered afterwards. It never attempted to bite when
it was held in the hands, only endeavouring to get loose by
stirring itself about. Above, and close under the eyes, were
several black, long, and stiff bristles, as in other nocturnal
birds. The Europeans eat it. Mr. Catesby says, the Indians
affirm, that they never saw these birds, or heard of them,
before a certain great battle, in which the Europeans killed
a great number of Indians. Therefore, they suppose that these
birds, which are restless, and utter their plaintive note at
night, are the souls of their ancestors who died in battle.

THE COUNT DE BUFFON

VII

THE COUNT DE BUFFON

*B*UFFON was one of the few truly *magnificent* personalities in science. He was the court zoögrapher to Louis XV, nobly born, personally handsome, proud, imperious, a complete man of the world, unable to endure criticism—everything that a zoölogist is almost never. Yet there is no denying his talents as a scientist, talents that rose at times, through the boldness and originality of his speculations, to those of some pioneering genius. Add to this a superhuman industry, the most superb facilities for carrying out his project of writing what was practically the Book of Everything, and great polish and charm as a stylist, and it is no wonder that he was recognized as the foremost writer on natural history in his century.

His contemporaries and some of his later countrymen have acknowledged him as something more. Geoffroy Saint-Hilaire believed Buffon an immortal genius, Rousseau threw himself down and kissed the threshold of Buffon's door, Mirabeau thought him the greatest man of many centuries, Cuvier modeled himself on Buffon (though he was a much better scientist than his model) and Saint-Beuve, of all aloof critics, praised Buffon's description of the swan as one of the finest specimens of French prose (though it is almost certain that de Montbéliard ghost-wrote the swan).

And, withal, Buffon is today more often mentioned than read. His encyclopedic *Natural History* is owned by almost every museum and great library, and yet it is seldom consulted as an authority, and cited chiefly as of historical interest only.

Behind such a downfall lies a story.

George Louis Leclerc, Comte de Buffon, was born in 1707 in the family château at Montbard, in Burgundy. He early showed a marked talent for physics and mathematics, and it is quite likely that the exact sciences, and not zoölogy, were his true calling. But owing to his winning personality, his high birth, and the many-faceted genius he so obviously possessed, he attained at the age of thirty-seven to the appointment of Intendant of the Jardin Du Roi and the Royal Museum. This placed him in possession of a magnificent collection of specimens, living and otherwise, of a great library, and at the head of a corps of naturalists. He improved these opportunities by beginning his *Histoire Naturelle*, intended to embrace the whole kingdom of Nature, from a glow-worm to a star, though botany was omitted or never reached owing to Buffon's distaste for the subject.

Buffon had complained, with justice, of his rival Linnaeus that the Linnaean system, though it clapped two Latin names on everything, adequately described nothing, was dull and repellent, and barren of any implication of the inter-relationships of life and the universe it inhabits. This deficiency Buffon proposed to correct by discoursing as *fully*, not as concisely, as possible, the length of the treatment to be proportional to the subject's importance to man. To his service Buffon could summon the best anatomists, artists, and printers, and he devoted his own life and all his sumptuous style to the undertaking. The first volume appeared in 1749 and the work continued for fifty years—beyond Buffon's lifetime, indeed, up to forty-four volumes.

Thus the conception of the *Histoire Naturelle* was magnificent, and would have been enough to make its editor renowned in any case. But the task was Herculean; we see as we read how weary Buffon grew of it.

At first he set about his labors with great zeal. As his anatomist to do dissections and draw up scientific descriptions, he had the gifted ornithologist Daubenton. Buffon supplied the library research, the synthesis of all the facts, the life histories, comment, and style. As long as he was treating of the nobler beasts or of the birds of Europe for which he had evident feeling, Buffon got off splendidly.

But only hearsay and derivation from others' writings could supply him with materials for foreign species, and small fry in all phyla he disdained as trivial vermin. Consequently, all the showier and easier parts of the work having come first (for he did not always take them up in a systematist's order, but in order of their importance in his judgment) he was put to it to sustain, unflagging, a sky-high reputation for saying fascinating things in the most resounding manner. By forcing his voice he wearied it beyond endurance, and came to lean upon one set of collaborators after another. Some mastered completely the trick of imitating the editor's style; others did purely mechanical work. By quarreling with Daubenton, Buffon lost a valuable scientific ally. Gradually the repute of the volumes fell off, to be refreshed from time to time as new talent was imported, or as the old master would revive for a while and suddenly do brilliant work again.

The volumes on birds were not reached for publication in their turn until 1770-1773, thirty-four years after the commencement. This does not mean, however, that the nightingale, which I have chosen for quotation, was not written many years before. The species would have been easily disposed of at the start, and there is every internal evidence from the style that it is Buffon's own work, and belongs to the height of his powers. Nor is it likely that he would have allowed any one else to touch the *diva* among birds!

To modern minds the most promising moment in Buffon's career was when, in one of his volumes, he startled the world by announcing a theory of evolution. It is stated with the utmost originality and boldness of speculation (though he never had any idea how to assemble facts in proof), and would raise him to a foremost pinnacle in science if he had not succumbed so abjectly to the outraged clergy of the University of Paris. He was under no medieval threat of torture and death; no censure they could have brought to bear could have jeopardized so powerful and wealthy a noble. Yet he published a complete retraction of his theories, and the following year was elected to the Académie Française. It would seem that he purchased this honor at the cost of his scientific honor. As his contemporaries did not believe in evolution, however, they were less critical of his action.

But in the meantime Buffon was embroiled with other difficulties. He had criticised Linnaeus' *Systema* bitterly and not without justice. But it appeared that his animosity was due to want of system in his own mind; in the end he had to come around to binomial nomenclature. Fellow scientists pointed out many errors in the *Histoire Naturelle*, but Buffon had not learned that a scientist can only save himself from criticism by admitting mistakes frankly and correcting them at once. He would admit nothing and change nothing.

Finally he went on the rocks over spontaneous generation, in which he superstitiously believed, although the times were getting late for that. Spallanzani, in experiment after experiment, simply demolished Buffon, who should have welcomed any proof of the truth and embraced it gladly.

So that is why science today does not join in the ecstatics of Buffon's one-time admirers. He is still reckoned a great man in his age, but not a timeless genius. No one, however, denies to Buffon his position as a stylist of Nature writing. At his best, and the passage of the nightingale is his best on the subject of birds, he was a master. The style is magniloquent, but we must not ask it to be otherwise; the translator must not tone it down, and the modern reader must not be embarrassed for Buffon. As Buffon himself said, "*Le style, c'est l'homme."*

I was the happier to translate Buffon's nightingale because the bird is one about which people all over the world feel the liveliest curiosity, yet I was unable to find in English any wholly satisfactory description of it—the poets aside. It must be that English ornithologists find that the poets have said it all, or the nightingale has left them speechless or, as I seem to divine, they are tired of hearing it praised while many other interesting fine birds go unpraised. Many writers belittle it, some are even quite hostile.

Yet in the British colonies, in America, the nightingale is the one European bird, except the skylark, that every descendant of the Mother Country longs to hear. John Burroughs went to England especially to hear it, arrived too late, and caught about five minutes of disjointed song altogether. Our excellent Dr. Frank Chapman, better qualified to find the bird, heard more of its song but gives us no very definite impression.

If I may be permitted to give my own, I may say, after hearing it for six consecutive years, that the nightingale's is the most magical, vivid, and varied voice known to me in the world of birds, nor can I conceive any other equal to it. I was never able to sleep when it sang, but would prop myself up on my elbow, though nodding with weariness, drinking in every note, until the song would be "buried deep in the next valley glades."

I do not deny the force of association; Keats and Matthew Arnold and Swinburne, the beautiful nightingale passage in the *Pastoral Symphony*, the Greek legends, the sense of history, of lovers, the spell of moonlit Mediterranean nights, all had their effect. But do we divorce any bird from its associations? When we think of eagles, sea gulls, stormy petrels, albatrosses, condors, ravens, doves, associations cluster thick about them and need not be blown away. Birds about which we have not collected at least some personal associations possess but little charm for us, however much we may be interested in them ornithologically. And I am only discussing here the beauty of the nightingale's song.

But I do deny what Shakespeare says, that the nightingale, if it should sing by day, would sound no better a musician than a wren. Nightingales sing constantly by day at the height of the breeding season. And though the effect is jarred by many mechanical sounds, and the performance interrupted by all sorts of birds, the nightingale is still the finest. The effect is altered, however. It is the truer one of cheery rapture and typical bird boldness, the intention to sing down everybody else in hearing.

If I must make a comparison with the birds of my own country, I would say that the nightingale has all the brilliance, dash, carrying power and versatility of the mockingbird. But the effect is not saucy. The piercing nostalgia of the tones is more like our white-throat sparrow's. The typical song mounts chromatically up and up into regions where it is obvious that the bird cannot clear a higher note—when, with effortless ease it soars serenely into realms of pitch that bring a gasp of astonishment from the listener. Contrary to Buffon's statement, it seems to me that the bird has a tremendous range, for the second part of the usual song is a descending cascade to a very deep slow warble, a note lower than any singing bird I know possesses.

I should add to my comparisons that the song of the nightingale is delivered, like our hermit thrush's, in separate melodic statements, with long pauses between. It is in these musical "rests" that the mind has time to dwell on the beauty of the foregoing, while, in expectation of the next phrase, no listener but will hold his breath with reverent excitement.

The true nightingale does not, according to Newton's *Dictionary of Birds*, occur in Scotland, Ireland, Wales, northern and western England, or peninsular Brittany, and references to it from those countries must intend some other bird. Nightingales have often been released in America. But it is seldom possible to naturalize a migratory insect-eating bird, and the only success in our country has been the freeing of nightingales in Florida in a vast outdoor aviary.

THE NIGHTINGALE

CHERE can be no properly constituted man to whom the name of the nightingale does not recall one of those beautiful spring evenings when, the night sky serene and clear, the air tranquil, and all nature silenced and listening, he has harkened, ravished, to the canticle of this woodland songster. One might name many another song bird whose voice rivals in some way the nightingale's—skylark and canary, chaffinch and warbler, linnet and goldfinch, blackbird and missel thrush, and the mockingbird of America; each is heard with admiration—as long as the nightingale is silent. Some have qualities as rich, others a timbre as pure and sweet, and others still an ear-flattering warble. But there is not one of them which our nightingale cannot shame, for it unites all these divers talents, and the variety of its repertoire is prodigious. So that the whole range of other birds' gifts is but as a couplet compared to the nightingale's ode.

The nightingale charms us, night after night, repeating itself never, or never in servile fashion, and should it re-state one passage, this is always given fresh brilliance by some delicate change of accent, embellished with new figures. In every mode the nightingale is master, and it can express all moods, it impersonates all rôles, and like a skillful artist knows how to heighten effect by contrast. This leader of spring's chorus carefully rehearses its part at Nature's psalmist. With a timid prelude it opens its song, in slender tones that are almost indecisive, as if it would try out its instrument and inveigle its listeners.

But soon gaining assurance, by degrees the song growing more lively, it warms to its performance and at last deploys the full powers and resources of its incomparable organ. Vi-

brant, fluting tones; light swift pluckings of the strings; bursts
of song, the clarity as astounding as the volubility; muted
murmurs, as to itself, that our ears scarce appreciate, yet
perfectly attuned to heighten the contrast of the more audible
tones; sudden trills, brilliant yet rapid, announced with decision and force and withal the most exquisite taste; plaintive
accents gently timed; tones drawn artlessly out yet swelling
with the swelling soul of the performers; enchanting, pene-
trant sounds; the true sighs of love and desire that seem to
issue from the very heart and to cause all hearts to throb
with it, awakening in every receptive listener the same sweet
tenderness, the same beseeching languorousness. It is in these
impassioned utterances that we recognize the very language of
the bridegroom's rapture in his possessed beloved, a rapture
such as only the beloved mate can inspire. Yet other phrases,
even more astounding, seem only designed to amuse or please
her passingly, or even merely to dispute, as with a prize song,
her judgment amid the rivals jealous of his glory and happiness.

These various phrases are spaced out with silence, those
rests that in every sort of melody underscore so tellingly the
grandest musical effects. In them one enjoys the lovely passage one has just heard, which still rings in the ears, and
enjoys it the more since the enjoyment is more intimate,
more contemplative, and is not troubled by a crowding of
fresh impressions upon the senses. This rest makes one more
expectant, yearning for the theme to be taken up once more.
One hopes that it will be a repetition of the passage that
has just flattered the ear. But even if one should be disappointed, the enchantment of the new melodic sentence for-
bids one to regret the older variation. And still the hope of
some repetition captivates the attentive listener.

More; it is because, as the Englishman Daines Barrington

so well points out,* our bird lifts his voice in favoring darkness, that we invariably attend up on it. Then that voice in all its brilliance is no whit obscured by any other. All others it simply effaces by its soft and fluting tones and by the long duration—often twenty seconds—of a single trill. The same observer distinguished in a single breath sixteen different melodic passages, each clearly set off by its opening and closing notes. And these the bird knew how to vary with artless taste by intermediary notes. Finally, he determined that the audible circle of a nightingale's voice is a mile in diameter, provided that the air be calm. That is at least the equal of the carrying power of the human voice.

It is astounding that so small a bird, weighing but a half-ounce, should have such powerful vocal organs. Mr. Hunter also observes that the muscles of the larynx or windpipe are stronger in proportion in this species than in any other bird, and stronger in the male, who is the singer, than in the silent female.

The nightingale's song begins in the normal course in April and is not over until the month of June, about the midsummer solstice. But the season of true song diminishes greatly as soon as the young begin to hatch. For the birds are then preoccupied in caring for and nourishing the offspring, since in the order of instincts Nature gives first place to the preservation of the race.

But the caged nightingales continue to sing for nine or ten months and their song is not only of longer duration, but is more perfect and well formed. From this Barrington wisely and truly draws the conclusion that in this species, as in so many other cases, the male does not sing to amuse the female or keep her content at incubation. The female, indeed, sits on the eggs out of a passion greater than the passion of love;

* A reference, undoubtedly, to Barrington's *Observations on the Singing of Birds*. [Ed.]

she takes internal satisfactions in this obedience to instinct
of which we can scarcely form a notion; but we can see how
keenly she feels them and we can hardly suppose that she is
in need of consolation. So as it is neither from any virtue of
love or duty that the female sits the eggs, there is no need
wherefrom the male should sing to her then. Indeed, during
the second nesting he sings not at all. With him it is love,
and above all, the first stages of his desire that inspire his
song. The need to sing and the hungers of love are vernal
affairs. It is the males who have the active part in the passion
of love; it is they who sing. They sing the greater part of the
year, if one knows how to make a sort of perpetual spring to
reign about them such as will constantly renew their ardors
without giving them any occasion to quench them. Here is
what happens to birds kept in a cage or those taken as adults.
Some are known which begin to sing with all their powers
but a few hours after capture. So that they must be well-
nigh insensible to the loss of their liberty, especially at first;
they would let themselves die of hunger in seven or eight
days if food were not put in the beak, and they would break
their heads against the cage, were their wings not secured;
but in the end the passion of song carries them away. The
songs of other birds, the sound of a viol, even the tones of
the human voice, if ringing and sonorous, instantly excite
them. They rush to the sides of the cage, drawn, stirred, listening. Duets seem especially to please them and they are sen-
sible to the effect of harmony. Nor are they silent auditors.
They join in and spare no effect to outsing the rival music,
as if they would drown out every voice and every other noise.
It is even claimed that they have been seen to fall dead at
the foot of someone singing. Another bird was observed, every
time a canary felt disposed to lift his voice, to swell its throat
and twitter with rage. This had the effect in the end of
silencing the overawed canary. So true is it that even acknowl-

edged superority is not above harboring jealousy.

All nightingales are not equally gifted artists. Fanciers distinguish and avoid what are clearly mediocre talents. Some even believe that the nightingales of one country do not sing as well as another. The connoisseurs of England prefer those of Surrey, for instance, to those of Middlesex. But it were difficult to assign valid reasons to such differences, since they are no more than accidental.

No sooner has June gone than the nightingale is finally silent. Of its voice there remains only a squawk, a sort of croaking in which none would recognize the melodious Philomel! It is not surprising that, in other days, in Italy they gave it another name, in this circumstance; it is withal another bird, an absolutely different bird, at least as to its voice, and a little in respect to the colors of its plumage.

Among nightingales, as in the case of many another bird, there are found sometimes females who have enough of the male in them to be rated as singers. I saw one of these singing females which was tame. Her warbling was quite of the male order, though it was not quite so strong or varied. She kept this unnatural talent until spring. Then abruptly she subordinated the exercise of this talent which was so foreign to her, to the true functions of her sex. She then fell silent and devoted herself to constructing her nest and to egg laying, although she had no mate. It seems that in the hot countries such as Greece it is a matter of common occurrence to encounter these singing hen birds both in this species and in many others. That at least is what one infers from a passage in Aristotle.

A musician, says Frisch, ought to study a nightingale's song. This is just what a Jesuit named Kircher actually did in his Musurgia and the same project tempted Barrington. But in the opinion of the latter, no attempt has been successful. Though the melodies were carefully written out in musical notation and then executed by the most skillful flute player, the result did not in the least resemble a nightingale's song.

Barrington suspects that the difficulty arises from the circumstances that one can scarcely appreciate the relative duration or value of each note.

It would scarcely be easy to determine the musical measure that the nightingale follows when it sings, or to capture the rhythm so varied in its movement, so delicately modulated in its transitions, so free in its progressions, so independent of all our conventional rules and thereby the more appropriate to this wild musician—in a word, a song made to be vividly felt by a delicate organ and not to be beaten out by a baton in an orchestral clash of sound. But it would seem to me to be even more difficult to imitate with any lifeless instrument the tones of a nightingale, its accents so full of soul and life, its warbled passages, its expressions and sighs.

To reproduce a nightingale's voice only some living instrument would serve, and that of a rare perfection, a ringing tone harmonious and light, a pure timbre, soft and yet brilliant; a vocal instrument of the utmost flexibility, and all this must be guided by a true ear supported by an infallible tact and an exquisite sensibility. Those, then, are the instruments with which one might render a nightingale's song.

I have encountered two persons who had never annotated a single passage, who were yet able to imitate it down to the last detail and in such a manner as to create the complete illusion. They were two men who whistled, rather than sang. One of them whistled so naturally that one could not distinguish from the lips, whether it was the performer or some neighbor to whom one was listening. The other whistled with more obvious effort, and was practically forced to take a constrained attitude, but as for the effect it was not less perfect. And not many years ago in London could be heard a man who, by his imitation, knew how to attract nightingales so

that they came and perched on him and allowed him to take
them in his hand.

Since so few can make the nightingale's song their own
by such a faithful imitation, and since everyone is eager to
enjoy that song, some have tried to possess it by the simpler
expedient of making themselves masters of the bird itself in
domesticating it. But as a domestic it is given to whimsical
moods. It renders service only if its character is humored.
Love and joy cannot be ordered at a command, still less the
songs that they inspire. To make a captive nightingale sing,
it must be accorded kind treatment in its prison; the walls
must be painted the color of its thickets; the cage must be
shaded by leaves, and moss spread beneath its feet. It must
be sheltered from cold and importunate visitors, and given
plenty of its preferred nourishment.

In a word, its captivity must be disguised as far as possible.
Under these conditions the nightingale will sing in its cage.
If it be an older bird, taken early in the spring, it will begin
to sing within eight days at the latest. Every year, in May
and December, it will begin again its song. But if they are
young, of the first laying, brought up with the feeding stick,
they will commence to twitter as soon as they can feed themselves. By degrees their voices will rise and take form; they
will be in full voice by the end of December, and will exercise their powers all year around save during the molt. These
sing far better than the wild birds. They embellish their natural song with all the figures that please them in the songs
of other birds that they are caused to hear and of all those
that inspire them with a desire to surpass them. If one has
the patience and the bad taste to teach them to whistle tunes
played on the *rossignolette* * they will learn to sing definite
airs. They will even come to sing alternatively with a chorus,

* Evidently a little pipe crudely imitating bird song, such as is still sold to
children and unwary persons at places of amusement. [Ed.]

repeating a phrase at the right time.

One would scarcely suspect that a song so varied as the nightingale's should be confined within the narrow limits of a single octave. Yet that is the conclusion of an observer of taste who combines with a true musical ear a delicate perception. True, he remarked certain piercing tones that mounted to the double octave, passing swift as a flash, but this happens but rarely, when the bird by a special exertion of the syrinx made the tone leap an octave as a flautist will do by forcing the breath.

This bird is, after a time, capable of forming an attachment for the person who takes care of it. Once it has learned to know its keeper, it recognizes him by his step and salutes him in advance with a cry of joy, and if it is molting, it is seen to weary itself in useless efforts at singing, and to seek to supplement by the gaiety of its movements, by the soul that it puts into its glances, the expression which its vocal organs refuse to utter. If it loses its benefactor, it sometimes dies of sorrow. Should it survive, it is often long before it accustoms itself to another.

Nightingales are solitary of habit; they travel alone, and arrive singly in April or May and still in their own company depart only in September. And when in the spring the male and female come together to make a home, this private union seems but to fortify still more their aversion to society in general.

For they do not suffer any of their kind in the terrain which they have appropriated unto themselves. It is believed that only in this way may they possess hunting preserves wide enough to sustain their familial needs. And the proof of this is that nests are not far distant, the one from another, in those regions blessed with abundance of provision. Further, it would seem that jealousy does not enter into their motive, for we know that jealousy finds no distance great enough, and abundance of provender cannot diminish either the umbrage of jealousy nor its minute precautions.

Each couple commences to make its nest toward the end of April or the beginning of May. These little creatures construct it of leaves and rushes, of twists of coarse grass on the outside; inwardly, of little fibres, rootlets, horse hair and a sort of woolly down. They settle it in a favorable exposure, one with somewhat of an aspect to the rising sun, and in the vicinage of waters. They place it either on the lowest branches of shrubs, such as gooseberry bushes, may, wild plums, or yoke-elms, etc., or else on a tuft of grass and even upon the earth at the foot of some bush, which results sometimes in the eggs, or even the mother and little ones, falling prey to coursing dogs, foxes, beech-martens and adders, etc.

In our clime the dam lays, ordinarily, five eggs, these of a uniform greenish brown, save that the brown dominates at the smaller end. The dam sits the eggs alone; she does not leave her post but to search out provender, and then only by night and when pressed by hunger. At the end of eighteen or twenty days of incubation, the little ones begin eclosion. The number of males is commonly twice that of the females. Also, should one capture in the month of April some male with connubial attachments, he is soon replaced at the side of the bereaved widow by a successor, and that one, if need be, by a third. So that despite the ravishing away of three or four consorts in succession, the hatching does not come off less well.

The mother bird disgorges the nutriment for her young ones, as the canary does. In this interesting function she is aided by the father. And it is from this cause that he abandons the art of music for the serious preoccupations of familial cares. It is said that beginning even from the incubation he seldom sings near the nest lest he discover its secret treasure. Yet should one approach the nest, paternal tenderness betrays him and he utters cries torn from him by anxiety for the clutch.

In less than fifteen days the chicks are covered with feathers and it is then that one must dissever them from the parents if they are to be reared in domestication. As soon as they can fly alone, the mother and father commence another laying, and after this a second and third. But for the success of this last it is essential that frosts should not too early supervene. In hot countries nightingales lay up to four clutches and everywhere in general the progeny of the last are less numerous.

Man, who does not feel himself truly in ownership until he can use and abuse that which he possesses, has devised means to lodge the nightingale in durance. The greatest obstacle to keeping these birds alive and content in captivity has ever been their love of liberty. But this natural sentiment their captors have understood how to counterbalance with other instincts as native—the need to gratify the passion of love, the love of geniture. So people take a mated pair and loose them in a great aviary or rather in a corner of a garden planted with yews, yoke-elms and other small trees through which is strung a wire netting. This is the gentlest and surest means of inducing them to propagate their race.

There have been trials, too, in establishing nightingales where none existed. For this people try to take the parents, the nest, and eggs all together, transporting the nest to some site which has been selected for its resemblance to the locality from which it has been bereft. The two cages containing the mother and father being placed by the nest, these are invisibly opened as soon as the young begin to cry. Thereupon the parents fall at once to continuing all their care. It is claimed that in the following season the birds return to the selfsame place, and no doubt they do so if there be the proper nourishment, and the proper materials for the nest.

As the male birds pass the whole night in singing, the ancients were persuaded that they never slept at this season, and from this erroneous idea arose that other, that their diet is an anti-soporific one, and that it were enough to put the heart and eyes of a nightingale under someone's pillow to render him a miserable insomniac. Finally, these ideas gaining ground and passing into the arts, the nightingale has become the very symbol of vigilance. But moderns, who have most closely observed these birds, find that in the season of song they sleep by day, and that the onset of this diurnal somnolence, above all in winter, announces that they will soon be in voice. Not only do they sleep, but they dream, too, it is said in the *Treatise upon the Nightingale*, because they have been heard in their sleep to twitter and sing in a low voice.

Nightingales hide them away in the thickest of coppices, where they nourish themselves upon aquatic and other insects, little worms, and ants and their eggs; they eat, also, figs and berries, but as it is a difficult thing to furnish them habitually with such fare when they are kept in cages, diverse little patties have been devised for them and on these they accommodate themselves full well.

All sorts of traps are good for catching nightingales; they are but little suspicious though so timid. They admire everything and are duped by everything (says Monsieur Linnaeus). So that one can take them by a bird-caller, by the limed twig, in bird-traps for titmice or in bird nets spread on newly turned earth where the larvæ of ants or meal worms have been scattered, or even morsels that resemble them, such as bits of the white of hard-boiled eggs. Sometimes they are found in such great numbers in a countryside, witnesses Belon, that in a village in the forest of Ardennes the little shepherd children took, each one, a score every day, along with many other small birds. It was a year of great drought "and all the pools," says Belon, "were already dried, so that they betook themselves to the forest wherever were moist humours." It is needful that the bird traps should be made of taffeta and not of wire, lest the captive should entangle his plumage in them and mayhap lose some pinions, which would retard his song.

These birds are very good eating when they are fat, and rival ortolans. They are fattened in Gascony for the table, which recalls the fantasy of Heliogabalus who ate the tongues of nightingales and peacocks, and the famous dish of Aesopus, which was composed of a hundred birds all renowned for their talents of song or speech.

Robert Cushman Murphy

VIII

ROBERT CUSHMAN MURPHY

*F*IFTEEN years ago, attending a meeting of the American Association for the Advancement of Science, I found myself seated next to a young man whose personality and appearance so pleased me that I ventured to talk to him. Presently a mutual friend, Wilson Popenoe, the agricultural explorer, came along and introduced us. It was an introduction that would only be remembered by myself, but I placed Dr. Murphy instantly as a brilliant younger ornithologist at the American Museum of Natural History in New York City, and as the authority upon oceanic birds.

Robert Cushman Murphy was born in Brooklyn Heights in 1887. Like so many of the modern naturalists, his interests were polarized by haunting museums and making the acquaintance of the curators. The Brooklyn Museum was the particular one in case, and Dr. F. A. Lucas was the curator. Their long talks were of whaling, polar faunas and deep sea life. And Dr. Lucas did not forget the dark-eyed youngster; when an opportunity came for the American Museum to place an able-bodied young naturalist on the whaler *Daisy* bound for the south polar seas, they settled upon Murphy, just graduated from Brown University. He declined the offer, having just become engaged to be married. But his fiancée who came from Providence, an old whaling town, telegraphed him, "Take that job. Letter follows." The result was that the two were united at once, and had a honeymoon on the *Daisy* as far as the West Indies where Mrs. Murphy disbarked, while her young husband set off for South Georgia which is an island without women.

Murphy returned after eleven months, having covered 17,000 miles, and began graduate work at Columbia. He was at once appointed curator of mammals and birds at the Brooklyn Museum, where once he used to press his nose against the show glass. In 1921 he became assistant curator of birds at the American Museum, for by this time, having led scientific expeditions into tropical and subantarctic waters of the Atlantic, into Lower California and Mexico after the remarkable sea-birds of those coasts, and to the coast of Peru, the greatest gathering ground of marine birds in the world, he was become an unsurpassed authority in his line. His honors include the award of the Brewster and John Burroughs medals for his splendid systematic work, *Oceanic Birds of South America* (1936) and he has been president of the National Association of Audubon Societies and a director of the Long Island Biological Association at Cold Spring Harbor.

From his first book, *Bird Islands of Peru* (1925) I have selected for quotation here the chapter entitled "The Most Valuable Bird in the World." Dr. Murphy refers thereby to the cormorant which has deposited through the ages its excreta or guano on the Chincha and many other islands off the coast of Peru. The cormorant is not the only bird that has contributed to the nitrate accumulations. He says:

"At the present time, four species, comprising one cormorant, one pelican and two gannets, belong in the category of important guano producers. One of the gannets is confined to the northern-most Peruvian islands, and is of much less value than any of the other three birds. In order of increasing economic importance, the members of this distinguished quartet, with their Peruvian and scientific names, are as follows:

1. The camanay (Sula nebouxi), a tropical gannet or booby.
2. The alcatraz (Pelecanus thagus), a pelican peculiar to the Humboldt Current.

3. The piquero (Sula variegata), a booby peculiar to the Humboldt Current.
4. The guanay (Phalacrocorax bougainvillei), a white-breasted cormorant peculiar to the Humboldt Current but of antarctic affinities."

Why the most valuable birds in the world should congregate on a group of bleak and rocky islands in a highly inaccessible quarter of the sea is no chance or accident, from a biological point of view. These birds wisely prefer to nest only on islands; they multiply in such incredible numbers only where there is an even more incredibly abundant fish life. And that fish life is dependent on smaller fry and invertebrates of the sea, which in turn live on microscopic animals, and the basic food of these, like that of all animals, must be plant life. The plant life which furnishes marine animals with nutriment is chiefly the microscopic diatoms. And diatoms, everywhere common in the ocean, reach a peak of their development where there is a cold current and an upwelling of waters from the deeps. Now all these conditions are perfectly exemplified where the Humboldt Current sweeps past the tropic islands of the Chinchas. So that, by a natural chain of biologic links, these lonely crags were predestined to draw the ships of the world, as if they were needles to a magnet.

The guano of the Chinchas was cautiously and wisely used by the stable government of the Peruvian Incas, and it was forbidden to kill the birds. Spanish conquest turned rather to the exploitation of Andean minerals. It was only at the opening of the last century that the Peruvian government, which was supporting itself on the exploitation of its phosphates on land, responded to the demands of expanding agriculture at home and on other continents, by leasing the rights to mine the island guano. Ships of twenty nations could be seen riding in the dangerous anchorages of the islands; the United States of America bid high for rights, for in no other country was such whirlwind agricultural expansion going on.

Anything but pleasant was the life of the humans engaged in this traffic, and it was a black era for the birds too. The goose that laid the golden egg was accorded no gratitude. Guanayes were driven from their nesting sites; the young were left to starve; the disturbance in the balance of nature simply opened the way for the ravages of predatory gulls and condors, and in a few decades, had there been any modern biologists to make predictions, the end of the source of all this wealth could have been forecast by the wise.

No thought was given to the birds, however. The sea captains engaged in the trade were of the most hard-bitten type of the old-fashioned sailing masters, and they were working for employers who cared for nothing but money getting. The idea was to charter the cheapest (and oldest and worst) of hulls for terrific loads of putrid guano to be put on board at the highest possible speed. The storms, the danger of the anchorage, the unseaworthiness of the ships, were of small account to the owners, who were only too pleased to collect the insurance on lost vessels and cargoes.

But the existence of the sailors was nothing compared with that of the coolies on the islands, who dug the fertilizer and loaded it under forced draft. They were Chinamen who quit the starvation and miseries of life at home under the promise of high pay on a foreign shore, and while their lot in the Flowery Kingdom may have been hard, the slavery to which they found themselves subjected on the Chinchas was probably worse than that of the builders of the pyramids. They lived in the perpetual stench of the guano, clad in rags, wretchedly housed, unattended in sickness, unable to leave or communicate with the outside world, and skillfully kept in debt. At their long hours of labor they were driven by pitiless negroes armed with huge whips. And though there were constant suicides and deaths from overwork, the ranks were filled by fresh arrivals in hulls sailing under the flags of civilized nations that had long ago prohibited slavery.

The Imperial Chinese Government was long in acting on this situation even after it became aware of it. It is not certain that conditions would ever have improved except in name or superficially, had not Peru suddenly awakened to the fact that the guano deposits, once thought inexhaustible, were nearing their end. The surface of the islands had been lowered a hundred feet and more by the exploitation; some were practically bared to the rock; on others the lower strata of fertilizer having been reached, it was found to be less valuable and no longer commanded the old high prices. There was not enough guano left to supply the needs even of Peru, and the contracts still had a long time to run.

But one by one as the contracts expired, the government took them over and began to administer the production of guano as a crop instead of a mine. The birds are now protected by law, and their predators are kept down. When an area is ready for cropping, the work is swiftly and scientifically carried out, and that area again fallowed. In this way the future of the guano and of the guanay is assured, and humanity, for once, has not been too late to prevent an ornithological tragedy such as was wrought in the case of the passenger pigeons.

THE GUANAY

"The Most Valuable Bird in the World"

*P*ICTURE to yourself the shining, rainless coast of Peru, washed by ocean waters to which storms are unknown, where the swells surge northward, from month to month and year to year, before winds that blow regularly from a southerly quarter. On such an ocean dark flocks of guanayes form rafts which can be spied miles away. Slowly the dense masses of birds press along the sea, gobbling up fish in their path, the hinder margins of the rafts continually rising into the air and pouring over the van in some such manner as the great flocks of passenger pigeons are said to have once rolled through open North American forests in which oak or beech mast lay thick upon the leafy floor.

At other times, when the guanayes are moving toward distant feeding grounds, they travel not in broad flocks but rather as a solid river of birds, which streams in a sharply-marked, unbroken column, close above the waves, until an amazed observer is actually wearied as a single formation takes four or five hours to pass a given point.

Equally impressive are the homeward flights of these cormorants, after a day of gorging upon anchovies, when in late afternoon slender ribbons, wedges, and whiplashes of guanayes in single file twist and flutter, high in air, toward the rounded plateaus of white islands which gradually turn black as the packed areas of birds swell out from clustered nuclei toward the borders of the available standing room.

Whence came this astounding sea bird, which has made the Peruvian coast its own?

In the northward extension of this representative of an

antarctic group to a point within six degrees of the equator, we recognize one of the profound effects of the Humboldt Current. The cool stream, lying between a tropical continent on the one hand and the heated surface waters of the open South Pacific on the other, forms, as it were, a tongue of littoral ocean in which the environment, and consequently the marine flora and fauna, is such as ordinarily holds for the subantarctic zone rather than for equatorial or even temperate seas.

Given, therefore, a belt of cool ocean waters replete with small organisms of more or less polar type, together with nesting sites upon islands which for climatic reasons could never become encumbered with vegetation, and the geographic stage was set for the northward emigration of the ancestors of the guanay. Furthermore, because of the normal superabundance of food, conditions seem to have been prearranged for the increase of the birds to numbers limited only by competition with other animals and by the amount of safe, insular space for reproduction. Although suitable islets are very numerous, the enormous food supply in the Humboldt Current is still out of all proportion to the area of the breeding places. This doubtless explains the excessively colonial nesting habit of the guanay, in which it surpasses all other birds, even the penguins, for in the middle of a bounteous sea there would be a constant tendency for the cormorant population to become more and more congested upon the islets. The doctrine of Malthus applies to birds as well as to men.

The guanay, unlike any other cormorant, "hawks" its food, that is it hunts exclusively by sight and from the air, locating the fishes which it seeks before descending to the water to catch them. Most cormorants search for their prey individually, swimming alone or in loose groups at the surface, then plunging in what seem to be favorable places and conducting the hunt as well as the capture while they are submerged. For the most part, moreover, they subsist upon bottom-living species of fish, often diving down many fathoms in pursuit of single victims. But the guanay feeds altogether upon surface-swimming fishes, such as anchovies, young herrings, and the toothsome silversides which the Peruvians call *pejerreyes* ("kingfish"). Such forms travel in tremendous schools which are assailed en masse by proportionately large flocks of birds.

The correlation between the numbers of the fishes and the extreme gregariousness of the cormorants results among the latter in a system of efficient coöperation which almost suggests certain customs of ants or other social insects. The vast flocks of guanayes which spend their nights upon the islands do not start hunting in a body when morning breaks. On the contrary, the birds first sally forth only in small scouting parties, which can be seen flying erratically above the ocean, usually keeping well in air, and frequently "back pedalling" or hovering when they see the silvery glint of schooling fish or the ruffled appearance of the sea which indicates the presence of fish below. The dropping of the scouts to the surface, and the shallow dives which mark the beginning of an orgy, are the signals that cause the approach of such rivers of birds as have been described above. The cohort of guanayes then spreads out as a great fan over the unfortunate anchovies, which are likely to be no less harried from beneath by bonitos and sea lions. Small wonder that the Peruvian fishermen, who are familiar with such sights, believe that the guanayes and the seals have a working understanding! However this may be, the gorging proceeds until both sea lions and birds must cease long enough to allow their rapid digestions to fit them for another meal. From the crop and gullet of a dead guanay the remains of no less than seventy-six anchovies, four or five inches in length, have been taken.

Sometimes the guanayes pursue the fishes to the very

beaches, so that a rare view of a one-sided fray may be enjoyed by a landsman. One morning during my sojourn at Independencia Bay shoals of silversides were packed in deep, glittering ranks close to the quiet shore, when a raft of guanayes, accompanied by a few pelicans and a horde of screaming gulls, drove the fishes before them against the shelving sand. Soon the water gleamed like flashing quicksilver, and in wild rioting the birds jammed and crowded each other until hundreds of them were pushed clear beyond the tideline by the scrambling mob behind.

The guanay stands and walks erect, somewhat after the manner of a penguin. Its height is in the neighborhood of twenty inches and the weight of a full-grown bird about four and a half pounds. It has a glossy green and blue-black neck and back, a white throat-patch which is a conspicuous mark in flight, a white under surface, and pinkish feet. During the courtship season a crest of plumes develops at the back of the head. The guanay's iris is brown, but an area of green, naked skin surrounding the orbit makes it look at close range like a veritable personification of envy. A second ring of turgid red skin, outside the staring "green eye," heightens its extraordinary expression.

Since the fame of the guanay proceeds chiefly from sheer numbers, it is not unnatural that observers have made extremely high estimates or guesses concerning the population of its colonies. The birds breed upon the plateaus and windward hillsides of the Peruvian islands in concentrated communities, the nests averaging three to each square yard of ground. Dr. Coker's measurements show that not fewer than a million adult birds dwelt within the limits of a single homogeneous colony on South Chincha Island during one of his visits. Another naturalist has written that these cormorants "congregate to the number of ten millions."

The breeding season, like that of many tropical ocean

birds, is practically continuous, but it reaches a climax during the southern summer months of December and January. Individual pairs of guanayes are believed commonly to rear two broods during a single year. The flight of the last families of the young of one season, in May or June, is at any rate followed hard by the courting and love-making of adults in preparation for the breeding season of the second spring.

At South Cincha Island in mid-October the breeding grounds were covered with just one year's accumulation of sun-baked guano, and the cormorants were getting ready to nest again. They stood in compact bodies, each comprising thousands of birds, on the flat top of the island, and, when a human being approached, all those on the nearer side began to stir—not en *bloc*, nor yet individually but in groups of a few hundred, each of which for the time constituted a unit. One group would move rapidly away, the birds carrying themselves bolt upright. Another group would advance toward the observer, so that this section of the army would gleam with white breasts instead of shiny, dark backs. Still another unit would rush to the right or to the left, so that both the dark backs and the white breasts showed at once, and the long bills and red nasal warts became conspicuous. Such closely huddled companies soon collided with others moving in different directions, producing much confusion about the margins. A few of the birds showed no fear at all, stolidly permitting a man to approach within a few feet. The greater proportion, however, frantically took to flight, rushing helter-skelter down the slope, and raising a cloud of dust with their whistling wings. The air became bewilderingly thick with birds as they circled overhead, but within a few moments the number returning to earth once more exceeded the number taking wing.

When an observer makes his way slowly and very quietly into the heart of a colony in which nesting has definitely begun, the guanayes gradually retreat, and one may sit down in a clear circle which is at first fifty or more feet in diameter. But almost imperceptibly the birds will edge in again, until the bare circle narrows to but three or four paces. From such a point of view it seems as though the ground were covered with as many pairs of sprawling webbed feet as there is room for, and yet new arrivals plump down by scores or hundreds every minute. Over the ocean, moreover, to the north, south, east, and west, one may commonly see endless black files still pouring in toward the island. The hum of wings is like the effect of an overdose of quinine upon the ears, and the combined voices seem like mutterings of the twelve tribes of Israel. It reminds me of all sorts of strange, oppressive roarings, such as the noise of railroad trains in river tunnels. The near-by voices, which can be distinguished individually, are merely sonorous bass grunts and screepy calls. It is the multiplication of such sounds by numbers almost too large to imagine that makes the outlandish and never-to-be-forgotten babel.

Toward evening of such October days, most of the guanayes would be courting, after strenuous hours at sea during which all their energies had doubtless been devoted to winning the sustenance of life. Privacy does not enter into their notion of fitness, and while six or seven birds occupy each square yard of ground, the love-making antics are often in full progress. These are in general not unlike the courtship habits of the closely related antarctic cormorants. Two guanayes stand side by side, or breast to breast, and ludicrously wave their heads back and forth or gently caress each other's necks. The crests upon their crowns are frequently erected, and the feathers of the nape puff out so that the velvety necks appear twice their normal thickness. Cheeks and chin-pouches continually tremble, and chattering bills are held wide open. Now and again one will bend its body forward and at the same time extend the head upside down along the spine and toward the tail, holding their curious, paralyzed attitude for several seconds. Sometimes the birds of a pair snap so much at one another that it is hard to judge whether they are making love or quarreling.

Indubitable quarrels between birds of different pairs also go on without cessation, and occasionally many join together in a mêlée. Every now and then, for example, some unfortunate guanay, which seems to be the butt of all bystanders, will go dashing through the throng, holding its head as high as possible in order to avoid the jabs and bites which all others direct at it. If the victim would but stop fleeing, perhaps the blows would cease, but it keeps more and more desperately running the gantlet, flapping its wings, bumping into innumerable neighbors, until eventually it bursts from the vicious crowd into a clear space, shakes itself with an abused air, and opens and shuts its mouth many times with an expression of having just swallowed an unpleasant dose.

In the early stages of courtship it often happens that several cocks select the same female for their addresses. In one instance, five assiduous suitors, all with necks expanded, were observed bowing around a single hen which crouched in their midst. But by no means all the birds are engaged in love-making at every moment, for they spend much time preening their feathers, frequently raising the coverts of the tail and thrusting the bill toward the oil gland. Then, after combing their heads and necks thoroughly with their claws—a real feat in balancing—they promenade in small troupes along the outer edge of the colony.

Visible actions, rather than unusual sounds, alarm the courting birds. A quick motion of the hand will start sudden pandemonium. Even when an observer rises to leave them as slowly, silently, and unostentatiously as possible, a small panic inevitably results, many of the nearer birds beginning to scamper about or to take flight. On the other hand, the firing of a gun straight into the air produces scarcely a stir provided the weapon is not brandished. The effect of human conversation is, however, most amusing. Whenever a man, sitting perfectly still, begins to talk to the guanayes in a loud voice, a silence falls over all the audience within hearing. Their mumbles and grunts die away, and they listen for a while as if in amazement.

During the course of a few hours' resting on any island, the birds get much befouled with fresh guano, which hardens upon their plumage. They periodically rid themselves of this by flying some distance off the lee side of the island where they plunge and violently beat the water with their wings. Sometimes most of the inhabitants of a colony will make their toilet in this way at one time, producing a thunderous roar which can be heard from afar. It is often audible during morning fogs, when the flocks are invisible, and as a boat draws near such a gathering it is easy to mistake the sound for the dreaded crashing of waves upon unseen rocky shores.

The grandest sight of the day, when the homeward flight is at its maximum, usually comes during the hour before sunset. From some point far away the birds make a bee line for the center of their island, but, as they near their destination, they invariably skirt the shores so as to come down across the wind. The instinct of following a leader is evidently strong; if, for any reason, a file is broken, and the rear birds turn toward the left coast instead of the right, those behind will obey the signal and all swing into the new course. Close over gulches and ridges of their home island the oncoming streams of birds flow, the separate "rivulets" cutting across each other like the blades of scissors. At the same time these files also rise and fall in beautiful undulations which can best be seen from the crest of a hill above them. Sometimes three or more such lines will flow along for a while ten or fifteen yards apart, but sooner or later one of them will make leeway until two files interweave. Then the soft, humming swish of wings is interjected with sharp clicks as the quills of two guanayes strike together in air. When one beholds the endless mingling, the crossing and recrossing and tangling of the lines, it seems incredible that more birds do not clash.

RICHARD JEFFERIES

IX

RICHARD JEFFERIES

*I*N THE fine old stone house of Coate Farm, near Swindon in Wiltshire, was born in 1848 John Richard, to gentleman Farmer Jefferies and his town wife, Elizabeth. From her, Richard Jefferies received, perhaps, his refinement and his love of books and poetry, his delicate hands that unsuited him to farm work from the first, and the delicate health that flawed all his happiness, tinged his writings with melancholy and heightened them with a sense of the briefness and beauty of life, and that finally destroyed him. From his father came his love of the country, the passion for bodily activity, the stomach that is required of a poet to be in childhood a ruthless robber of birds' nests and in boyhood an addicted hunter. His father early taught him to observe. He trained the lad's eyes and ears all day and every day, sharpening his sensitivity toward Nature until it was keen as his spaniel's nose, and wary as the wild duck's ears. Had he set out to make his son a poet of Nature this father could have done little better.

As it was, Coate Farm was already far too full of books on chivalry and magic, to make a good peasant of this boy. And the Jefferies family was moving on the predestined road of most of the English agricultural stock—off the land. This exodus might have been forced on them in any case; it was hastened by the fact that Richard's father was himself over-educated for his station. Absorbed in breeding fine strains of garden flowers, and raising specimen pears on the trees trained against the sunny wall, he neglected oats and barley. So, while their more illiterate neighbors drifted to the industrial centers, or emigrated to America, the Jefferies family relinquished their land acre by acre, dooming the house with debt.

Young Richard was remembered by his father's farm hands and dairy maids as a leggy, pale boy, with enormous blue eyes and a large, passionate mouth, who never did any work about the place as long as he could lie on a haycock and watch, under a shading hand, the ascending lark. When it was haying time, Dick was shooting moor hens; when it was plowing time he was studying sand martins nesting in the old quarry bank. When it was lesson time he was talking to one of those ragged girls that must have given him the memorable and pathetic character of "Lou" in *Bevis*. When the day was beautiful, he let all its gold spill by while he shut himself up, with his head drooping into a book of curious natural lore. He did nothing that the yeomanry could approve or understand, except for his skating. On the ice, the delicate, idle boy became a whirling snowflake whom no one could overtake.

The Wiltshire downs are at their loveliest about Coate Farm; they have breadth and wildness, contrasted with lowland Wiltshire, a heavy-soiled, too umbrageous dairy country with a bovine peasantry. On the windy downs the boy made his first acquaintance with bird life (unless the nesting of the house martins under the eaves and of the swallows in the chimney stacks preceded it). And there, in hedgerow and grass, he learned the ways of birds as only a curious and rather marauding country boy can know them. The great reservoir, that figures so delightfully in *Bevis*, that classic of boyhood, gave him moor hens and wild ducks, herons and crested grebes and divers. And Savernake Forest, full ten miles distant, was his regular walk. Hudson mentions it as the finest haunt for daws in all of England.

Precocious in everything, Richard fell in love early with his young cousin, the daughter of Day House Farm, across the down. She is, I think, the luscious Frances of *Bevis*, and the girlish heroine of *Amaryllis at the Fair*. They married improvidently, had a baby with the promptness of any country couple—and responsibilities, anxieties, poverty, and confinement were at once upon the young man. Newspaper work was the only sort of employment fitted to him which he could secure, and Jefferies was drawn into the maelstrom of Fleet Street. Reporting, editorial work, and hasty nature sketches designed to give the city-pent man a breath of the open air, were all the training, as a writer, that Jefferies ever had. He took a suburban "villa" in Surbiton, with a tiny yard around it, and suburban souls around his own. Between Fleet Street and the Surbiton house most of the rest of his life moved in a dutiful round.

What sort of Nature writing could come out of this? one may ask. But it must be remembered that Jefferies was a poet, and there is nothing so good for poetry as discontent, as idleness and joy remembered, as Nature passionately longed for, as pictures of childhood very far off and long ago, dancing bright before the eyes. Jefferies poured out his love of Nature like a caged blackbird, singing, in his unsatisfied desire, every month of the year, whereas it is probable that had he possessed the means to remain a country squire he would have gone on shooting pheasants and rabbits, as voicelessly as his ancestors had done for generations.

His first magazine articles to attract attention were a ringing if inconsistent defense of the English yeomanry whom he loved with passion, especially its children and young girls, though he loved them squire-fashion, not as one of them. Sheer Nature essays followed—very rambling at first, evocative and reminiscent. Many references to birds occur in them, but nothing one may lift from the general tissue of his deep poetic communion with Nature. Finally, having exhausted his Wiltshire notes, he turned his attention to Nature near

London. As he truly observes, there is a denser bird population in the suburbs than in the country. He had never heard
in Wiltshire so rapturous a morning chorus as the Maytime
symphony of missel thrush and blackbird, cuckoo and nightingale about Surbiton.

Jefferies' life would now seem to have been well on the
way toward fame, perhaps even financial security, if not happiness. But the forgotten flaw was in his destiny. A family
weakness, developed in him, no doubt, by gruelling London
work, poverty and neglect of the body, doomed him to tuberculosis. It invaded organ after organ; the record of his operations, his nervous destruction, his laboring breath, is almost
unreadable. He dictated his work to his wife in a whisper.
Yet that work was the crowning achievement of his life. To
this period belong *Bevis* (which my boy children read and
read again as I did when little) and *Amaryllis*, as well as his
introduction to *The Natural History of Selborne*, and the
two books of his finest, most mature Nature essays, from
which selection is here made, *The Life of the Fields* (1884),
and *Nature Near London* (1883). Jefferies, who loved health,
adored the wild wind and the bold children of the downs,
ripe fruit on sunny walls, young country women in their
flower, young men in their strength at the plow and among
beasts, sank, fighting, inch by inch, within the pall of London's smoke. He was like a song bird in a reeking coal chimney out of which he could find no escape. Even his last de-
spairing cries were song—since a poet, like a bird, can scarcely
utter any other note.

The selection called *Round a London Copse* is not without pathos, for it shows what Jefferies could do with what
he was forced to accept as Nature. The copse was a bit of
the wild left over by the growing suburb, right down his
street. (Even that is gone today, I understand.) Now, it is
easy enough to tell a rousing tale if you happen to have had

adventures with Andean condors, crested screamers, grey sea eagles, lyre birds or wild ostriches. It is a great deal harder to do anything with our common small sweet songsters of the civilized world, as I can assure the reader from having sought through hundreds of pages for just such material as this of Jefferies'. Many writers fail at it; among English authors only Hudson does as well as Jefferies. Jefferies, whose fate it was never to travel, even in so small a country as England, extracted the last sweetness from the little that he ever saw.

I am not proposing Jefferies as a great ornithologist, or even an amateur ornithologist in high scientific standing. Of scientific training or even attitude he was almost devoid. His only chance of overcoming this handicap (which he never realized) was to teach himself by the most minute, prolonged attention to bird behavior. And this his seemingly idle childhood and youth supplied him. How long, and how thoughtfully, he must have watched the soaring of birds one can judge from this specimen of his prose.

For the soaring of birds—rising abruptly and for a long time against gravity, without a single flap of the wings—seems to contradict all the laws of mechanics. More than one physicist has been quite unable to explain it; most of the explanations are so involved and wordy that after one has read and seemingly understood them, one cannot remember a word of the exposition or repeat even the principles involved. Jefferies may not have here the perfect or complete explanation, but it is the most concise and vivid that I know. It exhibits his style as it ought always to have been, had he had time to polish and select; it shows what a fine ornithologist he would have become if Fate had not wasted the privileges of bird watching upon so many who are blind and had instead conferred them for life upon the dreaming boy of Coate Farm, and the weary night commuter to Surbiton.

ROUND A LONDON COPSE

*I*N OCTOBER a party of wood-pigeons took up their residence in the little copse. It stands in the angle formed by two suburban roads, and the trees in it overshadow some villa gardens. This copse has always been a favourite with birds, and it is not uncommon to see a pheasant about it, sometimes within gunshot of the garden, while the call of the partridges in the evening may now and then be heard from the windows. But though frequently visited by wood-pigeons, they did not seem to make any stay till now when this party arrived.

There were eight of them. During the day they made excursions into the stubble fields, and in the evening returned to roost. They remained through the winter, which will be remembered as the most severe for many years. Even in the sharpest frost, if the sun shone out, they called to each other now and then.

At intervals the note of the wood-pigeon was heard in the adjacent house from October, all through the winter, till the nesting time in May. Sometimes towards sunset in the early spring they all perched together before finally retiring on the bare, slender tips of the tall birch trees, exposed and clearly visible against the sky.

Six once alighted in a row on a long birch branch, bending it down with their weight like a heavy load of fruit. The stormy sunset flamed up, tinting the fields with momentary red, and their hollow voices sounded among the trees. By May they had paired off, and each couple had a part of the copse to themselves. Instead of avoiding the house, they seemed, on the contrary, to come much nearer, and two or three couples built close to the garden.

These pigeons were new inhabitants; but turtle-doves had built in the copse since I knew it. They were late coming the last spring I watched them; but, when they did, chose a spot much nearer the house than usual.

While this nesting was going on I could hear five different birds at once either in the garden or from any of the windows. The doves cooed, and every now and then their gentle tones were over-powered by the loud call of the wood-pigeons. A cuckoo called from the top of the tallest birch, and a nightingale and a brook-sparrow (or sedge-reedling) were audible together in the common on the opposite side of the road. It is remarkable that one season there seems more of one kind of bird than the next. The year alluded to, for instance, in this copse was the wood-pigeons' year. But one season previously the copse seemed to belong to the missel-thrushes.

Early in the March mornings I used to wake as the workmen's trains went rumbling by to the great City, to see on the ceiling by the window a streak of sunlight, tinted orange by the vapour through which the level beams had passed. Something in the sense of morning lifts the heart up to the sun. The light, the air, the waving branches speak; the earth and life seem boundless at that moment. In this it is the same on the verge of the artificial City as when the rays come streaming through the pure atmosphere of the Downs. While thus thinking, suddenly there rang out three clear, trumpet-like notes from a tree at the edge of the copse by the garden. A softer song followed, and then again the same three notes, whose wild sweetness echoed through the wood.

The voice of the missel-thrush sounded not only close at hand and in the room, but repeated itself as it floated away, as the bugle-call does. He is the trumpeter of spring: Lord of March, his proud call challenges the woods; there are none who can answer. Listen for the missel-thrush: when he sings the snow may fall, the rain drift, but not for long; the violets are near at hand. The nest was in a birch visible from the garden, and that season seemed to be the missel-thrush's. Another year the cuckoos had possession.

There is a detached ash tree in the field by the copse; it stands apart, and about sixty or seventy yards from the garden. A cuckoo came to this ash every morning, and called there for an hour at a time, his notes echoing along the building, one following the other as wavelets roll on the summer sands. After a while two more used to appear, and then there was a chase round the copse, up to the tallest birch, and out to the ash tree again. This went on day after day, and was repeated every evening. Flying from the ash to the copse and returning, the birds were constantly in sight; they sometimes passed over the house, and the call became so familiar that it was not regarded any more than the chirp of a sparrow. Till the very last the cuckoos remained there, and never ceased to be heard till they left to cross the seas.

Even the starlings vary, regular as they are by habit. This season (1881) none have whistled on the house-top. In previous years they have always come, and only the preceding spring a pair filled the gutter with the materials of their nest. Long after they had finished a storm descended, and the rain, thus dammed up and unable to escape, flooded the corner. It cost half a sovereign to repair the damage, but it did not matter; the starlings had been happy.

Another time it was the season of the lapwings. Towards the end of November (1881), there appeared a large flock of peewits, or green plovers, which flock passed most of the day in a broad, level ploughed field of great extent. At this time I estimated their number as about four hundred; far exceeding any flock I had previously seen in the neighbourhood. Fresh parties joined the main body continually, until by December there could not have been less than a thousand. Still more and more arrived, and by the first of January (1882) even this number was doubled, and there were certainly fully two thousand there. It is the habit of green plovers to all move at once, to rise from the ground simultaneously, to turn in the air, or to descend—and all so regular that their very wings seem to flap together. The effect of such a vast body of white-breasted birds uprising as one from the dark ploughed earth was very remarkable.

When they passed overhead the air sang like the midsummer hum with the shrill noise of beating wings. When they wheeled a light shot down reflected from their white breasts, so that people involuntarily looked up to see what it could be. The sun shone on them, so that at a distance the flock resembled a cloud brilliantly illuminated. In an instant they turned and the cloud was darkened. Such a great flock had not been seen in that district in the memory of man.

Jays often come, magpies more rarely, to the copse; as for the lesser birds they all visit it. In the hornbeams at the verge blackcaps sing in spring a sweet and cultured song, which does not last many seconds. They visit a thick bunch of ivy in the garden. By these hornbeam trees a streamlet flows out of the copse, crossed at the hedge by a pole, to prevent cattle straying in. The pole is a robin's perch. He is always there, or near; he was there all through the terrible winter, all the summer, and he is there now.

There are a few inches, a narrow strip of sand, beside the streamlet under this pole. Whenever a wagtail dares to come to this sand the robin immediately appears and drives him away. He will bear no intrusion. A pair of butcher-birds built very near this spot one spring, but afterwards appeared to remove to a place where there is more furze, but beside the same hedge. The determination and fierce resolution of the shrike, or butcher-bird, despite his small size, is most marked. One day a shrike darted down from a hedge just before me, not a yard in front, and dashed a dandelion to the ground.

His claws clasped the stalk, and the flower was crushed in a moment; he came with such force as to partly lose his balance. His prey was probably a humble-bee which had settled on the dandelion. The shrike's head resembles that of the eagle in miniature. From his favourite branch he surveys the grass, and in an instant pounces on his victim.

Up in the oaks blackbirds whistle—you do not often see them, for they seek the leafy top branches, but once now and then while fluttering across to another perch. The blackbird's whistle is very human, like some one playing the flute; an uncertain player now drawing forth a bar of a beautiful melody and then losing it again. He does not know what quiver or what turn his note will take before it ends; the note leads him and completes itself. His music strives to express his keen appreciation of the loveliness of the days, the golden glory of the meadow, the light, and the luxurious shadows.

Such thoughts can only be expressed in fragments, like a sculptor's chips thrown off as the inspiration seizes him, not mechanically sawn to a set line. Now and again the blackbird feels the beauty of the time, the large white daisy stars, the grass with yellow-dusted tips, the air which comes so softly unperceived by any precedent rustle of the hedge. He feels the beauty of the time, and he must say it. His notes come like wild flowers not sown in order. There is not an oak here in June without a blackbird.

Thrushes sing louder here than anywhere else; they really seem to sing louder, and they are all around. Thrushes appear to vary their notes with the period of the year, singing louder in the summer, and in the mild days of October when the leaves lie brown and buff on the sward under their perch more plaintively and delicately. Warblers and willow-wrens sing in the hollow in June, all out of sight among the trees— they are easily hidden by a leaf.

At that time the ivy leaves which flourish up to the very

tops of the oaks are so smooth with enamelled surface, that high up, as the wind moves them, they reflect the sunlight and scintillate. Greenfinches in the elms never cease love-making; and love-making needs much soft talking. A nightingale in a bush sings so loud the hawthorn seems too small for the vigour of the song. He will let you stand at the very verge of the bough; but it is too near, his voice is sweeter across the field.

There are still, in October, a few red apples on the boughs of the trees in a little orchard beside the same road. It is a natural orchard—left to itself—therefore there is always something to see in it.

The trees lean this way and that, and they are scarred and marked as it were with lichen and moss. It is the home of birds. A blackbird had its nest this spring in the bushes on the left side, a nightingale another in the bushes on the right, and there the nightingale sang under the shadow of a horn-beam for hours every morning while "City" men were hurrying past to their train.

BIRDS CLIMBING THE AIR

TWO hawks come over the trees, and, approaching each other, rise higher into the air. They wheel about for a little without any apparent design, still rising, when one ceases to beat the air with his wings, stretches them to their full length, and seems to lean aside. His impetus carries him forward and upward, at the same time in a circle, something like a skater on one foot. Revolving round a centre, he rises in a spiral, perhaps a hundred yards across; screwing upwards, and at each turn ascending half the diameter of the spiral. When he begins this it appears perfectly natural, and nothing more than would necessarily result if the wings were held outstretched and one edge of the plane slightly elevated. The impulse of previous flight, the beat of strong pinions, and the swing and rush of the bird evidently suffice for two or three, possibly for four or five, winding movements, after which the retarding effects of friction and gravitation ought, according to theory, to gradually bring the bird to a stop. But up goes the hawk, round and round like a woodpecker climbing a tree; only the hawk has nothing tangible into which to stick his claws and to rest his tail against. Those winding circles must surely cease; his own weight alone must stop him, and those wide wings outstretched must check his course. Instead of which the hawk rises as easily as at first, and without the slightest effort—no beat of wing or flutter, without even a slip or jerk, easily round and round. His companion does the same; often, perhaps always, revolving the opposite way, so as to face the first. It is a fascinating motion to watch.

The graceful sweeping curl holds the eye: it is a line of beauty, and draws the glance up into the heights of the air. The darker upper part of one is usually visible at the same

time as the lighter under part of the other, and as the dark
wheels again the sunlight gleams on the breast and under
wing. Sometimes they take regular curves, ascending in an
equal degree with each; each curve representing an equal
height gained perpendicularly. Sometimes they sweep round
in wide circles, scarcely ascending at all. Again, suddenly one
will shoot up almost perpendicularly, immediately followed
by the other. Then they will resume the regular ascent. Up,
like the woodpecker round a tree, till now the level of the
rainy scud which hurries over in wet weather has long been
past; up till to the eye it looks as if they must soon attain
to the flecks of white cloud in the sunny sky to-day. They are
in reality far from that elevation; but their true height is none
the less wonderful. Resting on the sward, I have watched
them go up like this through a lovely morning atmosphere
till they seemed about to actually enter the blue, till they
were smaller in appearance than larks at their highest ascent,
till the head had to be thrown right back to see them. This
last circumstance shows how perpendicularly they ascend,
winding round a line drawn straight up. At their very highest
they are hardly visible, except when the under wing and
breast passes and gleams in the light.

All this is accomplished with outstretched wings held at
full length, without flap, or beat, or any apparent renewal
of the original impetus. If you take a flat stone and throw
it so that it will spin, it will go some way straight, then rise,
turn aside, describe a half-circle, and fall. If the impetus kept
in it, it would soar like the hawk, but this does not happen.
A boomerang acts much in the same manner, only more perfectly; yet, however forcibly thrown, the impetus soon dies
out of a boomerang. A skater gets up his utmost speed, suddenly stands on one foot, and describes several circles; but in
two minutes comes to a standstill, unless he "screws," or
works his skate, and so renews the impulse. Even at his best

he only goes round, and does not raise his weight an inch
from the ice. The velocity of a bullet rapidly decreases, and
a ball shot from an express rifle, and driven by a heavy charge,
soon begins to droop. When these facts are duly considered,
it will soon be apparent what a remarkable feat soaring really
is. The hawk does not always ascend in a spiral, but every
now and then revolves in a circle—a flat circle—and suddenly
shoots up with renewed rapidity. Whether this be merely
sportive wantonness or whether it is a necessity, is impossible
to determine; but to me it does not appear as if the hawk
did it from necessity. It has more the appearance of variation: just as you or I might walk fast at one moment and
slowly at another, now this side of the street and now the
other. A shifting of the plane of the wings would, however,
in all probability, give some impetus: the question is, would
it be sufficient? I have seen hawks go up in sunny and lovely
weather—in fact, they seem to prefer still, calm weather but,
considering the height to which they attain, no one can positively assert that they do or do not utilise a current. If they
do, they may be said to sail (a hawk's wings are technically his
sails) round half the circle with the wind fair and behind, and
then meet it the other half of the turn, using the impetus they
have gained to surmount the breeze as they breast it. Grant-
ing this mechanical assistance, it still remains a wonderful
feat, since the nicest adjustment must be necessary to get the
impetus sufficient to carry the birds over the resistance. They
do not drift, or very little.

My own impression is that a hawk can soar in a perfectly
still atmosphere. If there is a wind he uses it; but it is quite
as much an impediment as an aid. If there is no wind he
goes up with the greater ease and to the greater height, and
will of choice soar in a calm. The spectacle of a weight—for
of course the hawk has an appreciable weight—apparently
lifting itself in the face of gravitation and overcoming fric-

tion, is a very striking one. When an autumn leaf parts on a still day from the twig, it often rotates and travels some distance from the tree, falling reluctantly and with pauses and delays in the air. It is conceivable that if the leaf were animated and could guide its rotation, it might retard its fall for a considerable period of time, or even rise higher than the tree.

THOMAS NUTTALL

X

THOMAS NUTTALL

*Q*UIET as a hermit thrush in winter that, never uttering a sound, perpetually shuffles over old leaves with its claws, bends down its head to cock an eye at something interesting, moving with quick runs, slipping, dull of plumage, into thickets, and sleeping we never know where, Thomas Nuttall in the herbarium of the famous old Philadelphia Academy was known to all the American scientists of his day as a careful, thorough, rather pedantic systematic botanist, perpetually busied among sheets of dried specimens. But, personally, he was known to them scarcely at all. As some of them later remarked, they had no idea where he dwelt, or where he ate, whence he derived his evidently very modest little income. The appearance of this bachelor was, in general, quite untidy; he allowed, perhaps more from neglect than parsimony, his clothes to become worn and baggy. His associates knew that he was an Englishman, who had formerly been a printer; they were unaware that he had been born on a Yorkshire estate (in 1786) to which he was heir. They knew him as a botanist who had travelled in the then-unmapped West, up the Missouri to Fort Mandan. But they probably had little idea that he had all the time been keeping a knowing eye on the birds.

It was during his residence at Harvard (1825-1833) where he was curator of the botanical garden, that Nuttall seems to have formed the intention of writing his *Manual of Ornithology*, for in that book his earliest references to experiences with birds date to the period of his residence in Cambridge. In the botanic garden (so intimately known to me) the call of some passing bird voice from the trees would lure him from his plant specimens into the open. Here he studied birds not only as species, but as individuals, with identities and behaviors peculiar to each songster. He seems also to have kept a great many native birds in cages in his "cabinet," for more intimate study. This was something little practiced by Audubon or Wilson, and the excellent results were subsequently to appear.

At Harvard, Nuttall was just as much a recluse as in Philadelphia, perhaps more so since he was not surrounded by old friends. His house at that time stood where the Gray Herbarium is now; here Asa Gray lived after him, and when the building was removed across the street it was occupied by my late beloved teacher, Prof. B. L. Robinson, who has made some interesting remarks concerning the stamp which Nuttall left upon his residence:

"While living at the house in the Garden he kept himself much secluded in apartments reserved for him. He had a separate entrance by which he could enter and leave his study, and in the lower part of the Garden a particular small, locked gate, of which he alone had the key. Tradition states that he kept his valuable scientific collections over his study in a close, ill-smelling garret, which also served him as a bedroom. To avoid, so far as possible, any intercourse with other inmates of the house, he had a sort of slide cut, through which his meals could be passed."

Now all these details make Nuttall sound like a fearful or preposterous pedant, and a most unsociable and even morbid recluse, and possibly he was not untinged with these crabbed failings. But reserve, shyness, withdrawal, and unobserved movements, however censored by the gregarious and chattering simian that is man, are definitely popular virtues with birds. If they show any preference for one sort of a human,

it is usually for just such solitary and quiet souls. So as one
reads on in the *Manual of Ornithology*, which starts out
rather formally and is modelled upon Pennant and other di-
dactic ornithologists of a still earlier age, one slowly comes to
realize that Nuttall had found out an immense amount about
birds. He knew them very intimately, with a beautiful and
secret and sensitive appreciation and sympathy. It seems, too,
that Nuttall had unobtrusively established great friendships
with ornithologists of the time. He may have known Wilson;
he was certainly the friend of Audubon and Charles Lucien
Bonaparte. They mention him almost never—for they probably did all the talking and instructing. But he mentions them
often; he seems to have absorbed bird lore from them as a
clever child in a corner will absorb a wealth of adult information, making private deductions and judgments.

Already famous for his botanical journeys, Nuttall made
several expeditions entirely devoted to bird study. Apparently
they passed almost unobserved in scientific circles at the time.
Nuttall, whose presence was scarcely remarked, was gone before anyone noticed that he was not there; some of his trips
are only inferred from the internal evidence of the *Manual*.
At least twice (1829, 1830) he ransacked the southern states
—much the richest part of the country for bird life, and the
winter home of so many of our summer visitants. And many
are the references to his lonely journeys. For no companion
seems to have been at his side as he wandered the pine groves
and the cypress swamps, listening for the fine lisping notes
of very small shy *Aves*, or watching the ungainly dignity of
marsh birds at their rites.

The two volumes of the *Manual* appeared in 1832 and 1833
respectively. After his famous botanical trip across the Rockies
(1833-1836) in Captain Wyeth's expedition to the Columbia's mouth, and down the coast of California to San Diego,
he issued a new edition which included many western species

about which nothing, beside some specimens, had ever been known before. In this wise he became acquainted with birds about which Wilson could then have known nothing, while Audubon was only to familiarize himself with some of them many years later. His fellow-traveller, John K. Townsend, gives a glimpse of him when on the prairies of western Nebraska an absolutely new flora burst upon the sight of the expedition:

"Flowers of every hue were growing. It was a most enchanting sight; even the men noticed it, and more than one of our matter-of-fact people exclaimed, *beautiful, beautiful!* Mr. N. was here in his glory. He rode on ahead of the company, and cleared the passage with a trembling and eager hand, looking anxiously back at the approaching party, as though he feared it would come ere he had finished, and tread his lovely prizes under foot."

But in his experiences of bird life he took care, no doubt, that no one should be with him. His delights were solitary; only with restraint they emerge to us in the sensitive style of the *Manual*.

Of that style I would speak one shielding word. Nuttall was not a poet, like Alexander Wilson, and not an ebullient genius like Audubon. A man of science, it was his instinct to moderate his raptures; he probably admired Gilbert White, the precise and elegant. Nuttall's style must therefore be judged by a somewhat eighteenth century standard, and appreciated for its taste and discrimination. Romantic color must no more be asked of it than one would ask Gray to sound like Shelley.

So far as I know, Nuttall never described, in systematic ornithology, an original species or even a variety. He seems to have left that entirely to others, though he was perhaps the soundest botanical systematist of his time in America. He devoted his labors and love entirely to the life histories of his birds, and he got them into a far more concise compass than his great contemporaries. In transcribing by various syllables the approximate songs of birds, and their various signals, he was particularly successful. If Audubon and Wilson had such sensitive and accurate ears as he, they certainly do not show it in their writings. Wilson, though something of a musician, hardly makes the attempt, and Audubon's efforts are only fair or positively misleading and wretched.

A recent reprint and revision of the *Manual* in one volume, edited to bring the work up to date, is available now under the title *A Popular Handbook of the Birds of the United States and Canada* (Boston, 1921).

At the end of 1841, Nuttall left America for England. He had inherited Nut-Grove Hall, and the terms of the bequest demanded his residence there for nine months of every year. This seemed to prevent his return to America, in the days of sailing ships. Yet he contrived to circumvent these provisions once, by departing in September of one year and returning by March of the next. But at that season the flowers were dead in the fields, the birds silent or gone.

Nuttall died in 1859 at Nut-Grove Hall. It is said that he overstrained himself in his eagerness to open a case of rhododendrons (his favorite genus of flowers which he was monographing). His departure was scarcely remarked in his native country.

BALTIMORE ORIOLE

*T*HESE gay, lively, and brilliant strangers, leaving their hibernal retreat in South America, appear in New England about the first week in May, and more than a month earlier in Louisiana, according to the observations of Audubon. They were not seen, however, in West Florida by the middle of March, although vegetation had then so far advanced that the oaks were in leaf, and the white flowering cornel was in full blossom.

It is here that they pass the most interesting period of their lives; and their arrival is hailed as the sure harbinger of approaching summer. Full of life and activity, these fiery sylphs are now seen vaulting and darting incessantly through the lofty boughs of our tallest trees; appearing and vanishing with restless inquietude, and flashing at quick intervals into sight from amidst the tender waving foliage, they seem like living gems intended to decorate the verdant garment of the new-clad forest.

The mellow whistled notes which they are heard to trumpet from the high branches of our tallest trees and gigantic elms resemble, at times, *'tshippe-tshayïa too too*, and sometimes *'tshippee 'tshippee* (lispingly), *too too* (with the two last syllables loud and full). Another bird I have occasionally heard to call for hours, with some little variation, *tú tĕo tĕo tĕo tĕo too*, in a loud, querulous, and yet almost ludicrously merry strain. At other intervals the sensations of solitude seem to stimulate sometimes a loud and interrogatory note, echoed forth at intervals, as *k'rry kerry?* and terminating plaintively *k'rry k'rry k'rry, tū*; the voice falling off very slenderly in the last long syllable, which is apparently an imitation from the Cardinal Grosbeak, and the rest is derived from the Crested

Titmouse, whom they have already heard in concert as they passed through the warmer States.

There is nothing more remarkable in the whole instinct of our Golden Robin than the ingenuity displayed in the fabrication of its nest, which is, in fact, a pendulous cylindric pouch of five or seven inches in depth, usually suspended from near the extremities of the high, drooping branches of trees (such as the elm, the pear or apple tree, wild-cherry, weeping-willow, tulip-tree, or buttonwood). It is begun by firmly fastening natural strings of the flax of the silk-weed, or swamp-holyhock, or stout artificial threads, round two or more forked twigs, corresponding to the intended width and depth of the nest. With the same materials, willow down, or any accidental ravellings, strings, thread, sewing-silk, tow, or wool, that may be lying near the neighboring houses, or round the grafts of trees, it interweaves and fabricates a sort of coarse cloth into the form intended, towards the bottom of which is placed the real nest, made chiefly of lint, wiry grass, horse and cow hair, sometimes, in defect of hair, lining the interior with a mixture of slender strips of smooth vine-bark, and rarely with a few feathers, the whole being of a considerable thickness, and more or less attached to the external pouch. Over the top, the leaves, as they grow out, form a verdant and agreeable canopy, defending the young from the sun and rain. There is sometimes a considerable difference in the manufacture of these nests, as well as in the materials which enter into their composition. Both sexes seem to be equally adept at this sort of labor, and I have seen the female alone perform the whole without any assistance, and the male also complete this laborious task nearly without the aid of his consort,—who, however, in general, is the principal worker. I have observed a nest made almost wholly of tow, which was laid out for the convenience of a male bird, who with this aid completed his labor in a very short time, and frequently sang in a very ludicrous manner while his mouth was loaded with a mass larger than his head. So eager are these birds to obtain fibrous materials that they will readily tug at and even untie hard knots made of tow. In Audubon's magnificent plates a nest is represented as formed outwardly of the long-moss; where this abounds, of course, the labor of obtaining materials must be greatly abridged. The author likewise remarks that the whole fabric consists almost entirely of this material, loosely interwoven, without any warm lining,— a labor which our ingenious artist seems aware would be superfluous in the warm forests of the lower Mississippi. A female, which I observed attentively, carried off to her nest a piece of lamp-wick ten or twelve feet long. This long string, and many other shorter ones, were left hanging out for about a week before both the ends were wattled into the sides of the nest. Some other little birds, making use of similar materials, at times twitched these flowing ends, and generally brought out the busy Baltimore from her occupation in great anger.

I have had a male bird in a state of domestication raised from the nest very readily on fresh minced meat soaked in milk. When established, his principal food was scalded Indian cornmeal, on which he fed contentedly, but was also fond of sweet cakes, insects of all descriptions, and nearly every kind of fruit. In short, he ate everything he would in a state of nature, and did not refuse to taste and eat of everything but the condiments which enter into the multifarious diet of the human species: he was literally omnivorous.

No bird could become more tame, allowing himself to be handled with patient indifference, and sometimes with playfulness. The singular mechanical application of his bill was remarkable, and explains at once the ingenious art employed by the species in weaving their nest. If the folded hand was presented to our familiar Oriole, he endeavored to open it by inserting his pointed and straight bill betwixt the closed fingers, and then by pressing open the bill with great muscular force, in the manner of an opening pair of compasses, he contrived, if the force was not great, to open the hand and examine its contents. If brought to the face he did the same with the mouth, and would try hard to open the closed teeth. In this way, by pressing open any yielding interstice, he could readily insert the threads of his nest, and pass them through an infinity of openings, so as to form the ingenious net-work or basis of his suspensory and procreant cradle.

MOCKINGBIRD

THE Mocking Bird, like the Nightingale, is destitute of brilliant plumage; but his form is beautiful, delicate, and symmetrical in its proportions. His motions are easy, rapid, and graceful, perpetually animated with a playful caprice and a look that appears full of shrewdness and intelligence. He listens with silent attention to each passing sound, treasures up lessons from everything vocal, and is capable of imitating with exactness, both in measure and accent, the notes of all the feathered race. And however wild and discordant the tones and calls may be, he contrives, with an Orphean talent peculiarly his own, to infuse into them that sweetness of expression and harmonious modulation which characterize this inimitable and wonderful composer. With the dawn of morning, while yet the sun lingers below the blushing horizon, our sublime songster, in his native wilds, mounted on the topmost branch of a tall bush or tree in the forest, pours out his admirable song, which, amidst the multitude of notes from all the warbling host, still rises preeminent, so that his solo is heard alone, and all the rest of the musical choir appear employed in mere accompaniments to this grand actor in the sublime opera of Nature. Nor is his talent confined to imitation; his native notes are also bold, full, and perpetually varied, consisting of short expressions of a few variable syllables, interspersed with imitations and uttered with great emphasis and volubility, sometimes for half an hour at a time, with undiminished ardor. These native strains bear a considerable resemblance to those of the Brown Thrush, to whom he is so nearly related in form, habits, and manners; but, like rude from cultivated genius, his notes are distinguished by the rapidity of their delivery, their variety, sweetness, and energy. As if conscious of his unrivalled powers of song, and animated by the harmony of his own voice, his music is, as it were, accompanied by chromatic dancing and expressive gestures; he spreads and closes his light and fanning wings, expands his silvered tail, and with buoyant gaiety and enthusiastic ecstasy he sweeps around, and mounts and descends into the air from his lofty spray as his song swells to loudness or dies away in sinking whispers. While thus engaged, so various is his talent that it might be supposed a trial of skill from all the assembled birds of the country; and so perfect are his imitations that even the sportsman is at times deceived, and sent in quest of birds that have no existence around him. The feathered tribes themselves are decoyed by the fancied call of their mates, or dive with fear into the close thicket at the well-feigned scream of the Hawk.

Soon reconciled to the usurping fancy of man, the Mocking Bird often becomes familiar with his master; playfully attacks him through the bars of his cage, or at large in a room; restless and capricious, he seems to try every expedient of a lively imagination that may conduce to his amusement. Nothing escapes his discerning and intelligent eye or faithful ear. He whistles perhaps for the dog, who, deceived, runs to meet his master; the cries of the chicken in distress bring out the clucking mother to the protection of her brood. The barking of the dog, the piteous wailing of the puppy, the mewing of the cat, the action of a saw, or the creaking of a wheelbarrow, quickly follow with exactness. He repeats a tune of considerable length; imitates the warbling of the Canary, the lisping of the Indigo Bird, and the mellow whistle of the Cardinal, in a manner so superior to the originals that, mortified and astonished, they withdraw from his presence, or listen in silence as he continues to triumph by renewing his efforts.

In the cage also, nearly as in the woods, he is full of life and action while engaged in song, throwing himself round with inspiring animation, and, as it were, moving in time to the melody of his own accents. Even the hours of night, which consign nearly all other birds to rest and silence, like the Nightingale he oft employs in song, serenading the houseless hunter and silent cottager to repose, as the rising moon illumines the darkness of the shadowy scene. His capricious fondness for contrast and perpetual variety appears to deteriorate his powers. His imitations of the Brown Thrush are perhaps interrupted by the crowing of the cock or the barking of the dog; the plaintive warblings of the Bluebird are then blended with the chatter of the Swallow or the cackling of the hen; amid the simple lay of the native Robin we are surprised with the vociferations of the Whip-poor-will; while the notes of the garrulous Jay, Wren, and many others succeed with such an appearance of reality that we almost imagine ourselves in the presence of the originals, and can scarcely realize the fact that the whole of this singular concert is the effort of a single bird. Indeed, it is impossible to listen to these Orphean strains, when delivered by a superior songster in his native woods, without being deeply affected and almost riveted to the spot by the complicated feelings of wonder and delight in which, from the graceful and sympathetic action, as well as enchanting voice of the performer, the eye is no less gratified than the ear. It is, however, painful to reflect that these extraordinary powers of nature, exercised with so much generous freedom in a state of confinement, are not calculated for long endurance, and after this most wonderful and interesting prisoner has survived for 6 or 7 years, blindness often terminates his gay career; and thus shut out from the cheering light, the solace of his lonely but active existence, he now after a time droops in silent sadness and dies.

SNOWFLAKE

THIS messenger of cold and stormy weather chiefly inhabits the higher regions of the Arctic circle, whence, as the severity of the winter threatens, they migrate indifferently over Europe, eastern Asia, and the United States. On their way to the South they appear round Hudson Bay in September, and stay till the frosts of November again oblige them to seek out warmer quarters. Early in December they make their descent into the Northern States in whirling roving flocks, either immediately before or soon after an inundating fall of snow. Amidst the drifts, and as they accumulate with the blast, flocks of these *illwars fogel*, or bad-weather birds, of the Swedes, like the spirits of the storm are to be seen flitting about in restless and hungry troops, at times resting on the wooden fences, though but for an instant, as, like the congenial Tartar hordes of their natal regions, they appear now to have no other object in view but an escape from famine and to carry on a general system of forage while they happen to stay in the vicinity. At times, pressed by hunger, they alight near the door of the cottage and approach the barn, or even venture into the out-houses in quest of dormant insects, seeds, or crumbs wherewith to allay their hunger; they are still, however, generally plump and fat, and in some countries much esteemed for the table. In fine weather they appear less restless, somewhat more familiar, and occasionally even at this season they chant out a few unconnected notes as they survey the happier face of Nature. At the period of incubation they are said to sing agreeably, but appear to seek out the most desolate regions of the cheerless North in which to waste the sweetness of their melody, unheard by any ear but that of their mates.

The nest is here fixed on the ground in the shelter of low bushes, and formed nearly of the same materials as that of the Common Song Sparrow.

At times they proceed as far south in the United States as the State of Maryland. They are here generally known by the name of the *White* Snow Bird, to distinguish them from the more common dark-bluish Sparrow, so called. They vary in their color according to age and season, and have always a great predominance of white in the plumage.

The Snow Buntings are seen in spring to assemble in Norway and its islands in great numbers; and after a stay of about three weeks they disappear for the season, and migrate across the Arctic Ocean to the farthest known land. On their return in winter to the Scottish Highlands their flocks are said to be immense, mingling, by an aggregating close flight, almost into the form of a ball, so as to present a very fatal and successful mark for the fowler. They arrive lean, but soon become fat. In Austria they are caught in snares or traps, and when fed with millet become equal to the Ortolan in value and flavor. When caged they show a very wakeful disposition, instantly hopping about in the night when a light is produced. Indulgence in this constant train of action and perpetual watchfulness may perhaps have its influence on this species, in the selection of their breeding places within the Arctic regions, where for months they continue to enjoy a perpetual day.

The food of these birds consists of various kinds of seeds and the larvæ of insects and minute shell-fish; the seeds of aquatic plants are also sometimes sought by them, and I have found in their stomachs those of the *Ruppia*, species of *Polygonum*, and gravel. In a state of confinement they shell and eat oats, millet, hemp-seed, and green peas, which they split. They rarely perch, and, like Larks, live much on the ground.

This harbinger of winter breeds in the northernmost of the

American islands and on all the shores of the continent from Chesterfield Inlet to Behring's Straits. The most southerly of its breeding stations in America, according to Richardson, is Southampton Island, in the 62d parallel, where Captain Lyons found a nest, by a strange fatality, placed in the bosom of the exposed corpse of an Esquimaux child. Well clothed and hardy by nature, the Snow Bunting even lingers about the forts of the fur countries and open places, picking up grass-seeds, until the snow becomes deep. It is only during the months of December and January that it retires to the southward of Saskatchewan, and it is seen again there on its return as early as the middle of February, two months after which it arrives in the 65th parallel, and by the beginning of May it has penetrated to the coast of the Polar Sea. At this period it feeds upon the buds of the purple saxifrage (saxifraga oppositifolia), one of the most early of the Arctic plants.

YELLOW-LEGS

*C*HESE birds reside chiefly in the salt-marshes, and frequent low flats and estuaries at the ebb of the tide, wading in the mud in quest of worms, insects, and other small marine and fluviatile animals. They seldom leave these maritime situations, except driven from the coast by storms, when they may occasionally be seen in low and wet meadows as far inland as the extent of tide-water. The Yellow-Shanks have a sharp whistle of three or four short notes, which they repeat when alarmed and when flying, and sometimes utter a simple, low, and rather hoarse call, which passes from one to the other at the moment of rising on the wing. They are very impatient of any intrusion on their haunts, and thus often betray the approach of the sportsman to the less vigilant of the feathered tribes, by flying around his head, with hanging legs and drooping wings, uttering incessant and querulous cries.

At the approach of autumn small flocks here also accompany the Upland Plover (*Totanus bartramius*), flying high and whistling as they proceed inland to feed, but returning again towards the marshes of the sea-coast to roost. Sometimes, and perhaps more commonly at the approach of stormy weather, they are seen in small restless bands roving over the salt-marshes and tacking and turning along the meanders of the river, now crossing, then returning; a moment alighting, the next on the wing. They then spread out and reconnoitre; again closing in a loose phalanx, the glittering of their wings and snow-white tails are seen conspicuous as they mount into the higher regions of the air; and now intent on some more distant excursion, they rise, whistling on their way, high over the village spire and beyond the reach of danger, pursue their

184

way to some other clime or to explore new marshes and visit other coasts more productive of their favorite fare. While skimming along the surface of the neighboring river, I have been amused by the sociability of these wandering waders. As they course steadily along, the party, never very numerous, would be joined by some straggling Peeps, who all in unison pursue their route together like common wanderers or travellers, pleased and defended by the access of any company.

WILLIAM BEEBE

XI

WILLIAM BEEBE

*C*HE first scientific book on birds that I ever read was given me, when I was in my 'teens, by a person even younger than myself. The donor was my future wife, and the book was *The Bird* by William Beebe. I wonder if many other young readers have not, like myself, taken their step beyond the field identification of birds through this excellent book? For me it revealed the relationship of structure to function; it taught me my first (and still so incomplete) notions of anatomy which are, after all, the basis of those very systematics by which so many of us progress from esthetic to scientific appreciation.

And the first book that I ever bought with money earned on my twelve-dollar-a-week job was Dr. Beebe's *Jungle Peace* (1918) from which I have selected for quotation his now famous experience of that incredible South American bird, the hoatzin. These two books, still on the shelves behind me, constituted the starting point of my small library on ornithology.

Dr. Beebe is probably the most widely popular of American naturalists today. The brilliance of his popularizations and his feat of descent by bathysphere into the depths of the ocean account in part for his fame that is so firmly established even with those who know little of science. His public career, then, needs no comment here; his achievements in oceanography are outside the scope of these few lines; my concern will be with Dr. Beebe the ornithologist, and it will be understood that his learning of natural history in general and his accomplishments in many fields outside ornithology are assumed as acknowledged.

William Beebe was born in Brooklyn, N. Y., in 1877. His boyhood was spent in East Orange, and he was early fascinated by Nature. This interest was encouraged by his parents, while the romances of Jules Verne fostered his love of exploration and filled his young mind with visions of traveling forty thousand leagues under the sea and visiting incredible tropic isles. While the French novelist had to journey in the realms of imagination only, Dr. Beebe has been privileged to accomplish his dreams.

At the age of nineteen young Beebe entered Columbia and passed under the tutelage of Prof. Henry Fairfield Osborn who from the first believed him a pupil of outstanding brilliance. Soon after leaving college Beebe was appointed curator of birds at the then new Zoölogical Society's headquarters in Bronx Park (known to New Yorkers simply as "the Bronx zoo").

Dr. Beebe left very soon for Mexico in quest of birds. Again, he journeyed to Venezuela and British Guiana. Between trips he worked at the Bronx on the construction of the water bird, land bird, and ostrich houses.

One of the directors of the society, Col. Anthony R. Kuser, who owned a magnificent collection of living pheasants, interested Dr. Beebe in those kingly creatures. Between them the two men worked out plans for an expedition to Asia and the East Indies, where Dr. Beebe was to seek out in its native habitat every species of pheasant in the world. Specimens were to be taken, and eggs and nests; drawings and photographs were to be made, life history notes collected. And, in short, the result planned was a monumental monograph upon this gorgeous family of birds which disputes with parrots and hummingbirds and trogons and birds-of-paradise the royalty of the feathered phylum.

Col. Kuser acted as patron of the expedition, but the field

work was carried out by young Dr. Beebe quite alone. The conditions of travel were often extremely fatiguing and even dangerous; the task of collecting and study was sometimes difficult beyond anything that a bird student in a temperate country has to encounter. His travels took Dr. Beebe to Ceylon and the Himalayas, China, Japan, Java, Borneo, and other regions of southeastern Asia. The story of these labors may be read in a delightful book, *Pheasant Jungles*, and a popular ornithological account is given in *Pheasants—Their Lives and Homes*. But the *Monographs of the Pheasants* (1918) is of course the true scientific result of the arduous labors, and on it Dr. Beebe's reputation as an ornithologist is firmly founded. It won him the Elliot gold medal of the National Academy of Sciences.

During the preparation of the monographs, Dr. Beebe had made an exploring trip up the Amazon. He became impressed with the ignorance of tropical bird life, beyond systematic knowledge, prevalent even among scientists. On one occasion it is said, he spent one week under a fruiting tree, simply observing the birds that came to it. As a result of his absorption in tropical life, he planned and put through a field laboratory of tropical investigation in the British Guiana jungle, scene of Waterton's famous *Wanderings*. Dr. Beebe marked out one quarter square mile of this forest for intensive exploration. Not a nest was to escape observation, not a beetle or berry that might serve as food to a bird. At the end of a season's work it seemed that all their efforts, in Dr. Beebe's words, were "like the scratch of a single dredge along the bottom of an unknown ocean."

In 1923, Mr. Harrison Williams, a trustee of the Zoölogical Society, furnished a yacht for exploration of the Galapagos archipelago, whose curious life had awakened in Darwin's mind the first suggestion of the idea of natural selection. Much undoubtedly remained to be done in this field, and the expedition, headed by Dr. Beebe, cast anchor off these unearthly isles. Only one hundred hours were spent ashore, but many fascinating results were obtained. The record of this delightful sojourn may be read in *Galapagos—World's End*, which is rich in ornithological notes.

A return was planned in the now famous yacht *Arcturus*, but the scope of the plan widened until it included general oceanographic work on both shores of the two Americas. In this great project Dr. Beebe is still engaged, most recently in Templeton Crocker's yacht *Zaca*.

The hoatzins, of which Dr. Beebe speaks in the following pages, are birds belonging to a single species, which comprises a single genus, family, and sub-order. The skeletal structure is in many ways unique, and so are the soft internal parts, notably the immense gizzard-like, two-lobed crop. The food of the bird is almost entirely leaves!

But most remarkable of all is the behavior of the young who are able to climb and hang on to limbs not only by their hooked bills and big strong claws, but by the stiff terminals of the wings. They give thereby almost the impression of young arboreal reptiles; the use of the wing-tips recalls to us that the wing of a bird is after all a modified fore-leg, and in many ways the hoatzin young seem to recapitulate fossil Archaeopteryx itself, though the adult is not especially primitive, having been variously considered as related to pheasants, pigeons, rails, and plantain-eaters.

The name hoatzin, sometimes spelled hoactzin, is derived from a Nahuatl Indian word. The range of this species is in the northern and western portions of South America from Bolivia to Colombia and the Guianas, but especially in the valley of the Amazon.

HOATZINS AT HOME

*I*N NOVEMBER in New York City an Englishman from British Guiana said to me, "Go to the Berbice River, and at the north end of the town of New Amsterdam, in front of Mr. Beckett's house, you will find hoatzins." Six months later as I drove along a tropical river road I saw three hoatzins perched on a low thorn bush at the river's edge in front of a house. And the river was the Berbice, and the house that of Mr. Beckett.

We took a boat opposite Mr. Beckett's house, and paddled slowly with the nearly-flood tide up the Berbice River. It was two o'clock, the hottest time of the day. For three miles we drifted past the chosen haunts of the hoatzins. All were perched in the shade, quiet in the intense heat, squatting prostrate or sleepily preening their plumage. Now and then we saw a bird on her nest, always over the water. If she was sitting on eggs she sat close. If young birds were in the nest she half-crouched, or perched on the rim, so that her body cast a shadow over the young.

The vegetation was not varied. Muckamucka was here and there in the foreground, with an almost solid line of bunduri pimpler or thorn tree. This was the real home of the birds, and this plant forms the background whenever the hoatzin comes to mind. It is a growth which loves the water, and crowds down so that the rising of the tide, whether fresh or brackish, covers the mud in which it stands, so that it appears to be quite as aquatic as the mangrove which, here and there, creeps out alongside it.

The pimpler bears thorns of the first magnitude, often double, recurved and at such diabolically unexpected places that, like barbed wire, it is impossible to grasp anywhere with-

out drawing blood. Such a chevaux-de-frise would defend a
trench against the most courageous regiment. The stems were
light gray, greening toward the younger shoots, and the foliage
was pleasantly divided into double lines of locust-like leaflets.

The plants were in full flower,—dainty, upright panicles of
wisteria-like pea-blooms, pale violet and white with tiny buds
of magenta. A faint, subdued perfume drifted from them
through the tangle of branches. The fruit was ripening on
many plants, in clusters of green, semi-circular, flat, kidney
pods. The low branches stretched gracefully waterwards in
long sweeping curves. On these at a fork or at the crossing
of two distinct branches, the hoatzins placed their nests, and
with the soft-tissued leaflets they packed their capacious crops
and fed their young.

Besides these two plants, which alone may be considered
as forming the principal environment, two blooms were conspicuous at this season; a deep-calyxed, round blossom of rich
yellow,—an hibiscus, which the Indians called makoe, and
from the bark of which they made most excellent rope. The
other flower was a vine which crept commonly up over the
pimpler trees, regardless of water and thorns, and hung out
twin blossoms in profusion, pink and pinkish-white, trumpet-
shaped, with flaring lips.

The mid-day life about this haunt of hoatzins was full of
interest. Tody-flycatchers of two species, yellow-breasted and
streaked, were the commonest birds, and their little homes,
like bits of tide-hung drift, swayed from the tips of the pimpler branches. They dashed to and fro regardless of the heat,
and whenever we stopped they came within a foot or two,
curiously watching our every motion. Kiskadees hopped along
the water's edge in the shade, snatching insects and occasionally splashing into the water after small fish. Awkward Guinea
green herons, not long out of the nest, crept like shadow sil-
houettes of birds close to the dark water. High overhead, like

flecks of jet against the blue sky, the vultures soared. Green dragonflies whirled here and there, and great blue-black bees fumbled in and out of the hibiscus, yellowed with pollen and too busy to stop a second in their day-long labor.

This little area held very strange creatures as well, some of which we saw even in our few hours' search. Four-eyed fish skittered over the water, pale as the ghosts of fish, and when quiet, showing only as a pair of bubbly eyes. Still more weird hairy caterpillars wriggled their way through the muddy, brackish current—aquatic larvæ of a small moth which I had not seen since I found them in the trenches of Pará.

The only sound at this time of day was a drowsy but penetrating tr-r-r-r-p! made by a green-bodied, green-legged grasshopper of good size, whose joy in life seemed to be to lie lengthwise upon a pimpler branch, and skreek violently at frequent intervals, giving his wings a frantic flutter at each utterance, and slowly encircling the stem.

In such environment the hoatzin lives and thrives, and, thanks to its strong body odor, has existed from time immemorial in the face of terrific handicaps. The odor is a strong musky one, not particularly disagreeable. I searched my memory at every whiff for something of which it vividly reminded me, and at last the recollection came to me—the smell, delectable and fearfully exciting in former years—of elephants at a circus, and not altogether elephants either, but a compound of one-sixth sawdust, another part peanuts, another of strange animals and three-sixths swaying elephant. That, to my mind, exactly describes the odor of hoatzins as I sensed it among these alien surroundings.

As I have mentioned, the nest of the hoatzin was invariably built over the water, and we shall later discover the reason for this. The nests were sometimes only four feet above high water, or equally rarely, at a height of forty to fifty feet. From six to fifteen feet included the zone of four-fifths of the nests of these birds. They varied much in solidity, some being frail and loosely put together, the dry, dead sticks which composed them dropping apart almost at a touch. Usually they were as well knitted as a heron's, and in about half the cases consisted of a recent nest built upon the foundations of an old one. There was hardly any cavity at the top, and the coarse network of sticks looked like a precarious resting place for eggs and an exceedingly uncomfortable one for young birds.

When we approached a nest, the occupant paid no attention until we actually came close to a branch, or shook it. She then rose, protesting hoarsely, and lifting wings and tail as she croaked. At the last moment, often when only a yard away, she flew off and away to a distance of fifty feet or more. Watching closely, when she realized that we really had intentions on her nest, she returned and perched fifteen or twenty feet away, croaking continually, her mate a little farther off, and all the hoatzins within sight or hearing joining in sympathetic disharmony, all with synchronous lifting of tail and wings at each utterance.

The voice of the female is appreciably deeper than that of the male, having more of a gurgling character, like one of the notes of a curassow. The usual note of both sexes is an unwritable, hoarse, creaking sound, quite cicada or frog-like.

Their tameness was astounding, and they would often sit unmoved, while we were walking noisily about, or focusing the camera within two yards. If several were sitting on a branch and one was shot, the others would often show no symptoms of concern or alarm, either at the noise of the gun or the fall of their companion. A hoatzin which may have been crouched close to the slain bird would continue to preen its plumage without a glance downward. When the young had attained their first full plumage it was almost impossible to distinguish them from the older members of the flock except by their generally smaller size.

But the heart of our interest in the hoatzins centered in the nestlings. Some kind Providence directed the time of our visit, which I chose against the advice of some of the very inhabitants of New Amsterdam. It turned out that we were on the scene exactly at the right time. A week either way would have yielded much poorer results. The nestlings, in seven occupied nests, observed as we drifted along shore, or landed and climbed among the thorns, were in an almost identical stage of development. In fact, the greatest difference in size occurred between two nestlings of the same brood. Their down was a thin, scanty, fuzzy covering, and the flight feathers were less than a half-inch in length. No age would have showed to better advantage every movement of wings or head.

When a mother hoatzin took reluctant flight from her nest, the young bird at once stood upright and looked curiously in every direction. No slacker he, crouching flat or awaiting his mother's directing cries. From the moment he was left alone he began to depend upon the warnings and signs which his great beady eyes and skinny ears conveyed to him. Hawks and vultures had swept low over his nest and mother unheeded. Coolies in their boats had paddled underneath with no more than a glance upward. Throughout his week of life, as through his parents' and their parents' parents' lives, no danger had disturbed their peaceful existence. Only for a sudden windstorm such as that which the week before had upset nests and blown out eggs, it might be said that for the little hoatzin chicks life held nothing but siestas and munchings of pimpler leaves.

But one little hoatzin, if he had any thoughts such as these, failed to count on the invariable exceptions to every rule, for this day the totally unexpected happened. Fate, in the shape of enthusiastic scientists, descended upon him. He was not for a second nonplussed. If we had concentrated upon him a thousand strong, by boats and by land, he would have fought the good fight for freedom and life as calmly as he waged it against us. And we found him no mean antagonist, and far from reptilian in his ability to meet new and unforeseen conditions.

His mother, who a moment before had been packing his capacious little crop with predigested pimpler leaves, had now flown off to an adjoining group of mangroves, where she and his father croaked to him hoarse encouragement. His flight feathers hardly reached beyond his finger-tips, and his body was covered with a sparse coating of sooty black down. So there could be no resort to flight. He must defend himself, bound to earth like his assailants.

Hardly had his mother left when his comical head, with thick, blunt beak and large intelligent eyes, appeared over the rim of the nest. His alert expression was increased by the suspicion of a crest on his crown where the down was slightly longer. Higher and higher rose his head, supported on a neck of extraordinary length and thinness. No more than this was needed to mark his absurd resemblance to some strange, extinct reptile. A young dinosaur must have looked much like this, while for all that my glance revealed, I might have been looking at a diminutive Galapagos tortoise. Indeed this simile came to mind often when I became more intimate with nestling hoatzins.

Sam, my black tree-climber, kicked off his shoes and began creeping along the horizontal limbs of the pimplers. At every step he felt carefully with a calloused sole in order to avoid the longer of the cruel thorns, and punctuated every yard with some gasp of pain or muttered personal prayer, "Pleas' doan' stick me, Thorns!"

At last his hand touched the branch, and it shook slightly. The young bird stretched his mittened hands high above his head and waved them a moment. With similar intent a boxer or wrestler flexes his muscles and bends his body. One or two uncertain, forward steps brought the bird to the edge of the nest at the base of a small branch. There he stood, and raising one wing leaned heavily against the stem, bracing himself. My man climbed higher and the nest swayed violently.

Now the brave little hoatzin reached up to some tiny side twigs and, aided by the projecting ends of dead sticks from the nest, he climbed with facility, his thumbs and forefingers apparently being of more aid than his feet. It was fascinating to see him ascend, stopping now and then to crane his head and neck far out, turtle-wise. He met every difficulty with some new contortion of body or limbs, often with so quick or so subtle a shifting as to escape my scrutiny. The branch ended in a tiny crotch and here perforce, ended his attempt at escape by climbing. He stood on the swaying twig, one wing clutched tight, and braced himself with both feet.

Nearer and nearer crept Sam. Not a quiver on the part of the little hoatzin. We did not know it, but inside that ridiculous head there was definite decision as to a deadline. He watched the approach of this great, strange creature—this Danger, this thing so wholly new and foreign to his experience, and doubtless to all the generations of his forbears. A black hand grasped the thorny branch six feet from his perch, and like a flash he played his next trick—the only remaining one he knew, one that set him apart from all modern land birds, as the frog is set apart from the swallow.

The young hoatzin stood erect for an instant, and then both wings of the little bird were stretched straight back, not folded, bird-wise, but dangling loosely and reaching well beyond the body. For a considerable fraction of time he leaned forward. Then without effort, without apparent leap or jump he dived straight downward, as beautifully as a seal, direct as a plummet and very swiftly. There was a scarcely-noticeable splash, and as I gazed with real awe, I watched the widening ripples which undulated over the muddy water—the only trace of the whereabouts of the young bird.

It seemed as if no one, whether ornithologist, evolutionist, poet or philosopher could fail to be profoundly impressed at the sight we had seen. Here I was in a very real, a very modern boat, with the honk of motor horns sounding from the river road a few yards away through the bushes, in the shade of this tropical vegetation in the year nineteen hundred and sixteen; and yet the curtain of the past had been lifted and I had been permitted a glimpse of what must have been common in the millions of years ago. It was a tremendous thing, a wonderful thing to have seen, and it seemed to dwarf all the strange sights which had come to me in all other parts of the earth's wilderness. I had read of these habits and had expected them, but like one's first sight of a volcano in eruption, no reading or description prepares one for the actual phenomenon.

I sat silently watching for the re-appearance of the young bird. We tallied five pairs of eyes and yet many minutes passed before I saw the same little head and emaciated neck sticking out of the water alongside a bit of drift rubbish. The only visible thing was the protruding spikes of the bedraggled tail feathers. I worked the boat in toward the bird, half-heartedly, for I had made up my mind that this particular brave little bit of atavism deserved his freedom, so splendidly had he fought for it among the pimplers. Soon he ducked forward, dived out of sight and came up twenty feet away among an inextricable tangle of vines. I sent a little cheer of well wishing after him and we salvaged Sam.

Then we shoved out the boat and watched from a distance. Five or six minutes passed and a skinny, crooked, two-fingered mitten of an arm reared upward out of the muddy flood and the nestling, black and glistening, hauled itself out of water.

Thus must the first amphibian have climbed into the thin air. But the young hoatzin neither gasped nor shivered, and seemed as self-possessed as if this was a common occurrence in its life. There was not the slightest doubt however, that this was its first introduction to water. Yet it had dived from a height of fifteen feet, about fifty times its own length, as cleanly as a seal leaps from a berg. It was as if a human child should dive two hundred feet!

In fifteen minutes more it had climbed high above the water, and with unerring accuracy directly toward its natal bundle of sticks overhead. The mother now came close, and with hoarse rasping notes and frantic heaves of tail and wings lent encouragement. Just before we paddled from sight, when the little fellow had reached his last rung, he partly opened his beak and gave a little falsetto cry,—a clear, high tone, tailing off into a guttural rasp. His splendid courage had broken at last; he had nearly reached the nest and he was aching to put aside all this terrible responsibility, this pitting of his tiny might against such fearful odds. He wanted to be a helpless nestling again, to crouch on the springy bed of twigs with a feather comforter over him and be stuffed at will with delectable pimpler pap. Such is the normal right destiny of a hoatzin chick, and the whee-og! wrung from him by the reaction of safety seemed to voice all this.

PHILIP HENRY GOSSE

XII

PHILIP HENRY GOSSE

*I*T IS not easy to charm most of us who have positively patriotic feelings about our familiar birds, with descriptions of exotic song and plumage. I know that, for myself, I have long reached a stage of contentment with the bird world about which I still know all too little—the avifauna of North America and Europe. Towards the stranger and often more gorgeous creatures of nearly fabulous places, I have reservations. So that it was with some cool skepticism that I first opened Gosse's *Birds of Jamaica*. But my languor was short. I was presently delivered over to the writer, and still more to West Indian birds, which he has made me long to see and hear. The spell of island life, the beauty of wild tropical scenery, and the adventure of toiling through mountain jungles to hear the mysterious notes of some unseen singer, he made me feel. And since, except among ornithologists aware of the history of their science, Gosse has been so nearly forgotten, it gives me pleasure to bring him forward, without claiming anything extravagant for him, to the attention of modern readers.

Philip Henry Gosse was born in Worcester, England, in 1810. From his father, a miniature painter, the future naturalist inherited, no doubt, his talent for drawing, that went so far to make him the most popular of popularizers of science in a former generation.

Gosse's earliest employment was in a whaler's office in Newfoundland. There he beguiled the tedium of his life by making his first acquaintance with the northern birds of the New World and a little later he tried, unsuccessfully, to farm in Canada and then taught school in Alabama. His *Letters from Alabama* are marked by much humor and appreciation; we see the man in the full ebullience of youth, his style still unformed and not yet quite satisfactory but already vivid and popular. Many notices of birds occur in these letters, but the debt he owes to Wilson and Audubon, not apparent to English readers, is a little too great.

Before long Gosse had either had enough of Alabama or it of him (he is a critical guest) and he returned to England, writing on the voyage his *Canadian Naturalist*, soon followed by an *Introduction to Zoölogy*. But *The Ocean* (1844) definitely established him as a remarkable writer on natural history, and, receiving a teaching appointment at the British Museum, he was assured, after much penury, of some income.

This was an era when great movements were afoot in English science; the air tingled with a coming battle of titans; the public too was eager for popularizations of natural science, and the collecting mania (which is not really scientific at all) had just discovered in tree and pond, on the shore and in the tidal pools, an untouched field where the objects of collection cost nothing and might, as they became rare, sell dear. Gosse was the cabinet god and encyclopedia of these people. His personal approach, his easy narration and his style deeply tinged with appreciation of Nature, as well as his high repute as a sound naturalist, destined him to great success.

To this happy period we owe *The Birds of Jamaica* (1847) from which my quotations are made. For Gosse had been sent to that island by the British Museum to collect specimens, and there had remained two years. The book reveals him as an excellent ornithologist of the time, a keen observer, and a most fluent and yet unaffected describer. In particular Gosse seems to have had an ear for bird song and the rarer ability to make us *feel* the song even when we do not know how it goes.

On his return Gosse labored on many books at once, both technical and popular. He injured his health, withdrew from London and the association of scientific men, and met and married Emily Bowes. Partly under her influence, perhaps, his naturally conscience-searching and emotional nature was drawn in conversion to a small religious sect more Calvinist than Calvin.

To this couple was born in 1849 the future poet and critic, Edmund Gosse. The naturalist disposes of the event in his diary thus:

"E. delivered of a son. Received green swallows from Jamaica."

Mrs. Gosse died while the boy was young. The father with the best of intentions now charged himself with the lad's upbringing and attacked it with appalling zeal. At heart the boy was a creative artist, in need of mental liberty. The atmosphere at home was one of a revival meeting relieved only by the disciplines of science. So began a struggle of two temperaments, made not less poignant by their mutual love and dependence for society.

The fearful record of these years has been told by Edmund Gosse, in *Father and Son*. This astounding biography concerns us here only so far as it records the falling star of an eminent naturalist.

For the Darwinian controversy had begun to rage. And as Gosse's sect demanded a literal interpretation of the Bible, and all his training demanded that he accept the evidence for evolution written upon the very rocks, Gosse's mental conflict was terrible. In the end he decided to save his soul.

Other scientists—Agassiz and Fabre for instance—have denied evolution, continued splendid work without it, and retained the esteem of fellow workers. But Gosse committed a fatal blunder. He tried to reconcile science and religion by two books embodying an explanation in scientific terms of the way in which even the most complex organisms could have sprung from the dust in a twinkling, and the very fossils have taken their place in the rocks at once.

His friend Darwin forbore to comment. Huxley's scorn was acid. Even the approval of the pious was no consolation, for they imagined that Gosse had claimed that God put the fossils in the rocks to tempt geologists to infidelity.

From this time dates the downfall of Gosse as a scientist. But his capacities as an interpreter of Nature were not abated. Turning to further popular works, always illustrated with exquisite draftsmanship, he hastened, by his very success, the stripping of the tidal pools of England of all their rarities, at the hands of collectors fired by his beautiful descriptions.

Finally, disappointed on all counts, Gosse abandoned authorship and devoted himself to a second wife and to the raising of orchids. To this date belongs a letter I happen to own, which illustrates, though but a scrap, the irreconcilable currents in his nature:

Sandhurst, 8 Sept. 1887

WM. LAVERS, *Esq.*

Accept, my very kind Friend my best thanks for the beautiful little Nepenthes * you so generously left for me just now; it is unfortunate that it occurred during my Scripture Reading. We unite in true affection to you all.

Yours ever,

P. H. GOSSE

I would draw attention to a detail in the excerpts which follow, a detail that illustrates the scientific times. I refer to his attempts to capture alive and transplant for possible acclimatizing in England, some West Indian hummingbirds. We note the same desire on Wallace's part, with respect to birds of paradise. How difficult a task was this Gosse did not well understand. It seems that a bird must have some undesirable

* Pitcher-plant. [Ed.]

features, like starlings and house sparrows, to make its way in a new environment. The western and eastern hemispheres cannot readily exchange their hummingbirds and nightingales. And today our understanding and appreciation of Nature have so altered that the idea of transplanting even beautiful birds that belong elsewhere hardly seems interesting or in good taste. But the Victorian drawing-room was notoriously over-ornamented.

LONG-TAILED HUMMINGBIRD

CHIS is the gem of Jamaican Ornithology. Its slender form, velvet crest, emerald bosom, and lengthened tail-plumes, render it one of the most elegant even of this most brilliant family. Though peculiar, as far as I am aware, to Jamaica, it has long been known, though it would seem from received figures and descriptions very imperfectly.

In the latter part of February, a friend showed me a nest of this species in a singular situation, but which I afterwards found to be quite in accordance with its usual habits. It was at Bognie, situated on the Bluefields mountain, but at some distance from the scenes above described. About a quarter of a mile within the woods, a blind path, choked up with bushes, descends suddenly beneath an overhanging rock of limestone, the face of which presents large projections, and hanging points, encrusted with a rough, tuberculous sort of stalactite. At one corner of the bottom there is a cavern, in which a tub is fixed to receive water of great purity, which perpetually drips from the roof, and which in the dry season is a most valuable resource. Beyond this, which is very obscure, the eye penetrates to a larger area, deeper still, which receives light from some other communication with the air. Round the projections and groins of the front, the roots of the trees above have entwined, and to a fibre of one of these hanging down, not thicker than whipcord, was suspended a Humming-bird's nest, containing two eggs. It seemed to be composed wholly of moss, was thick, and attached to the rootlet by its side. One of the eggs was broken. I did not disturb it, but after about three weeks, visited it again. It had been apparently handled by some curious child, for both eggs were broken, and the nest was evidently deserted.

But while I lingered in the romantic place, picking up some of the landshells which were scattered among the rocks, suddenly I heard the whirr of a Humming-bird, and, looking up, saw a female Polytmus hovering opposite the nest, with a mass of silk-cotton in her beak. Deterred by the sight of me, she presently retired to a twig, a few paces distant, on which she sat. I immediately sunk down among the rocks as quietly as possible, and remained perfectly still. In a few seconds she came again, and after hovering a moment disappeared behind one of the projections, whence in a few seconds she emerged again and flew off. I then examined the place, and found to my delight, a new nest, in all respects like the old one, but unfinished, affixed to another twig not a yard from it. I again sat down among the stones in front, where I could see the nest, not concealing myself, but remaining motionless, waiting for the petite bird's reappearance. I had not to wait long: a loud *whirr*, and there she was, suspended in the air before her nest: she soon espied me, and came within a foot of my eyes, hovering just in front of my face. I remained still, however, when I heard the whirring of another just above me, perhaps the mate, but I durst not look towards him lest the turning of my head should frighten the female. In a minute or two the other was gone, and she alighted again on the twig, where she sat some little time preening her feathers, and apparently clearing her mouth from the cotton-fibres, for she now and then swiftly projected the tongue an inch and a half from the beak, continuing the same curve as that of the beak. When she arose, it was to perform a very interesting action; for she flew to the face of the rock, which was thickly clothed with soft dry moss, and hovering on the wing, as if before a flower, began to pluck the moss, until she had a large bunch of it in her beak; then I saw her fly to the nest, and *having seated herself in it*, proceed to place the new material, pressing, and arranging, and interweaving the whole with her beak, while she fashioned the cup-like form of the interior, by the pressure of her white breast, moving round and round as she sat. My presence appeared to be no hindrance to her proceedings, though only a few feet distant; at length she left again, and I left the place also. On the 8th of April I visited the cave again, and found the nest perfected, and containing two eggs, which were not hatched on the 1st of May, on which day I sent Sam * to endeavour to secure both dam and nest. He found her sitting, and had no difficulty in capturing her, which, with the nest and its contents, he carefully brought down to me. I transferred it, having broken one egg by accident, to a cage, and put in the bird; she was mopish, however, and quite neglected the nest, as she did also some flowers which I inserted; sitting moodily on a perch. The next morning she was dead.

The tongue of this species, (and doubtless others have a similar conformation) presents, when recent, the appearance of two tubes laid side by side, united by half their length, but separate for the remainder. Their substance is transparent in the same degree as a good quill, which they much resemble: each tube is formed by a lamina rolled up, yet not so as to bring the edges into actual contact, for there is a longitudinal fissure on the outer side, running up considerably higher than the junction of the tubes; into this fissure the point of a pin may be inserted and moved up and down the length. Near the tip the *outer* edge of each lamina ceases to be convoluted, but is spread out, and split at the margin into irregular fimbriæ, which point backward, somewhat like the vane of a feather; these are not barbs, however, but simply soft and flexible points, such as might be produced by snipping diagonally the edge of a strip of paper. I conjecture that the nectar of flowers is pumped up the tubes, and that minute

* Samuel Campbell, Gosse's young negro collector, a boy of great talent for his work. [Ed.]

insects are caught, when in flowers, in these spoon-like tips, their minute limbs being perhaps entangled in the fimbriæ, when the tongue is retracted into the beak, and the insects swallowed by the ordinary process, as doubtless those are which are captured with the beak in flight. I do not thoroughly understand the mode by which liquids are taken up by a Humming-bird's tongue, though I have carefully watched the process. If syrup be presented to one in a quill, the tongue is protruded for about half an inch into the liquor, the beak resting in a pen, as it is held horizontal: there is a slight but rapid and constant projection and retraction of the tubes, and the liquor disappears very fast, perhaps by capillary attraction, perhaps by a sort of pumping, certainly not by licking.

When I left England, I had laid myself out for the attempt to bring these radiant creatures alive to this country. Very many were caught by myself and my lads: the narrow path on Bluefields peak already mentioned, was the locality to which we resorted on these expeditions. A common gauze butterfly-net, on a ring of a foot in diameter and a staff of three or four feet, we found the most effective means of capture. The elaborate traps recommended by some authors, I feel would suit the natural history of the closet, better than that of the woods. We often found the curiosity of these little birds stronger than their fear; on holding up the net near one, he frequently would not fly away, but come and hover over the mouth, stretching out his neck to peep in, so that we could capture them with little difficulty. Often too, one when struck at unsuccessfully, would return immediately, and suspend itself in the air just above our heads, or peep into our faces, with unconquerable familiarity. Yet it was difficult to bring these sweet birds, so easily captured, home; they were usually dead or dying when we arrived at the house, though not wounded or struck. And those which did arrive in apparent health, usually died the next day. At my first attempt in the spring of 1845, I transferred such as I succeeded in bringing alive, to cages immediately on their arrival at the house, and though they did not beak themselves, they soon sunk under the confinement. Suddenly they would fall to the floor of the cage, and lie motionless with closed eyes; if taken into the hand, they would perhaps seem to revive for a few minutes; then throw back the pretty head, or toss it to and fro as if in great suffering, expand the wings, open the eyes, slightly puff up the feathers of the breast, and die: usually without any convulsive struggle. This was the fate of my first attempts.

From that time to the end of May, I obtained about twenty-five more, nearly all males. Many of those which were found alive, were in a dying state, and of those which were turned out into the room, several more died in the first twenty-four hours; so that out of the twenty-five, only seven were domesticated. These, however, became quite at home; and I may here observe that there was much difference in the tempers of individuals; some being moody and sulky, others very timid, and others gentle and confiding from the first. I have noticed this in other birds also; Doves, for instance, which manifest individuality of character, perhaps as much as men, if we were competent to appreciate it. My ordinary plan of accustoming them to the room, and teaching them to feed, was very simple. On opening the basket in which one or more newly-caught Humming-birds were brought home, they would fly out, and commonly soar to the ceiling, rarely seeking the window; there for awhile, or against the walls, as above mentioned, they would flutter, not beating themselves, but hanging on rapidly vibrating wings, lightly touching the plaster with the beak or breast, every second, and thus slightly rebounding. By keeping a strict watch on them while so occupied, we could observe when they became exhausted, and sunk rapidly down to alight; commonly, they would then suffer themselves to be raised, by passing the finger under the breast, to which they would apply their little feet. Having thus raised one on my finger, and taken a little sugar into my mouth, I inserted its beak between my lips. Sometimes it would at once begin to suck eagerly; but at other times it was needful to invite it thus many times, before it would notice the sugar: by persevering, however, they commonly learned. And when one had once fed from the mouth, it was always ready to suck afterwards, and frequently, as above narrated, voluntarily sought my lips. Having given one his first lesson, I gently presented him to the line, and drawing my finger from under him, he would commonly take to it, but if not, the proceeding had to be repeated: and even when perched, the repetition of the feeding and placing on the line was needful to induce the habit. If the bird's temper were kindly, it soon began to perch on the line of its own accord; when I ceased to feed it from my lips, presenting to it, instead, the glass of syrup. After it had sucked thus a time or two, it found it as it stood at the edge of a table; and I considered it domesticated. Their ordinary mode of coming down to drink was curious. Instead of flying down soberly in a direct line, which would have been far too dull for the volatile genius of a Hummingbird, they invariably made a dozen or twenty distinct stages of it, each in a curve descending a little, and ascending nearly to the same plane, and hovering a second or two at every angle; and sometimes when they arrived opposite the cup more quickly than usual, as if they considered it reached too soon, they would make half a dozen more horizontal traverses before they would bring their tiny feet to the edge of the glass and insert their sucking tongue. They were rather late in retiring to roost, frequently hawking and sporting till dusk; and when settled for the night, were restless, and easily disturbed. The entrance of a person with a candle, at any hour, was liable to set one or two upon the wing; and this was always a matter

of regret with me, because of the terror which they seemed
to feel, incapacitating them from again finding the perching
line. After having inhabited my specimen-room for some time,
(those first caught almost four weeks,) I transferred them, five
in number, all males, to a large cage with a wired front, and
two transverse perches; I had much dreaded this change, and
therefore did it in the evening, hoping that the intervening
night would calm them. I had in some measure prepared
them for the change by placing the cage (before the front was
affixed) upon the table some days previously, and setting their
syrup-cup first close to the cage, then a little within, then a
little farther, until at length it stood at the remotest corner.
And I was pleased to observe that the birds followed the cup
every day, flying in and out of the cage to sip, though at
first very shyly and suspiciously, many times flying in and suddenly darting out without tasting the fluid. After I had shut
them in, they beat and fluttered a good deal; but by the next
day I was gratified to find that all had taken their places
quietly on the perches, and sipped at the syrup, though rather
less than usual. I had now high hopes of bringing them alive
to England, thinking the most difficult task was over; especially as within a day or two after, I added to them two more
males, one of which presently learned both to perch and to
find the cup, and also a female. The latter interested me
much, for on the next day after her introduction, I noticed
that she had seated herself by a long-tailed male, on a perch
occupied only by them two, and was evidently courting his
caresses. She would hop sideways along the perch by a series
of little quick jumps, till she reached him, when she would
gently peck his face, and then recede, hopping and shivering
her wings, and presently approach again to perform the same
actions. Now and then she would fly over him, and make as
if she were about to perch on his back, and practise other
little endearments; to which, however, I am sorry to say, he

seemed most ungallantly indifferent, being, in fact, the dullest of the whole group. I expected to have them nidificate in the cage, and therefore affixed a very inviting twig of lime-tree to the cage wall, and threw in plenty of cotton, and perhaps should have succeeded, but for the carelessness of my servant. For he having incautiously left open the cage door, the female flew out and effected her escape.

But all my hopes of success were soon to be quashed; for after they had been in cage but a week, they began to die, sometimes two in a day; and in another week, but a solitary individual was left, which soon followed the others. I vainly endeavoured to replace them, by sending to the mountain; for where the species was so numerous two months before, they were now (beginning of June) scarcely to be seen at all. The cause of the death of my caged captives, I conjecture to have been the want of insect food; that, notwithstanding their frequent sipping at the syrup, they were really starved to death. I was led to this conclusion, by having found, on dissecting those which died, that they were excessively meagre in flesh, and that the stomach, which ordinarily is as large as a pea, and distended with insects, was, in these, shrunken to a minute collapsed membrane, with difficulty distinguished.

ALEXANDER WILSON

XIII

ALEXANDER WILSON

W HEN America was almost an unbroken wilderness from the Appalachians to the Pacific, when Daniel Boone was harrying the Indians of Kentucky, when passenger pigeons darkened the sky in their flights, and the whooping cranes shook the ground with their chorus, there met by sheerest chance in all that vast wilderness two who lived only for birds, who loved them with a love surpassing that of women. If there is Destiny, it guided Alexander Wilson and John James Audubon together in Louisville, Kentucky, that March day in 1810. They could have missed each other so easily; instead, with the fateful attraction of celestial bodies, these two lights of early American ornithology came swiftly together.

Audubon was then unknown to science, to art, or to his later glittering fame. Wilson took him for a country storekeeper with a French accent and a collection of bird drawings, but no science. Audubon says Wilson wore a perpetual surprised expression; he took the stranger for a peddler of some sort. And that is just what he was.

Born in 1776 near Glasgow, Alexander Wilson, after years of bitter slavery at the thrumming looms, betook himself to peddling cloth, to which, like a ballad singer of old, he added the sale of his verses. As a dialect poet Wilson is a sort of minor Burns, not without humor, bitterness, and heartiness; his poems were often mistaken for Burns' by those who did not know genius or miss the lack of it. But minor though Wilson's poetry, it must be mentioned for it had two profoundly important results. Just because Wilson was a poet he wrote a great deal better than an ornithologist could be expected to write. And because he was a poet with a democratic conscience he got himself into hot water with his rhymed attack on the master weavers; this resulted in his being thrown in jail and compelled to burn his poems in public; and the result of that, on his sensitive proud soul, was to drive him to America.

He was then just attaining manhood, and seems to have known nothing much about ornithology; he considered himself a poet and a journeyman weaver, and also, at times, he practised the trade of village dominie. There was some little of the pedant in his temperament, and even this had its value. It made him, later, a very precise ornithologist, eager to verify, to correct predecessor authorities. So he did not fall into the blunders of his rival Audubon, through exuberance of temperament and incautious utterance.

Wilson turned his attention to ornithology at the suggestion of the Philadelphia naturalists William Bartram, Benjamin Barton and George Ord. For they found Wilson despondent over the failure of his third love affair, and they persuaded him to lay down his melancholy flute and take up the inspiriting study of the Class of Aves. All this sounds like the setting for a thoroughly dilettante career. But the love-sick minor poet whose soul was daily ground by the drudgery of swingeing lessons into country children, had unsuspected stuff in him. Alexander Wilson was one of those rare poets who is also a scientist. In fact, he was a better scientist than poet, and he set himself with zeal to become the historian and the portraitist of all the birds in America. Travelling, bird-watching, collecting specimens, seeking subscribers for his volumes (to cost the unheard sum of one hundred dollars) he made himself past master of American bird life in its heroic age. Never again will there be fowl in the air such as flew and cried there then. Untrodden swamps, lakes never yet shot over, beech forests the size of a European kingdom, where the axe had not yet rung—this last hardwood wilderness of the temperate world awaited Alexander Wilson. He was not the first naturalist who ever set foot in it, by any means; but he was much the best so far.

And then his path crossed Audubon's.

Their meeting was not wholly happy. Though they had never then heard of each other, each sensed in the other a dangerous rival. Both men were vain—Audubon with the undisguised child-like hearty vanity of the artist, Wilson vain as is the pedagogue and the self-educated man, with reserve, silence, touchiness. Audubon flourished his marvelous drawings, snatched from the very attitudes of wilderness life. Beside them Wilson's drawings were wooden. Says one of Wilson's biographers: "A man who has given his heart to the accomplishment of an object, believing that he has no rival, must be somewhat more than human, if he be delighted to find that another is engaged in the same purpose with equal energy and advantages far greater than his own."

Wilson calls Audubon's drawings "very good," in his diary, and Audubon in his memoirs records that he showed Wilson birds (whooping cranes and others) he had never seen before, and that despite all he could do to cheer him, Wilson seemed despondent. Wilson remarks that here he parted to the landlord of the inn with his little wild parakeet which had accompanied him on all his travels perched on his shoulder. Not long after, Wilson died in his forty-eighth year, his frail frame worn away by prodigious efforts to find subscribers for his book, and by dysentery contracted, no doubt, in his wilderness travels.

The American Ornithology began to appear in 1808 and was still not completed when Wilson died. Prince Charles Lucien Bonaparte, the international ornithologist, brought it up to date in subsequent editions. Indeed these appeared in

England just in time to do great damage to Audubon who was then in Britain seeking subscribers and seeing his work through the press.

Americans know Wilson as the father of American ornithology, just as they consider Audubon its "golden boy." He was practically the first writer to do anything worthy of notice with the life histories of some four hundred North American birds. To have first-hand acquaintance with the lives of so great a number is well-nigh unsurpassed. Today if you want to spend a lifetime monographing the barred owl, there is a great literature on the owl to assist you; there are immense collections of specimens in museums; you can see motion picture films of owls, with accompanying sound tracks. Colleagues will help you. Wilson, untrained in any science, working alone, confronted by an immense fauna about which there was nothing worthy written or known, accomplished miracles.

It has seemed to me very appropriate that the first of our great bird writers should be permitted to speak for two species that are now almost extinct with us. The Carolina parrot, generally known now as the parakeet, was Wilson's little familiar. He should certainly have known about it if anyone did. In his times it was still a common bird, popular with plume hunters, but not at all popular with farmers, who took no sentimental view of its harsh voice and lousy plumage. Its depredations among crops were so serious and persistent that the expansion of pioneer agriculture practically foredoomed it to banishment. Further, the stupidity of the bird in immediately settling on the same spot after being momentarily driven up by gun-fire, shows that this curious northern representative of a great tropical family was one without great survival value. One regrets its absence, but it is not the most precious creature that has ever suffered at the hands of man.

More keenly one feels the loss of ivory-billed woodpeckers. Here was one of those fabulous creatures in which we can hardly believe even with Audubon's portrait and Wilson's account before us. But these fierce, vasty, noisy hewers of wood belong in the class of creatures that, like buffalo, are out-size for present times. The ivory-bills were like some species out of another geologic age—kings, but kings of an order that may not stay. Wilson's experience with these woodpeckers sufficiently explains how this is so.

CAROLINA PARROT

O F ONE hundred and sixty-eight kinds of parrots, enumerated by European writers as inhabiting the various regions of the globe, this is the only species found native within the territory of the United States. The vast and luxuriant tracts lying within the torrid zone, seem to be the favourite residence of those noisy, numerous, and richly plumaged tribes. The Count de Buffon has, indeed, circumscribed the whole genus of parrots to a space not extending more than twenty-three degrees on each side of the equator: but later discoveries have shewn this statement to be incorrect, as these birds have been found on our continent as far south as the Straits of Magellan, and even on the remote shores of Van Diemen's Land, in Terra Australasia. The species now under consideration is also known to inhabit the interior of Louisiana, and the shores of Mississippi and Ohio, and their tributary waters, even beyond the Illinois river, to the neighbourhood of Lake Michigan, in lat. 42 deg. north; and, contrary to the generally received opinion, is chiefly *resident* in all these places. Eastward, however, of the great range of the Alleghany, it is seldom seen farther north than the state of Maryland; though straggling parties have been occasionally observed among the valleys of the Juniata; and, according to some, even twenty-five miles to the north-west of Albany, in the state of New York.* But such accidental visits furnish no certain criteria, by which to judge of their usual extent of range; those aërial voyagers, as well as others who navigate the deep, being subject to be cast away, by the violence of the elements, on distant shores and unknown countries.

* Barton's *Fragments*, &c., p. 6, Introduction.

From these circumstances of the northern residence of this species, we might be justified in concluding it to be a very hardy bird, more capable of sustaining cold than nine-tenths of its tribe; and so I believe it is; having myself seen them, in the month of February, along the banks of the Ohio, in a snow-storm, flying about like pigeons, and in full cry.

The preference, however, which this bird gives to the western countries, lying in the same parallel of latitude with those eastward of the Alleghany mountains, which it rarely or never visits, is worthy of remark; and has been adduced, by different writers, as a proof of the superior mildness of climate in the former to that of the latter. But there are other reasons for this partiality equally powerful, though hitherto overlooked; namely, certain peculiar features of country to which these birds are particularly and strongly attached: these are, low rich alluvial bottoms, along the borders of creeks, covered with a gigantic growth of sycamore trees, or button-wood; deep, and almost impenetrable swamps, where the vast and towering cypress lift their still more majestic heads; and those singular salines, or, as they are usually called, licks, so generally interspersed over that country, and which are regularly and eagerly visited by the paroquets. A still greater inducement is the superior abundance of their favourite fruits. That food which the paroquet prefers to all others is the seeds of the cockle bur, a plant rarely found in the lower parts of Pennsylvania or New York; but which unfortunately grows in too great abundance along the shores of the Ohio and Mississippi, so much so as to render the wool of those sheep that pasture where it most abounds, scarcely worth the cleaning, covering them with one solid mass of burs, wrought up and imbedded into the fleece, to the great annoyance of this valuable animal. The seeds of the cypress tree and hackberry, as well as beech nuts, are also great favourites with these birds; the two former of which are not commonly found in Pennsylvania, and the latter by no means so general or so productive. Here, then, are several powerful reasons, more dependent on soil than climate, for the preference given by these birds to the luxuriant regions of the west. Pennsylvania, indeed, and also Maryland, abound with excellent apple orchards, on the ripe fruit of which the paroquets occasionally feed. But I have my doubts whether their depredations in the orchard be not as much the result of wanton play and mischief, as regard for the seeds of the fruit, which they are supposed to be in pursuit of. I have known a flock of these birds alight on an apple tree, and have myself seen them twist off the fruit, one by one, strewing it in every direction around the tree, without observing that any of the depredators descended to pick them up. To a paroquet, which I wounded and kept for some considerable time, I very often offered apples, which it uniformly rejected; but burs, or beech nuts, never. To another very beautiful one, which I brought from New Orleans, and which is now sitting in the room beside me, I have frequently offered this fruit, and also the seeds separately, which I never knew it to taste. Their local attachments, also, prove that food, more than climate, determines their choice of country. For even in the states of Ohio, Kentucky, and the Mississippi territory, unless in the neighbourhood of such places as have been described, it is rare to see them. The inhabitants of Lexington, as many of them assured me, scarcely ever observe them in that quarter. In passing from that place to Nashville, a distance of two hundred miles, I neither heard nor saw any, but at a place called Madison's lick. In passing on, I next met with them on the banks and rich flats of the Tennessee river: after this, I saw no more till I reached Bayo St. Pierre, a distance of several hundred miles: from all which circumstances, I think we cannot, from the residence of these birds, establish with propriety any correct standard by which to judge of the comparative temperatures of different climates.

In descending the river Ohio, by myself, in the month of February, I met with the first flock of paroquets, at the mouth of the Little Sioto. I had been informed, by an old and respectable inhabitant of Marietta, that they were sometimes, though rarely, seen there. I observed flocks of them, afterwards, at the mouth of the Great and Little Miami, and in the neighbourhood of numerous creeks that discharge themselves into the Ohio. At Big Bone lick, thirty miles above the mouth of Kentucky river, I saw them in great numbers. They came screaming through the woods in the morning about an hour after sunrise, to drink the salt water, of which they, as well as the pigeons, are remarkably fond. When they alighted on the ground, it appeared at a distance as if covered with a carpet of the richest green, orange, and yellow: they afterwards settled, in one body, on a neighbouring tree, which stood detached from any other, covering almost every twig of it, and the sun, shining strongly on their gay and glossy plumage, produced a very beautiful and splendid appearance. Here I had an opportunity of observing some very particular traits of their character: having shot down a number, some of which were only wounded, the whole flock swept repeatedly around their prostrate companions, and again settled on a low tree, within twenty yards of the spot where I stood. At each successive discharge, though showers of them fell, yet the affection of the survivors seemed rather to increase; for, after a few circuits around the place, they again alighted near me, looking down on their slaughtered companions with such manifest symptoms of sympathy and concern, as entirely disarmed me. I could not but take notice of the remarkable contrast between their elegant manner of flight, and their lame crawling gait among the branches. They fly very much like the wild pigeon, in close compact bodies,

and with great rapidity, making a loud and outrageous screaming, not unlike that of the red-headed woodpecker. Their
flight is sometimes in a direct line; but most usually circuit-
ous, making a great variety of elegant and easy serpentine
meanders, as if for pleasure. They are particularly attached
to the large sycamores, in the hollow of the trunks and
branches of which they generally roost, thirty or forty, and
sometimes more, entering at the same hole. Here they cling
close to the sides of the tree, holding fast by the claws and
also by the bills. They appear to be fond of sleep, and often
retire to their holes during the day, probably to take their
regular *siesta*. They are extremely sociable with, and fond of
each other, often scratching each other's heads and necks,
and always, at night, nestling as close as possible to each
other, preferring, at that time, a perpendicular position, supported by their bill and claws. In the fall, when their favourite cockle burs are ripe, they swarm along the coast, or high
grounds of the Mississippi, above New Orleans, for a great
extent. At such times, they are killed and eaten by many of
the inhabitants; though, I confess, I think their flesh very
indifferent. I have several times dined on it from necessity,
in the woods: but found it merely passable, with all the sauce
of a keen appetite to recommend it.

A very general opinion prevails, that the brains and intestines of the Carolina paroquet are a sure and fatal poison
to cats. I had determined, when at Big Bone, to put this to
the test of experiment; and for that purpose collected the
brains and bowels of more than a dozen of them. But after
close search, Mistress Puss was not to be found, being engaged perhaps on more agreeable business. I left the medicine
with Mr. Colquhoun's agent, to administer it by the first opportunity, and write me the result; but I have never yet heard
from him. A respectable lady near the town of Natchez, and
on whose word I can rely, assured me, that she herself had

made the experiment, and that, whatever might be the cause, the cat had actually died either on that or the succeeding day. A French planter near Bayo Fourche pretended to account to me for this effect by positively asserting, that the seeds of the cockle burs on which the paroquets so eagerly feed, were deleterious to cats; and thus their death was produced by eating the intestines of the bird. These matters might easily have been ascertained on the spot, which, however, a combination of trifling circumstances prevented me from doing. I several times carried a dose of the first description in my pocket till it became insufferable, without meeting with a suitable *patient*, on whom, like other professional gentlemen, I might conveniently make a fair experiment.

I was equally unsuccessful in my endeavours to discover the time of incubation or manner of building among these birds. All agreed that they breed in hollow trees; and several affirmed to me that they had seen their nests. Some said they carried in no materials; others that they did. Some made the eggs white; others speckled. One man assured me that he cut down a large beech tree, which was hollow, and in which he found the broken fragments of upwards of twenty paroquet eggs, which were of a greenish yellow colour. The nests, though destroyed in their texture by the falling of the tree, appeared, he said, to be formed of small twigs glued to each other, and to the side of the tree, in the manner of the chimney swallow. He added, that if it were the proper season, he could point out to me the weed from which they procured the gluey matter. From all these contradictory accounts nothing certain can be deduced, except that they build in companies, in hollow trees. That they commence incubation late in summer, or very early in spring, I think highly probable, from the numerous dissections I made in the months of March, April, May, and June; and the great variety which I found in the colour of the plumage of the head and neck of both sexes, during the two former of these months, convinces me, that the young birds do not receive their full colours until the early part of the succeeding summer.

While parrots and paroquets, from foreign countries, abound in almost every street of our large cities, and become such great favourites, no attention seems to have been paid to our own, which in elegance of figure and beauty of plumage is certainly superior to many of them. It wants indeed that disposition for perpetual screaming and chattering that renders some of the former pests, not only to their keepers, but to the whole neighbourhood in which they reside. It is alike docile and sociable; soon becomes perfectly familiar; and, until equal pains be taken in its instruction, it is unfair to conclude it incapable of equal improvement in the language of man.

As so little has hitherto been known of the disposition and manners of this species, the reader will not, I hope, be displeased at my detailing some of these, in the history of a particular favourite, my sole companion in many a lonesome day's march.

Anxious to try the effects of education on one of those which I procured at Big Bone lick, and which was but slightly wounded in the wing, I fixed up a place for it in the stern of my boat, and presented it with some cockle burs, which it freely fed on in less than an hour after being on board. The intermediate time between eating and sleeping was occupied in gnawing the sticks that formed its place of confinement, in order to make a practicable breach; which it repeatedly effected. When I abandoned the river, and travelled by land, I wrapt it up closely in a silk handkerchief, tying it tightly around, and carried it in my pocket. When I stopped for refreshment, I unbound my prisoner, and gave it its allowance, which it generally despatched with great dexterity, unhusking the seeds from the bur in a twinkling; in doing which it always employed its left foot to hold the bur, as did several others that I kept for some time. I began to think that this might be peculiar to the whole tribe, and that they all were, if I may use the expression, left-footed; but by shooting a number afterwards while engaged in eating mulberries, I found sometimes the left, sometimes the right foot stained with the fruit; the other always clean; from which, and the constant practice of those I kept, it appears, that like the human species in the use of their hands, they do not prefer one or the other indiscriminately, but are either left or right footed. But to return to my prisoner: In recommitting it to "durance vile" we generally had a quarrel; during which it frequently paid me in kind for the wound I had inflicted, and for depriving it of liberty, by cutting and almost disabling several of my fingers with its sharp and powerful bill. The path through the wilderness between Nashville and Natchez is in some places bad beyond description. There are dangerous creeks to swim, miles of morass to struggle through, rendered almost as gloomy as night by a prodigious growth of timber, and an underwood of canes and other evergreens; while the descent into these sluggish streams is often ten or fifteen feet perpendicular into a bed of deep clay. In some of the worst of these places, where I had, as it were, to fight my way through, the paroquet frequently escaped from my pocket, obliging me to dismount and pursue it through the worst of the morass before I could regain it. On these occasions I was several times tempted to abandon it; but I persisted in bringing it along. When at night I encamped in the woods, I placed it on the baggage beside me, where it usually sat, with great composure, dozing and gazing at the fire till morning. In this manner I carried it upwards of a thousand miles in my pocket, where it was exposed all day to the jolting of the horse, but regularly liberated at meal times and in the evening, at which it always expressed great satisfaction. In passing through the Chickasaw and Chactaw nations, the Indians, wherever I stopped to feed, collected around me, men, women, and children, laughing and seeming wonderfully amused with the novelty of my companion. The Chickasaws called it in their language "*Kelinky*"; but when they heard me call it Poll, they soon repeated the name; and wherever I chanced to stop among these people, we soon became familiar with each other through the medium of Poll. On arriving at Mr. Dunbar's, below Natchez, I procured a cage, and placed it under the piazza, where by its call it soon attracted the passing flocks; such is the attachment they have for each other. Numerous parties frequently alighted on the trees immediately above, keeping up a constant conversation with the prisoner. One of these I wounded slightly in the wing, and the pleasure Poll expressed on meeting with this new companion was really amusing. She crept close up to it as it hung on the side of the cage, chattering to it in a low tone of voice, as if sympathizing in its misfortune, scratched about its head and neck with her bill; and both at night nestled as close as possible to each other, sometimes Poll's head being thrust among the plumage of the other. On the death of this companion, she appeared restless and inconsolable for several days. On reaching New Orleans, I placed a looking glass beside the place where she usually sat, and the instant she perceived her image, all her former fondness seemed to return, so that she could scarcely absent herself from it a moment. It was evident that she was completely deceived. Always when evening drew on, and often during the day, she laid her head close to that of the image in the glass, and began to doze with great composure and satisfaction. In this short space she had learnt to know her name; to answer and come when called on; to climb up my clothes, sit on my shoulder, and eat from my mouth. I took her with me to sea, determined to persevere in her education; but, destined to another fate, poor Poll, having one morning, about daybreak wrought her way through the cage, while I was asleep, instantly flew overboard, and perished in the Gulf of Mexico.

The Carolina, or Illinois parrot, (for it has been described under both these appellations,) is thirteen inches long, and twenty-one in extent; forehead and cheeks, orange red; beyond this, for an inch and a half, down and round the neck, a rich and pure yellow; shoulder and bend of the wing, also edged with rich orange red. The general colour of the rest of the plumage is a bright yellowish silky green, with light blue reflections, lightest and most diluted with yellow below; greater wing-coverts and roots of the primaries, yellow, slightly tinged with green; interior webs of the primaries, deep dusky purple, almost black, exterior ones, bluish green; tail, long, cuneiform, consisting of twelve feathers, the exterior one only half the length, the others increasing to the middle ones, which are streaked along the middle with light blue; shafts of all the larger feathers, and of most part of the green plumage, black; knees and vent, orange yellow; feet, a pale whitish flesh colour; claws, black; bill, white, or slightly tinged with pale cream; iris of the eye, hazel; round the eye is a small space without feathers, covered with a whitish skin; nostrils placed in an elevated membrane at the base of the bill, and covered with feathers; chin, wholly bare of feathers, but concealed by those descending on each side; from each side of the palate hangs a lobe or skin of a blackish colour; tongue, thick and fleshy; inside of the upper mandible near the point, grooved exactly like a file, that it may hold with more security.

The female differs very little in her colours and markings from the male. After examining numerous specimens, the following appear to be the principal differences. The yellow on the neck of the female does not descend quite so far; the interior vanes of the primaries are brownish, instead of black, and the orange red on the bend and edges of the wings is considerably narrower; in other respects, the colours and markings are nearly the same.

The young birds of the preceding year, of both sexes, are generally destitute of the yellow on the head and neck, until about the beginning or middle of March, having those parts wholly green, except the front and cheeks, which are orange red in them as in the full grown birds. Towards the middle of March the yellow begins to appear, in detached feathers, interspersed among the green, varying in different individuals. In some which I killed about the last of that month, only a few green feathers remained among the yellow; and these were fast assuming the yellow tint: for the colour changes without change of plumage. A number of these birds, in all their grades of progressive change from green to yellow, have been deposited in Mr. Peale's museum.

What is called by Europeans the Illinois parrot (*psittacus pertinax*) is evidently the young bird in its imperfect colours. Whether the present species be found as far south as Brazil, as these writers pretend, I am unable to say; but, from the great extent of country in which I have myself killed and examined these birds, I am satisfied that the present species, now described, is the only one inhabiting the United States.

Since the foregoing was written, I have had an opportunity, by the death of a tame Carolina paroquet, to ascertain the fact of the poisonous effects of their head and intestines to cats. Having shut up a cat and her two kittens, (the latter only a few days old,) in a room with the head, neck, and whole intestines of the paroquet, I found, on the next morning, the whole eaten except a small part of the bill. The cat exhibited no symptom of sickness; and, at this moment, three days after the experiment has been made, she and her kittens are in their usual health. Still, however, the effect might have been different, had the daily food of the bird been cockle burs, instead of Indian corn.

IVORY-BILLED WOODPECKER

THIS majestic and formidable species, in strength and magnitude, stands at the head of the whole class of woodpeckers hitherto discovered. He may be called the king or chief of his tribe; and nature seems to have designed him a distinguished characteristic in the superb carmine crest and bill of polished ivory with which she has ornamented him. His eye is brilliant and daring; and his whole frame so admirably adapted for his mode of life, and method of procuring subsistence, as to impress on the mind of the examiner the most reverential ideas of the Creator. His manners have also a dignity in them superior to the common herd of woodpeckers. Trees, shrubbery, orchards, rails, fence posts, and old prostrate logs, are alike interesting to those, in their humble and indefatigable search for prey; but the royal hunter now before us, scorns the humility of such situations, and seeks the most towering trees of the forest; seeming particularly attached to those prodigious cypress swamps, whose crowded giant sons stretch their bare and blasted or moss-hung arms mid-way to the skies. In these almost inaccessible recesses, amid ruinous piles of impending timber, his trumpet-like note and loud strokes resound through the solitary savage wilds, of which he seems the sole lord and inhabitant. Wherever he frequents he leaves numerous monuments of his industry behind him. We there see enormous pine trees with cartloads of bark lying around their roots, and chips of the trunk itself in such quantities as to suggest the idea that half a dozen of axe-men had been at work there for the whole morning. The body of the tree is also disfigured with such numerous and so large excavations, that one can hardly conceive it possible for the whole to be the work

237

of a woodpecker. With such strength, and an apparatus so powerful, what havoc might he not commit, if numerous, on the most useful of our forest trees! and yet with all these appearances, and much of vulgar prejudice against him, it may fairly be questioned whether he is at all injurious; or, at least, whether his exertions do not contribute most powerfully to the protection of our timber. Examine closely the tree where he has been at work, and you will soon perceive, that it is neither from motives of mischief nor amusement that he slices off the bark, or digs his way into the trunk.— For the sound and healthy tree is the least object of his attention. The diseased, infested with insects, and hastening to putrefaction, are *his* favourites; there the deadly crawling enemy have formed a lodgement between the bark and tender wood, to drink up the very vital part of the tree. It is the ravages of these vermin which the intelligent proprietor of the forest deplores, as the sole perpetrators of the destruction of his timber. Would it be believed that the larvæ of an insect, or fly, no larger than a grain of rice, should silently, and in one season, destroy some thousand acres of pine trees, many of them from two to three feet in diameter, and a hundred and fifty feet high! Yet whoever passes along the high road from Georgetown to Charleston, in South Carolina, about twenty miles from the former place, can have striking and melancholy proofs of this fact. In some places the whole woods, as far as you can see around you, are dead, stripped of the bark, their wintry-looking arms and bare trunks bleaching in the sun, and tumbling in ruins before every blast, presenting a frightful picture of desolation. And yet ignorance and prejudice stubbornly persist in directing their indignation against the bird now before us, the constant and mortal enemy of these very vermin, as if the hand that probed the wound to extract its cause, should be equally detested with that which inflicted it; or as if the thief-catcher should be

confounded with the thief. Until some effectual preventive
or more complete mode of destruction can be devised against
these insects, and their larvae, I would humbly suggest the
propriety of protecting, and receiving with proper feelings
of gratitude, the services of this and the whole tribe of woodpeckers, letting the odium of guilt fall to its proper owners.

In looking over the accounts given of the ivory-billed woodpecker by the naturalists of Europe, I find it asserted, that
it inhabits from New Jersey to Mexico. I believe, however,
that few of them are ever seen to the north of Virginia, and
very few of them even in that state. The first place I observed this bird at, when on my way to the south, was about
twelve miles north of Wilmington in North Carolina. Having wounded it slightly in the wing, on being caught, it
uttered a loudly reiterated, and most piteous note, exactly
resembling the violent crying of a young child; which terri-
fied my horse so, as nearly to have cost me my life. It was
distressing to hear it. I carried it with me in the chair, under
cover, to Wilmington. In passing through the streets, its affecting cries surprised every one within hearing, particularly
the females, who hurried to the doors and windows with
looks of alarm and anxiety. I drove on, and, on arriving at
the piazza of the hotel, where I intended to put up, the
landlord came forward, and a number of other persons who
happened to be there, all equally alarmed at what they heard;
this was greatly increased by my asking, whether he could
furnish me with accommodations for myself and my baby.
The man looked blank and foolish, while the others stared
with still greater astonishment. After diverting myself for a
minute or two at their expense, I drew my woodpecker from
under the cover, and a general laugh took place. I took him
up stairs and locked him up in my room, while I went to
see my horse taken care of. In less than an hour I returned,
and, on opening the door, he set up the same distressing

shout, which now appeared to proceed from grief that he had been discovered in his attempts at escape. He had mounted along the side of the window, nearly as high as the ceiling, a little below which he had begun to break through. The bed was covered with large pieces of plaster; the lath was exposed for at least fifteen inches square, and a hole, large enough to admit the fist, opened to the weather-boards; so that in less than another hour he would certainly have succeeded in making his way through. I now tied a string round his leg, and, fastening it to the table, again left him. I wished to preserve his life, and had gone off in search of suitable food for him. As I reascended the stairs, I heard him again hard at work, and on entering had the mortification to perceive that he had almost entirely ruined the mahogany table to which he was fastened, and on which he had wreaked his whole vengeance. While engaged in taking a drawing, he cut me severely in several places, and, on the whole, displayed such a noble and unconquerable spirit, that I was frequently tempted to restore him to his native woods. He lived with me nearly three days, but refused all sustenance, and I witnessed his death with regret.

The head and bill of this bird is in great esteem among the southern Indians, who wear them by way of amulet or charm, as well as ornament; and, it is said, dispose of them to the northern tribes at considerable prices. An Indian believes that the head, skin, or even feathers of certain birds, confer on the wearer all the virtues or excellencies of those birds. Thus I have seen a coat made of the skins, heads, and claws of the raven; caps stuck round with heads of butcher-birds, hawks, and eagles; and as the disposition and courage of the ivory-billed woodpecker are well known to the savages, no wonder they should attach great value to it, having both beauty, and, in their estimation, distinguished merit to recommend it.

This bird is not migratory, but resident in the countries where it inhabits. In the low countries of the Carolinas it usually prefers the large timbered cypress swamps for breeding in. In the trunk of one of these trees, at a considerable height, the male and female alternately, and in conjunction, dig out a large and capacious cavity for their eggs and young. Trees thus dug out have frequently been cut down, with sometimes the eggs and young in them. This hole, according to information,—for I have never seen one myself,—is generally a little winding, the better to keep out the weather, and from two to five feet deep. The eggs are said to be generally four, sometimes five, as large as a pullet's, pure white, and equally thick on both ends—a description that, except in size, very nearly agrees with all the rest of our woodpeckers. The young begin to be seen abroad about the middle of June. Whether they breed more than once in the same season is uncertain.

So little attention do the people of the countries where these birds inhabit, pay to the minutiæ of natural history, that, generally speaking, they make no distinction between the ivory-billed and pileated woodpecker; and it was not till I shewed them the two birds together, that they knew of any difference. The more intelligent and observing part of the natives, however, distinguish them by the name of the large and lesser logcocks. They seldom examine them but at a distance, gunpowder being considered too precious to be thrown away on woodpeckers; nothing less than a turkey being thought worth the value of a load.

The food of this bird consists, I believe, entirely of insects and their larvæ. The pileated woodpecker is suspected of sometimes tasting the Indian corn: the ivory-billed never. His common note, repeated every three or four seconds, very much resembles the tone of a trumpet, or the high note of a clarionet, and can plainly be distinguished at the distance of more than half a mile; seeming to be immediately at hand, though perhaps more than one hundred yards off. This it utters while mounting along the trunk or digging into it. At these times it has a stately and novel appearance; and the note instantly attracts the notice of a stranger. Along the borders of the Savannah river, between Savannah and Augusta, I found them very frequently; but my horse no sooner heard their trumpet-like note, than, remembering his former alarm, he became almost ungovernable.

The ivory-billed woodpecker is twenty inches long, and thirty inches in extent; the general colour is black, with a considerable gloss of green when exposed to a good light; iris of the eye, vivid yellow; nostrils, covered with recumbent white hairs; fore part of the head, black; rest of the crest of a most splendid red, spotted at the bottom with white, which is only seen when the crest is erected; this long red plumage being ash-coloured at its base, above that white, and ending in brilliant red; a stripe of white proceeds from a point, about half an inch below each eye, passes down each side of the neck, and along the back, where they are about an inch apart, nearly to the rump; the first five primaries are wholly black; on the next five the white spreads from the tip higher and higher to the secondaries, which are wholly white from their coverts downward. These markings, when the wings are shut, make the bird appear as if his back were white; hence he has been called by some of our naturalists the large white-backed woodpecker. The neck is long; the beak an inch broad at the base, of the colour and consistence of ivory, prodigiously strong and elegantly fluted. The tail is black, tapering from the two exterior feathers, which are three inches shorter than the middle ones, and each feather has the singularity of being greatly concave below; the wing is lined with yellowish white; the legs are about an inch and a quarter long, the exterior toe about the same length, the claws exactly semi-circular and remarkably powerful, the whole of a light blue or lead colour. The female is about half an inch shorter, the bill rather less, and the whole plumage of the head black, glossed with green; in the other parts of the plumage, she exactly resembles the male. In the stomachs of three which I opened, I found large quantities of a species of worm called borers, two or three inches long, of a dirty cream colour, with a black head; the stomach was an oblong pouch, not muscular like the gizzards of some others. The tongue was worm-shaped, and for half an inch at the tip as hard as horn, flat, pointed, of the same white colour as the bill, and thickly barbed on each side.

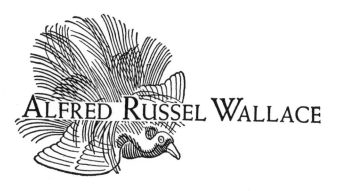

ALFRED RUSSEL WALLACE

XIV

ALFRED RUSSEL WALLACE

O THE theory of natural selection Darwin was led in part by a study of the birds of the Galapagos islands, each island with a different species of thrush, of creeper, of ground finch, and of flycatcher. Wallace, studying birds of paradise, parrots, bee-eaters and pigeons of the East Indies, was first astonished, and then enlightened, by the high degree of endemism which the avifauna of each archipelago possessed. Simultaneously from their studies of island faunas, they reached the same momentous conclusions, and they share the honors of their joint discovery.

Alfred Russel Wallace was born in 1823 at Usk in south Wales. His schooling was very brief and he never had any formal training in his future profession. He used to assist his brother who was a surveyor, and as he trudged with the transit he would note the beauty of the wildflowers, without knowing their names or that he might learn more of them. He was eighteen when he saw and purchased a shilling book on British wildflowers, and, having a great deal of leisure, began to use it. A world of enchantment seemed to open to him. His delight in collecting and his appreciation of the beauty of flora were only equaled by the fascination of the science he guessed at behind the sketchy systematics of his book. Later he purchased Lindley's splendid old classic on the elements of botany and Loudon's ever excellent encyclopedia of plants. With these he soon made himself not only a good field botanist but developed a flair for classification (with its implications of relationship and evolution) and a strong sense of the geographical distribution of species. These

principles, no matter with what group of organisms one begins to apply them, carry over perfectly in any other group,
and tinge one's thinking for life.

A friendship with H. W. Bates, the famous collector and
author of the theory of protective mimicry, definitely decided
him on a naturalist's career. His ambition was to become a
collector for museums and amateurs of natural history, and
his was an era when rare and exotic species commanded such
high prices that it was possible to find a ready market and
earn a good competence in this fashion.

Wallace's first expedition was with Bates to the valley of
the Amazon. He was able to sell his specimens through a
London agent, and on his return to England he was welcomed at the museums as a collector of great promise. In
1854 he set out on his memorable journey to the East Indies.

His travels, now under idyllic conditions, again under great
hardship, took him to Singapore (whose birds were well
known from a collector's point of view) and Java, which he
found overcivilized, to Borneo and Celebes, wondrously rich
in birds, to Ceram, wondrously poor in them, to Amboyna
(an ornithological museum), and to New Guinea and to the
Aru Islands where he found his birds of paradise, so in demand with collectors.

One of his shipments of birds, shells and insects consisted
in a consignment of 16,000 specimens. What part birds played
in them may be judged from the following:

"There were numbers of gorgeous lories, parrots, and par-
rakeets, white and black cockatoos, exquisite fruit-pigeons of
a great variety of colours, many fine king-fishers from the
largest to the most minute, as well as the beautiful racquet-
tailed species, beautiful black, green, and blue ground-
thrushes, some splendid specimens of the Papuan and King
paradise-birds, and many beautiful bee-eaters, rollers, fly-
catchers, grakles, sun-birds, and paradise crows, making alto-

gether such an assemblage of strange forms and brilliant colours as no one of my visitors had ever imagined to exist so
near them."

It was while he was lying ill with intermittent fever at
Ternate that there flashed into Wallace's mind the idea that
species are not immutable but have evolved through the
ages by natural selection. In his rather exalted frame of mind
attendant on his fever, the whole subject seemed to precipi-
tate out of a murky solution and crystallize. As soon as he
was well, he wrote out his ideas, sent them to Darwin, and
requested him to have them published.

Darwin, who had been amassing evidence for twenty years
and planning a book that he never seemed to complete, was
delighted at confirmation of his beliefs and aghast at finding
his discovery forestalled. Hooker, the botanist, urged Darwin
and Wallace to present joint papers to the scientific world,
and this was done (though Wallace was still in the isles of
the Orient), with what memorable results everyone knows.
Wallace offered to put himself and all his findings entirely
under Darwin's captaincy, a gesture unsurpassed in generos-
ity, though scientists are habitually generous to each other.
Darwin assumed that leadership, but never without complete
acknowledgment of Wallace's great and original contribution.

On his return to England, after eight years in the East,
Wallace found himself well off as a result of the sale of his
specimens. He spent years in the museums "working up" his
collections and enjoying the society of all the leading British
scientists. His fame called him to lecturing and authorship.
Among his most delightful books are the wondrously sugges-
tive Island Life, and The Malay Archipelago (1869) from
which I have made my selection. The Geographical Distribution of Animals is probably his greatest written monument.

Wallace, at the age of forty-three, married the young

daughter of William Mitten, a well known specialist on the mosses. The rest of his very long life was passed in tranquillity and honor. He received the first Darwin medal of the Royal Society, the Royal medal, and a government pension in recognition of his services. On one of his American trips, he visited the mountains of Colorado, and the forests and peaks of California. His lectures all over the United States attracted large audiences and fired the minds of young students of natural history on the Kansas plains as in the atmosphere of Boston. His engaging personality swayed all who heard him.

The last years of his life were taken up with inquiries into the supernatural, as well as in furthering idealistic tax and land reforms and projects for the betterment of human misery through a revival of Christianity. In these necessarily extrascientific endeavors he was sincerely absorbed.

Birds of paradise, of which Wallace writes so vividly in the following excerpt, are confined to the Australasian faunal province and belong to some sixty species of a family whose relationships are with the beautiful bower birds on the one hand and on the other with the crows—not all of which are of a forbidding monotone.

The first birds of paradise were brought to Europe by Magellan's followers. Speedily their plumage grew in great demand in Europe, both for wear and in the collections of wealthy amateurs. Wallace found that the natives were themselves indifferent to creatures they beheld daily, but they well understood their monetary value. So intensive had been previous collecting (of an unscientific sort) that he was put to it to find, even seventy-five years ago, the very species he had, above all, come so far to collect. As he says:

"It must be considered as somewhat extraordinary that, during five years' residence and travel in Celebes, the Moluccas, and New Guinea, I should never have been able to purchase skins of half the species which Lesson,* forty years ago, obtained during a few weeks in the same countries. I believe that all, except the common species of commerce, are now much more difficult to obtain than they were even twenty years ago; and I impute it principally to their having been sought after by the Dutch officials through the Sultan of Tidore. . . .

"The birds of paradise are an article of commerce, and are the monopoly of the chiefs of the coast villages, who obtain them at a low rate from the mountaineers, and sell them to the Bugis traders. A portion is also paid every year as tribute to the Sultan of Tidore. The natives are therefore very jealous of a stranger, especially a European, interfering in their trade, and above all of going into the interior to deal with the mountaineers themselves."

As a result of the habit of native collectors of cutting off the feet of the birds before shipment, it was long believed in Europe that birds of paradise had none, and spent their entire lives upon the wing. Whether jokingly or not, Linnaeus named one *Paradisea apoda* (the "footless"). Others believed that the birds fed only on dew, or not at all. The females being seldom sent in commercial channels, they were long unknown to European collections, and even today their nestings and life histories are none too well known.

If paradise birds were growing scarce in Wallace's time, they were rarer in the decades that followed. The millinery trade kept up a constant demand for them, which was satisfied by natives not in the least touched by sentiment. It was not until 1913 in the United States that, through the exertions of the Audubon Societies, the importation for sale of bird of paradise plumes was forbidden by act of Congress.

* The author of the excellent *Traité d'Ornithologie*. [Ed.]

This date seems very late indeed; it is much earlier, so far as I know, than that of any similar law in any other country, if indeed there are any so thorough-going. The Netherlands government did not seek even to regulate the exportation of birds of paradise until 1924.

KING BIRD OF PARADISE

The Aru Islands, March to May, 1857:—One of my first
objects was to inquire for the people who are accustomed to
shoot the paradise birds. They lived at some distance in the
jungle, and a man was sent to call them. When they arrived,
we had a talk by means of the orang-kaya as interpreter, and
they said they thought they could get some. They explained
that they shoot the birds with a bow and arrow, the arrow
having a conical wooden cap fitted to the end as large as a
tea-cup, so as to kill the bird by the violence of the blow without making any wound or shedding any blood. The trees frequented by the birds are very lofty; it is therefore necessary
to erect a small leafy covering or hut among the branches, to
which the hunter mounts before daylight in the morning and
remains the whole day, and whenever a bird alights they are
almost sure of securing it. They returned to their homes the
same evening, and I never saw any thing more of them, owing,
as I afterward found, to its being too early to obtain birds in
good plumage.

The first two or three days of our stay here were very wet,
and I obtained but few insects or birds, but at length, when
I was beginning to despair, my boy Baderoon returned one
day with a specimen which repaid me for months of delay
and expectation. It was a small bird, a little less than a thrush.
The greater part of its plumage was of an intense cinnabar
red, with a gloss as of spun glass. On the head the feathers
became short and velvety, and shaded into rich orange. Beneath, from the breast downward, was pure white, with the
softness and gloss of silk, and across the breast a band of
deep metallic green separated this color from the red of the
throat. Above each eye was a round spot of the same metallic

green; the bill was yellow, and the feet and legs were of a fine cobalt blue, strikingly contrasting with all the other parts of the body. Merely in arrangement of colors and texture of plumage this little bird was a gem of the first water, yet these comprised only half its strange beauty. Springing from each side of the breast, and ordinarily lying concealed under the wings, were little tufts of grayish feathers about two inches long, and each terminated by a broad band of intense emerald green. These plumes can be raised at the will of the bird, and spread out into a pair of elegant fans when the wings are elevated. But this is not the only ornament. The two middle feathers of the tail are in the form of slender wires about five inches long, and which diverge in a beautiful double curve. About half an inch of the end of this wire is webbed on the outer side only, and colored of a fine metallic green, and being curled spirally inward, forms a pair of elegant glittering buttons.

My transports of admiration and delight quite amused my Aru hosts, who saw nothing more in the "burong raja" than we do in the robin or the goldfinch.

RED BIRD OF PARADISE

Waigiou, July to September, 1860:—When I first arrived I was surprised at being told that there were no paradise birds at Muka, although there were plenty at Bessir, a place where the natives caught them and prepared the skins. I assured the people I had heard the cry of these birds close to the village, but they would not believe that I could know their cry. However, the very first time I went into the forest I not only heard but saw them, and was convinced there were plenty about; but they were very shy, and it was some time before we got any. My hunter first shot a female, and I one day got very close to a fine male. He was, as I expected, the rare red species (Paradisea rubra) which alone inhabits this island, and is found nowhere else. He was quite low down, running along a bough searching for insects, almost like a woodpecker, and the long black ribband-like filaments in his tail hung down in the most graceful double curve imaginable. I covered him with my gun, and was going to use the barrel which had a very small charge of powder and number eight shot, so as not to injure his plumage, but the gun missed fire, and he was off in an instant among the thickest jungle. Another day we saw no less than eight fine males at different times, and fired four times at them; but though other birds at the same distance almost always dropped, these all got away, and I began to think we were not to get this magnificent species. At length the fruit ripened on the fig-tree close by my house, and many birds came to feed on it; and one morning as I was taking my coffee, a male paradise bird was seen to settle on its top. I seized my gun, ran under the tree, and, gazing up, could see it flying across from branch to branch, seizing a fruit here and another there, and then, be-

255

fore I could get a sufficient aim to shoot at such a height (for it was one of the loftiest trees of the tropics), it was away into the forest. They now visited the tree every morning; but they staid so short a time, their motions were so rapid, and it was so difficult to see them, owing to the lower trees, which impeded the view, that it was only after several days' watching, and one or two misses, that I brought down my bird—a male in the most magnificent plumage.

This bird differs very much from the two large species which I had already obtained, and, although it wants the grace imparted by their long golden trains, is in many respects more remarkable and more beautiful. The head, back, and shoulders are clothed with a richer yellow, the deep metallic green color of the throat extends farther over the head, and the feathers are elongated on the forehead into two little erectile crests. The side-plumes are shorter, but are of a rich red color, terminating in delicate white points, and the middle tail feathers are represented by two long rigid glossy ribbands, which are black, thin, and semi-cylindrical, and droop gracefully in a spiral curve.

I had only shot two male Paradiseas on my tree when they ceased visiting it, either owing to the fruit becoming scarce, or that they were wise enough to know there was danger. We continued to hear and see them in the forest, but after a month had not succeeded in shooting any more; and as my chief object in visiting Waigiou was to get these birds, I determined to go to Bessir, where there are a number of Papuans who catch and preserve them. I hired a small outrigger boat for this journey, and left one of my men to guard my house and goods. We had to wait several days for fine weather, and at length started early one morning, and arrived late at night, after a rough and disagreeable passage. The village of Bessir was built in the water at the point of a small island.

My first business was to send for the men who were accustomed to catch the birds of paradise. Several came, and I showed them my hatchets, beads, knives, and handkerchiefs; and explained to them, as well as I could by signs, the price I would give for fresh-killed specimens. It is the universal custom to pay for every thing in advance; but only one man ventured on this occasion to take goods to the value of two birds. The rest were suspicious, and wanted to see the result of the first bargain with the strange white man, the only one who had ever come to their island. After three days, my man brought me the first bird—a very fine specimen, and alive, but tied up in a small bag, and consequently its tail and wing feathers very much crushed and injured. I tried to explain to him, and to the others that came with him, that I wanted them as perfect as possible, and that they should either kill them, or keep them on a perch with a string to their leg. As they were now apparently satisfied that all was fair, and that I had no ulterior designs upon them, six others took away goods; some for one bird, some for more, and one for as many as six. They said they had to go a long way for them, and that they would come back as soon as they caught any. At intervals of a few days or a week, some of them would return, bringing me one or more birds; but though they did not bring any more in bags, there was not much improvement in their condition.

Some few were brought me the same day they were caught, and I had an opportunity of examining them in all their beauty and vivacity. As soon as I found they were generally brought alive, I set one of my men to make a large bamboo cage with troughs for food and water, hoping to be able to keep some of them. I got the natives to bring me branches of a fruit they were very fond of, and I was pleased to find they ate it greedily, and would also take any number of live grasshoppers I gave them, stripping off the legs and wings, and then swallowing them. They drank plenty of water, and

were in constant motion, jumping about the cage from perch
to perch, clinging on the top and sides, and rarely resting a
moment the first day till nightfall. The second day they were
always less active, although they would eat as freely as before; and on the morning of the third day they were almost
always found dead at the bottom of the cage, without any
apparent cause. Some of them ate boiled rice as well as fruit
and insects; but after trying many in succession, not one out
of ten lived more than three days. The second or third day
they would be dull, and in several cases they were seized with
convulsions, and fell off the perch, dying a few hours afterward. I tried immature as well as full-plumaged birds, but
with no better success, and at length gave it up as a hopeless
task, and confined my attention to preserving specimens in
as good a condition as possible.

The red birds of paradise are not shot with blunt arrows,
as in the Aru Islands and some parts of New Guinea, but are
snared in a very ingenious manner. A large climbing Arum
bears a red reticulated fruit, of which the birds are very fond.
The hunters fasten this fruit on a stout forked stick, and
provide themselves with a fine but strong cord. They then
seek out some tree in the forest on which these birds are
accustomed to perch, and climbing up it fasten the stick to
a branch and arrange the cord in a noose so ingeniously that
when the bird comes to eat the fruit its legs are caught, and
by pulling the end of the cord, which hangs down to the
ground, it comes free from the branch and brings down
the bird. Sometimes, when food is abundant elsewhere, the
hunter sits from morning till night under his tree with the
cord in his hand, and even for two or three whole days in
succession, without even getting a bite; while, on the other
hand, if very lucky, he may get two or three birds in a day.
There are only eight or ten men at Bessir who practice this
art, which is unknown anywhere else in the island. I deter-

mined, therefore, to stay as long as possible, as my only chance of getting a good series of specimens; and although I was nearly starved, every thing eatable by civilized man being scarce or altogether absent, I finally succeeded.

Thus one of my objects in coming to the far East was accomplished. I had obtained a specimen of the King Bird of Paradise (Paradisea regia), which had been described in Linnaeus from skins preserved in a mutilated state by the natives.

I knew how few Europeans had ever beheld the perfect little organism I now gazed upon, and how very imperfectly it was still known in Europe. The remote island in which I found myself situated, in an almost unvisited sea, far from the tracks of merchant-fleets and navies; the wild luxuriant tropical forest, which stretched far away on every side; the rude uncultured savages who gathered round me—all had their influence in determining the emotions with which I gazed upon this "thing of beauty."

After the first king-bird was obtained, I went with my men into the forest, and we were not only rewarded with another in equally perfect plumage, but I was enabled to see a little of the habits of both it and the larger species. It frequents the lower tree of the less dense forests, and is very active, flying strongly with a whirring sound, and continually hopping or flying from branch to branch. It eats hard stone-bearing fruits as large as a gooseberry, and often flutters its wings after the manner of the South American manakins, at which time it elevates and expands the beautiful fans with which its breast is adorned. The natives of Aru call it "goby-goby."

THE GREAT BIRD OF PARADISE

CHE Great Bird of Paradise (Paradisea apoda of Linnaeus) is the largest species known, being generally seventeen or eighteen inches from the beak to the tip of the tail. The body, wings, and tail are of a rich coffee-brown, which deepens on the breast to a blackish-violet or purple-brown. The whole top of the head and neck is of an exceedingly delicate straw-yellow, the feathers being short and close set, so as to resemble plush or velvet; the lower part of the throat up to the eye is clothed with scaly feathers of an emerald green color, and with a rich metallic gloss, and velvety plumes of a still deeper green extend in a band across the forehead and chin as far as the eye, which is bright yellow. The beak is pale lead blue; and the feet, which are rather large and very strong and well formed, are of a pale ashy-pink. The two middle feathers of the tail have no webs, except a very small one at the base and at the extreme tip, forming wire-like cirrhi, which spread out in an elegant double curve, and vary from twenty-four to thirty-four inches long. From each side of the body, beneath the wings, springs a dense tuft of long and delicate plumes, sometimes two feet in length of the most intense golden-orange color and very glossy, but changing toward the tips into a pale brown. This tuft of plumage can be elevated and spread out at pleasure, so as almost to conceal the body of the bird.

These splendid ornaments are entirely confined to the male sex, while the female is really a very plain and ordinary-looking bird of a uniform coffee-brown color which never changes; neither does she possess the long tail wires, nor a single yellow or green feather about the head.

The Great Bird of Paradise is very active and vigorous, and

seems to be in constant motion all day long. It is very abundant, small flocks of females and young males being constantly met with; and though the full-plumaged birds are less plentiful, their loud cries, which are heard daily, show that they also are very numerous. Their note is "Wawk-wawk-wawk—Wŏk, wŏk-wŏk," and is so loud and shrill as to be heard a great distance, and to form the most prominent and characteristic animal sound in the Aru Islands. The mode of nidification is unknown; but the natives told me that the nest was formed of leaves placed on an ant's nest, or on some projecting limb of a very lofty tree, and they believe that it contains only one young bird. The egg is quite unknown, and the natives declared they had never seen it; and a very high reward offered for one by a Dutch official did not meet with success. They moult about January or February, and in May, when they are in full plumage, the males assemble early in the morning to exhibit themselves in dancing-parties, in certain trees in the forest, which are not fruit-trees, as I at first imagined, but which have an immense head of spreading branches and large but scattered leaves, giving a clear space for the birds to play and exhibit their plumes. On one of these trees a dozen or twenty full-plumaged male birds assemble together, raise up their wings, stretch out their necks, and elevate their exquisite plumes, keeping them in a continual vibration. Between whiles they fly across from branch to branch in great excitement, so that the whole tree is filled with waving plumes in every variety of attitude and motion. The bird itself is nearly as large as a crow, and is of a rich coffee-brown color. The head and neck is of a pure straw yellow above, and rich metallic green beneath. The long plumy tufts of golden-orange feathers spring from the sides beneath each wing, and when the bird is in repose are partly concealed by them. At the time of its excitement, however, the wings are raised vertically over the back, the head is bent down and stretched out, and the long plumes are raised up and expanded till they form two magnificent golden fans, striped with deep red at the base, and fading off into the pale brown tint of the finely divided and softly waving points. The whole bird is then overshadowed by them, the crouching body, yellow head, and emerald-green throat forming but the foundation and setting to the golden glory which waves above. When seen in this attitude, the bird of paradise really deserves its name, and must be ranked as one of the most beautiful and most wonderful of living things.

This habit enables the natives to obtain specimens with comparative ease. As soon as they find that the birds have fixed upon a tree on which to assemble, they build a little shelter of palm leaves in a convenient place among the branches, and the hunter ensconces himself in it before daylight, armed with his bow and a number of arrows terminating in a round knob. A boy waits at the foot of the tree, and when the birds come at sunrise, and a sufficient number have assembled, and have begun to dance, the hunter shoots with his blunt arrow so strongly as to stun the bird, which drops down, and is secured and killed by the boy without its plumage being injured by a drop of blood. The rest take no notice, and fall one after another till some of them take the alarm.

The native mode of preserving them is to cut off the wings and feet, and then skin the body up to the beak, taking out the skull. A stout stick is then run up through the specimen coming out at the mouth. Round this some leaves are stuffed, and the whole is wrapped up in a palm spathe and dried in the smoky hut. By this plan the head, which is really large, is shrunk up almost to nothing, the body is much reduced and shortened, and the greater prominence is given to the flowing plumage. Some of these native skins are very clean, and often have wings and feet left on; others are dreadfully

stained with smoke, and all give a most erroneous idea of the
proportions of the living bird.

The true paradise birds are omnivorous, feeding on fruits
and insects—of the former preferring the small figs; of the
latter, grasshoppers, locusts, and phasmas, as well as cockroaches and caterpillars. When I returned home, in 1862, I
was so fortunate as to find two adult males of this species
in Singapore; and as they seemed healthy, and fed voraciously
on rice, bananas, and cockroaches, I determined on giving
the very high price asked for them—£100—and to bring them
to England by the overland route under my own care. On
my way home I staid a week at Bombay, to break the journey, and to lay in a fresh stock of bananas for my birds. I
had great difficulty, however, in supplying them with insect
food, for in the Peninsular and Oriental steamers cockroaches
were scarce, and it was only by setting traps in the store-
rooms, and by hunting an hour every night in the forecastle,
that I could secure a few dozen of these creatures—scarcely
enough for a single meal. At Malta, where I staid a fortnight,
I got plenty of cockroaches from a bakehouse, and when I
left, took with me several biscuit-tins full, as provision for
the voyage home. We came through the Mediterranean in
March, with a very cold wind; and the only place on board
the mail-steamer where their large cage could be accommo-
dated was exposed to a strong current of air down a hatch-
way which stood open day and night, yet the birds never
seemed to feel the cold. During the night journey from Mar-
seilles to Paris it was a sharp frost; yet they arrived in London
in perfect health, and lived in the Zoölogical Gardens for
one, and two years, often displaying their beautiful plumes to
the admiration of the spectators.

ELLIOTT COUES

XV

ELLIOTT COUES

*I*N THE compilation of this book nothing more surprised me than the difficulty of finding any adequate literature upon the great bird life of western North America. Splendid systematic work there is. Indeed precisely because in the Far West discoveries of new species or varieties is still going on, the energies of western ornithologists have been absorbed in systematics, and though many life histories have been carefully worked out, there have been very few among those historians dowered with the gift of tongues.

Certainly the western bird life does not lack for color or fascination. On the high prairies and plains rolling up to the Rockies, flies and drums that gamey bird, the prairie grouse. There the western meadowlark pours out his song, so much richer and happier than that of the eastern species. The magpies course above the sandy streams, the rough-winged swallows nest in burrows along the bluffs of the wandering Missouri.

On the Rockies themselves dwell the snowy ptarmigan; the dipper builds its nest behind the waterfalls, the lovely little rosy linnet and the Rocky Mountain bluebird vie in song.

Westward lies the great desert basin and here the lizard-eating road-runner scuttles, the stately Gambel's quail paces and cries, the canyon wrens and the sage thrashers pour out their melodies. Pinyon jays and ravens scream; the silky fly-snapper or phainopepla dives from the bushes at sight of the passing horseman.

Beyond, in Californian sunlight flash the hummingbirds; the mockers serenade the moon; the wren-tit bubbles forth his song, and in the coastal ranges wheel the condors. On the Pacific's shore is met another oceanic bird life, where willets teeter and sanderlings feed at the lip of the wave, while out on the kelp beds fish the pelicans, and murrelets and puffins nest upon the islands.

Here then is an avifauna as varied as that of the eastern region, related to it, but on the heroic scale. Yet aside from some lovely passages in Muir's writings, elsewhere quoted, this world of birds has had no Homer worthy of its epic save only Elliott Coues.

Elliott Coues is the commanding figure in the historical middle of American ornithology. He bestrides the great gap between the old heroic age of Audubon's time and the modern era. He belongs to the moderns because he was a sound anatomist, systematist, critic and self-critic; he had the true scientific spirit. Yet he partakes of Audubon's era because he too knew bird life in an almost primeval condition. Although in his day the birds of the eastern states were rather thoroughly known, Coues found a gloriously fresh field in the avifauna of the Far West and, widely exploring it, became its historian.

Coues was born in 1842 in the seaport town of Portsmouth, New Hampshire (and how memorable its boy life has been made by Thomas Bailey Aldrich's classic *The Story of a Bad Boy!*) When childhood was almost over, young Elliott was taken to live in Washington. The bird life of the Capital is peculiarly rich; it has left a deep impression upon many men —John Burroughs prominent among them. Here Coues, at the age of nineteen, published an important monograph on the genus of the sandpipers and came early to the attention of older naturalists at the Smithsonian.

Meantime he was attending Columbia College (now George Washington University) and trained as a physician. He entered under age, as a medical cadet in the Civil War,

and soon rose to be an assistant army surgeon, a rank he
held actively from 1864 to 1881.

In his army life Coues was stationed variously at Fort
Whipple, Arizona, at Fort Macon, North Carolina, and Fort
Randall in the Territory of Dakota. He was appointed naturalist and secretary to the Boundary Commission surveying the
frontier with Canada from the Lake-of-the-Woods to the
Pacific. Later he became secretary and naturalist for the Geological Survey of the Territories or what are now the western
states.

Coues made the most of his matchless opportunities. He
collected constantly, adding many new species to our avifauna. But more important, he mastered the life histories of
western birds, hitherto known at best as skins, skeletons and
feathers.

Ornithology at Fort Whipple in 1864 and 1865 must have
been exciting. Coues was frequently, on account of the war
with the Apache Indians, unable to go out of sight of the fort.
It was not too much to imagine that while he watched the
birds, Apaches watched him. Often when he wanted a specimen, it was unsafe to fire off his gun; when he might shoot,
the birds were often too wary. Ornithology under these conditions "was sometimes too spicy for comfort." His memories
of the gentle little titmouse and the beautiful phainopepla
or flysnapper were forever after colored by the discovery, made
while following these birds, of the still bleeding naked bodies
of soldiers from the fort.

In 1874 he wrote his *Birds of the Northwest* which revealed
him not only as a keen field worker and absolutely sound
anatomist, but a writer of abilities in popularization which
were astonishing in a man of such highly disciplined science.
He followed this with *Birds of the Colorado Valley* (1878),
and it is from these two books that my selections have been
made.

Hundreds of technical papers followed. Coues' *Key to North American Birds* ran through many editions, and well into our century and is even now not really superseded. The introduction itself forms a concise treatise on ornithology, and the book has guided many careers. He also contributed forty thousand zoölogical definitions to the *Century Dictionary*, and taught anatomy at Columbia.

Coues' personality was hardly less influential. His enthusiasm was electrifying, his presence commanding and handsome. True, he was more than a slight eccentric; he was often unpredictable and emotional, but never a bore and seldom unjust. He had several marked aversions; one of them was Buffon as an ornithologist. His associates were endlessly delighted by his humor, which extended (most unusually for an impeccable scientist) to a keen sense of nonsense. Humor and much literary cultivation crop up delightfully and without warning in the soberest of his life histories.

When well along in life Dr. Coues startled his scientific friends by joining and actively propagating Theosophy. On a European trip he had come under the sway of Helena Blavatsky and Henry Steel Orcott, and he returned to found the Gnostic Branch of the Theosophical Society in Washington. He was soon President of the American Board of Control of the Theosophical Society, and seemed scheduled, and ambitious, to become the acknowledged leader of the cult in America. This ambition clashed with that of William Juan Judge, while his refusal to accept the Mahatmic messages brought him into conflict with the whole society. In 1882 Coues could call Mme. Blavatsky "the greatest woman of this age, who is born to redeem her times." Yet the next year he published an article titled "Mme. Blavatsky's Famous Hoax," and was promptly expelled from the society.

To his scientific friends this was something in the nature of an honor. One cannot judge of others' convictions of faiths or the motives behind either conversion or apostasy. Coues had a strong moral nature which drew him to what seemed for a time like a redeeming movement. He had also a strong scientific conscience, and quite evidently he discovered something which that conscience could not permit him to accept as veracious. Or else his persuasion was only under the magnetism of one woman, and when something broke the spell, the movement itself had no appeal to him.

The last years of Coues' life were spent in collecting, editing and annotating, with ethnological, zoölogical, botanical, and historical notes, the most famous documents of western exploration. He was particularly indignant over the wretched first editions of the Lewis and Clarke narrative, and undertook to restore and revise the whole great mass of material, with the result that Coues' editions of the Lewis and Clarke and the Zebulon Pike narratives are far more valuable than the original issues.

While on an arduous journey in Arizona and New Mexico, studying the trail of the old Spanish explorers, his health broke down. He returned to Washington and lingered some months in the year 1899. At the end, it is said, he sat up suddenly in his bed and cried, "Welcome, oh, welcome, beloved death!"

In the following selections from Coues' writings I have chosen birds famous in the annals of western life and exploration, birds about which Indian and Spanish and cowboy legends have grown by the natural accretion of all folk lore. Although three of them are not unknown in the eastern states, they reach the climax of their lives in the West.

The cowbird of which Coues writes is, as he says, remarkable for sharing with the European cuckoo the parasitic habit in regard to raising its young, although it belongs to the New World family of the troupials, while our eastern cuckoos are not at all parasitic. Coues hardly touches upon the origin of the cowbird's name, which is derived from the habit that these polygamous flocks once had of following the bison herds in order to feed upon their ticks. Today, on the prairies, they are often associated with domestic cows, having altered their habits slightly with their characteristic adaptability and intelligence.

Far different from this association of a gregarious bird with a gregarious mammal is the apparent society formed by the burrowing owls, prairie dogs, and rattlesnakes. As Coues points out, bird, rodent, and reptile are bound together in a strange subterranean life in the pattern of the hunt or chase; there is a relationship between the three, but it is not a symbiosis, but what ecologists call a "food relation."

The cliff swallow whose pottery nests Coues describes so vividly, is one of the few western birds whose habits are almost affectionate toward man. Originally a cliff dweller like some of the western Indians, these swallows today come right into the cities to build. Their great colonies adorn the picturesque ruins of Capistrano Mission in California, and legend has adorned the birds in its turn—something unusual in New World Nature.

The bush-tits of the West are related to no bird of the eastern states but rather to the long-tailed tits of Europe, and like them they build exquisitely artificed nests. One that I gathered on my own grounds here in California is before me as I write, all wrought of lichens, cunningly suspended, and furnished with an entrance on the side incapable of admitting anyone larger than its minute owner. For the bush-tit is, in an avifauna of eagles and ravens, ibises and condors, an almost laughably small bird.

PLUMBEOUS BUSH-TIT

*U*P TO the present time, no one seems to have found the nest of the Plumbeous Bush-tit, though several naturalists besides myself have collected diligently in regions where the bird abounds. Not to pass over so extraordinary a specimen of bird-architecture as the genus *Psaltriparus* has invented and successfully introduced, I shall refer to the nests of *P. minimus*,* from which those of the scarcely distinct *P. plumbeus* cannot be presumed to differ. The order of architecture is thoroughly composite; in its execution, the qualities of skill, ingenuity, good taste and laborious perseverance are exhibited on the part of the builders; while the wee creatures seem possessed of no little ambition to make a monument, which, if not so lasting as brass, is infinitely more comfortable and convenient. This nest belongs in the category of pensile structures, being suspended from twigs of trees or bushes, but it is not a simple cup or basket, open at the top. It resembles the old-fashioned silken purse (which I recall from tradition rather than by actual memory) more than many of the nests called "purse-like" do, the entrance being a circular orifice at the side—nothing but the rings which slipped along these old purses being wanting to render the simile complete. One hardly knows which to admire most— the industry with which such a great feat is executed, or the cunning with which so curious a fabric is wrought—and no one certainly would suspect the owners of the nest to be such pygmies. As Dr. Cooper says, it seems as if it would take a whole flock to get up one such structure. The nest

---

* The Least Bush-tit. The nest of the plumbeous species is of course well known since Coues' day. As he surmised, it does not differ from that of the Least. [Ed.]

measures in length from six to eight or nine inches, with a diameter of three or three and a half; the general shape is cylindrical, not perfectly expressed however, for the ends are rounded and the top contracted. The orifice is about an inch in diameter. The substance is closely woven of lichens, mosses, very soft plant-fibre, or cottony vegetable matter, slender spears of grass and fibrous rootlets, and lined with the downiest, softest possible material, and a great mass of feathers, some of which may appear at the entrance, or be felted in the substance of the walls. The weaving is usually so well executed that the walls appear pretty firm and smooth from the outside; while their thickness reduces the cavity about one-half. The nest retains the greenish-gray color of the mosses and lichens of which it is principally composed, and the whole affair resembles a natural product. The reader will find, on Audubon's plate already cited, an artistic representation of a nest presented to him by Mr. Nuttall, and as the birds are drawn alongside, in spirited attitudes, the striking disparity in size is illustrated. In this wonderfully elaborate structure, eggs are deposited to the number of six to nine—an egg to every inch of nest; they are pure white, without markings, and measure scarcely or not three-fifths of an inch in length.

These queer little elfs were very numerous about Fort Whipple, where I saw them all the year round, and learned as much about them as any one seems to know. Though living in a coniferous region, they avoided the pine forests, keeping in the oak scrub of the hillsides, and the undergrowth along the creek bottoms and through the numerous ravines that make down the mountain sides. They endured, without apparent inconvenience, an extreme of cold which sometimes proved fatal to birds of much more seeming hardihood, like Ravens for instance; and were as active and sprightly in the depth of winter as at any other time. I used to wonder how they managed, in such tiny animal furnaces, to generate heat enough to stand such a climate, and speculated whether their incessant activity might not have something to do with it. They always seemed to me model store-houses of energy—conserved to a degree in cold weather, with consumption of no more than was needed to keep them a-going, and thus accumulated for the heavier draft required when, in the spring, the arduous duties of nest-building and rearing a numerous family devolve upon them. Their food at this season consists of various seeds that persist through the winter; during the rest of the year, different insects contribute to their subsistence, and foraging for the minute bugs, larvæ and eggs that lurk in the crevices of bark seems to be their principal business. They are very industrious in this pursuit, and too much absorbed in the exciting chances of the chase to pay attention to what may be going on around them. They are extremely sociable—the gregarious instinct common to the Titmice reaches its highest development in their case, and flocks of forty or fifty—some say even of a hundred—may be seen after the breeding season has passed, made up of numerous families, which, soon after leaving the nest, meet kindred spirits, and enter into intimate friendly relations. Often, in rambling through the shrubbery, I have been suddenly surrounded by a troop of the busy birds, perhaps unnoticed till the curious chirping they keep up attracted my attention; they seemed to pervade the bushes. If I stood still, they came close around me, as fearless as if I were a stump, ignoring me altogether. At such times, it was pleasant to see the earnestness with which they conducted affairs, and the energy they displayed in their own curious fashion, as if it were the easiest thing in the world to work hard, and quite proper to attend to serious matters with a thousand antics. They are droll folk, quite innocent of dignity, superior to the trammels of decorum, secure in the consciousness that their wit will carry off any extravagance. I used to call them my merry little philosophers—for they took the weather as it came, and evidently knew how much better it is to laugh at the world than cry with it. When fretted with the friction of garrison-life, I have often sought their society, and amused myself like another Gulliver among the Liliputians.

CLIFF SWALLOW

T HE Swallows, as a rule, are birds of local distribution in the breeding season, notwithstanding their pre-eminent migratory abilities; they tend to settle in particular places, and return year after year; and nothing is better known than that one town may be full of Swallows of several kinds unknown in another town hard by.

A happy conjunction of circumstances is required to satisfy these birds. Not only are cliffs or their substitutes necessary, but these must be situated where clayey mud, possessing some degree of adhesiveness and plasticity, can be procured. The indication is met at large in the West, along unnumbered streams, where the birds most do congregate; and their very general dispersion in the West, as compared with their rather sporadic distribution in the East, is thus readily explained. The great veins of the West—the Missouri, the Columbia, and the Colorado,—and most of their venous tributaries, re-turning the humors from the clouds to their home in the sea, are supplied in profusion with animated congregations of the Swallows, often vastly more extensive than those gatherings of the feathered Sons of Temperance beneath our eaves, where the sign of the order,—a bottle, neck downward, —is set for our edification.

It is generally understood that the most perfect nest, that is, a nest fully finished and furnished with a neck, resembling a decanter tilted over,—that such a "bottle-nosed" or "retort-shaped" nest, is the typical one, indicating the primitive fashion of building. It was probably not until they had served a long apprenticeship that they acquired the sufficient skill to stick a nest against a perfectly smooth, vertical support. Some kind of domed nest was still requisite, to carry out the idea of hole-breeding, a trait so thoroughly ingrained in Hirundine nature, and implying perfect covering for the eggs; and the indication is fully met in one of the very commonest forms of nests, namely, a hemispherical affair, quite a "breastwork" in fact, with a hole at the most protuberant part, or just below it. The running on of a neck to the nest, as seen in those nests we consider the most elaborate, seems to merely represent a surplusage of building energy, like that which induces a House Wren, for example, to accumulate a preposterous quantity of trash in its cubby-holes. Such architecture reminds me of the Irishman's notion of how cannon are made—by taking a hole and pouring the melted metal around it. It is the rule, when the nest is built in any exposed situation. But since the Swallows have taken to building under eaves, or other projections affording a degree of shelter, the bottle-necked, even the simply globular nests, seem to be going out of fashion; and thousands of nests are now built as open as those of the Barn Swallow, being simply half-cups attached to the wall, and in fact chiefly distinguished from those of Barn Swallows by containing little or no hay.

Considering how sedulously most birds strive to hide their nests, and screen themselves during incubation, it becomes a matter of curious speculation why these Swallows should ever build beneath our eaves, in the most conspicuous manner, and literally fly in the face of danger. Richardson * speaks of a colony that persisted in nesting just over a frequented promenade, where they had actually to graze people's heads in passing to and from their nests, and were exposed to the curiosity and depredations of the children; yet they stuck to their first choice, even though there were equally eligible and far safer locations just at hand. I think such obstinacy is due to the bird's reluctance to give up the much-needed shelter

* Sir John Richardson (1787-1865), the famous Scottish naturalist, surgeon to Franklin's first Arctic expedition. [Ed.]

which the eaves provide against the weather—indeed, this may have had something to do with the change of habit in the beginning. The Cliff Swallow's nest is built entirely of mud, which, when sun baked into 'adobe,' is secure enough in dry weather, but liable to be loosened or washed away during a storm. In fact, this accident is of continual occurrence, just as it is in the cases of the Chimney Swifts. The birds' instinct—whatever that may mean; I despise the word as a label of our ignorance and conceit—say rather, their reason, teaches them to come in out of the rain. This may also have something to do with the clustering of nests, commonly observed when the birds build on the faces of cliffs, for obviously such a mass would withstand the weather better than a single edifice.

It is pleasant to watch the establishment and progress of a colony of these birds. Suddenly they appear—quite animated and enthusiastic, but undecided as yet; an impromptu debating society on the fly, with a good deal of sawing the air to accomplish, before final resolutions are passed. The plot thickens; some Swallows are seen clinging to the slightest inequalities beneath the eaves, others are couriers to and from the nearest mud-puddle; others again alight like feathers by the water's side, and all are in a twitter of excitement. Watching closely these curious sons and daughters of Israel at their ingenious trade of making bricks, we may chance to see a circle of them gathered around the margin of the pool, insecurely balanced on their tiny feet, tilting their tails and ducking their heads to pick up little "gobs" of mud. These are rolled round in their mouths till tempered, and made like a quid into globular form, with a curious working of their jaws; then off go the birds, and stick the pellet against the wall, as carefully as ever a sailor, about to spin a yarn, deposited his chew on the mantel-piece. The birds work indefatigably; they are busy as bees, and a steady stream flows back and forth for several hours a day, with intervals for rest and refreshment, when the Swallows swarm about promiscuously a-flycatching. In an incredibly short time, the basement of the nest is laid, and the whole form becomes clearly outlined; the mud dries quickly, and there is a standing place. This is soon occupied by one of the pair, probably the female, who now stays at home to welcome her mate with redoubled cries of joy and ecstatic quivering of the wings, as he brings fresh pellets, which the pair in closest consultation dispose to their entire satisfaction. In three or four days, perhaps, the deed is done; the house is built, and nothing remains but to furnish it. The poultry-yard is visited, and laid under contribution of feathers; hay, leaves, rags, paper, string—Swallows are not very particular—may be added; and then the female does the rest of the "furnishing" by her own particular self. Not impossibly, just at this period, a man comes with a pole, and demolishes the whole affair; or the *enfant terrible* of the premises appears, and removes the eggs to enrich his sanded tray of like treasures; or a tom-cat reaches for his supper. But more probably matters are so propitious that in due season the nest decants a full brood of Swallows—and I wish that nothing more harmful ever came out of the bottle.

Seeing how these birds work the mud in their mouths, some have supposed that the nests are agglutinated, to some extent at least, by the saliva of the birds. It is far from an unreasonable idea—the Chimney Swift sticks her bits of twigs together, and glues the frail cup to the wall with viscid saliva; and some of the Old World Swifts build nests of gummy spittle, which cakes on drying, not unlike gelatine. Undoubtedly some saliva is mingled with the natural moisture of the mud; but the readiness with which these Swallows' nests crumble on drying shows that saliva enters slightly into their composition—practically not at all—and that this fluid possesses no special viscosity. Much more probably, the moisture of the birds' mouths helps to soften and temper the pellets, rather than to agglutinate the dried edifice itself.

In various parts of the West, especially along the Missouri and the Colorado, where I have never failed to find clustering nests of the Cliff Swallow, I have occasionally witnessed some curious associates of these birds. In some of the navigable cañons of the Colorado, I have seen the bulky nests of the Great Blue Heron on flat ledges of rock, the faces of which were stuccoed with Swallow-nests. How these frolicsome creatures must have swarmed around the sedate and imperturbable Herodias, when she folded up her legs and closed her eyes, and went off into the dreamland of incubation, undisturbed, in a very Babel! Again, I have found a colony of Swallows in what would seem to be a very dangerous neighborhood—all about the nest of a Falcon, no other than the valiant and merciless *Falco polyagrus*, on the very minarets and buttresses of whose awe-inspiring castle, on the scowling face of a precipice, a colony of Swallows was established in apparent security. The big birds seemed to be very comfortable ogres, with whom the multitude of hop-o'-my-thumbs had evidently some sort of understanding, perhaps like that which the Purple Grackles may be supposed to have with the Fish-hawks when they set up housekeeping in the cellar of King Pandion's palace. If it had only been a Fish-hawk in this case instead [of] *Falco polyagrus*, we could understand such amicable relations better—for Cliff Swallows are cousins of Purple Martins, and, if half we hear be true, *Progne* was Pandion's daughter.

COW-BIRD

$\mathcal{P}$ARASITISM, in the zoölogical sense of the term a frequent condition of lower forms of life, is sufficiently rare among higher animals to excite special interest; and the exceptional absence of the strong parental instincts of birds is particularly noteworthy. Considering that conscious volition—that choice, in a word—determines the whole process of perpetuation of the species in the Cow-bird, denying all but the purely sexual of conjugal relations, abrogating parental relations, and rendering family relations impossible, we must concede a case of parasitism having almost an ethical significance, to such an extreme is it pushed.

It is singular that this particular kind of parasitism should occur in the isolated cases of birds so unlike, as Cuckoos and Cow-birds, and only there, so far as we know.

It does not appear that the Cow-bird ever attempts to take forcible possession of a nest. She watches her chance while the owners are away, slips in by stealth, and leaves the evidence of her unfriendly visit to be discovered on their return, in the shape of the ominous egg. The parents hold anxious consultation in this emergency, as their sorrowful cries and disturbed actions plainly indicate. If their nest was empty before, they generally desert it, and their courage in giving up a cosy home results in one Cow-bird the less. Sometimes even after there is an egg of their own in the nest, they have nerve enough to let it go, rather than assume the hateful task of incubating the strange one. But if the female has already laid an egg or two, the pair generally settle into the reluctant conviction that there is no help for it; they quiet down after awhile, and things go on as if nothing had happened. Not always, however, will they desert even an empty nest; some birds have discovered a way out of the difficulty—it is the most ingenious device imaginable, and the more we think about it the more astonishing it seems. They build a two-story nest, leaving the obnoxious egg in the basement.

The Cow-bird's foster-parents are numerous; the list of those so determined is already large, and when completed will probably comprise pretty much all of the species nesting within the Cow-bird's breeding range, from the size of a Thrush down to that of the Gnatcatcher. It is unnecessary to recite the long list; I will mention, however, the Wood Thrush, Yellow-breasted Chat, and Towhee Bunting, as showing that the foster-birds are not always smaller than the Cow-bird itself. The Summer Yellowbird, the Maryland Yellow-throat, and the Red-eyed Vireo, are among those most persistently victimized. On the prairies of the west, where the Cow-birds are very numerous, and breeding birds restricted in number of species if not of individuals, I had almost said that in a majority of the nests taken in June will be found a Cow-bird's egg.

It is interesting to observe the female Cow-bird ready to lay. She becomes disquieted; she betrays unwonted excitement, and ceases her busy search for food with her companions. At length she separates from the flock, and sallies forth to reconnoitre, anxiously indeed, for her case is urgent, and she has no home. How obtrusive is the sad analogy! She flies to some thicket, or hedge-row, or other common resort of birds, where, something teaches her—perhaps experience—nests will be found. Stealthily and in perfect silence she flits along, peering furtively, alternately elated or dejected, into the depths of the foliage. She espies a nest, but the owner's head peeps over the brim, and she must pass on. Now, however, comes her chance; there is the very nest she wishes, and no one at home. She disappears for a few minutes, and it is almost another bird that comes out of the bush. Her business done, and trouble over, she chuckles her self-gratulations, rustles her plumage to adjust it trimly, and flies back to her associates. They know what has happened, but are discreet enough to say nothing—charity is often no less wise than kind.

Polygamy is rare among higher birds; in no creatures are the parental and conjugal instincts more strongly developed or beautifully displayed. But the Cow-bird illustrates this mode of life, and not in the lordly manner of the barn-yard cock, so devoted to his harem, so gallant and just to all. As in this species there is no love of offspring, neither can there be conjugal affection; all family ties are dispensed with. The association is a mere herding together in quest of food in similar resorts. The Cow-birds never mate; their most intimate relations are no sooner effected than forgotten; not even the decent restrictions of a seraglio are observed; it is a perfect community of free-lovers, who do as the original Cynics did. The necessary courtship becomes in consequence a curiously mixed affair. During the period corresponding to the mating season of orderly birds, the patriarchs of the sorry crew mount up the trees and fences, to do what they call their singing. They posture and turn about, and ruffle their feathers to look bigger than Nature made them; if their skins were not tough they would certainly burst with vanity. They puff out their throats and pipe the most singular notes, perhaps honestly wishing to please their companions of the other sex—at any rate, to their own satisfaction. Meanwhile the females are perched near by, but without seeming very enthusiastic—rather taking it all as a matter of course, listening at times, it may be, but just as likely preening their plumage, with other thoughts and an ulterior purpose. The performance over, it is a very little while afterward when the whole band goes trooping after food in the nearest cattle-yard or pasture.

Cow-birds appear to be particularly abundant in the West; more so, perhaps, than they really are, for the numbers that in the East spread equally over large areas are here drawn within small compass, owing to lack of attractions abroad.

Every wagon-train passing over the prairies in summer is attended by flocks of the birds; every camp and stock-corral, permanent or temporary, is besieged by the busy birds, eager to glean subsistence from the wasted forage. Their familiarity under these circumstances is surprising. Perpetually wandering about the feet of the draught-animals, or perching upon their backs, they become so accustomed to man's presence that they will hardly get out of the way. I have even known a young bird to suffer itself to be taken in hand, and it is no uncommon thing to have the birds fluttering within a few feet of one's head. The animals appear to rather like the birds, and suffer them to perch in a row upon their back-bones, doubtless finding the scratching of their feet a comfortable sensation, to say nothing of the riddance from insect parasites.

A singular point in the history of this species is its unexplained disappearance, generally in July, from many or most localities in which it breeds. Where it goes, and for what purpose, are unknown; but the fact is attested by numerous observers. Sometimes it reappears in September in the same places, sometimes not. Thus, in North Dakota, I saw none after early in August.

BURROWING OWL

CHE Burrowing Owl is the only bird of its family inhabiting in any numbers, the entirely treeless regions of the West. Wherever it can find shelter in the holes of such animals as wolves, foxes, and badgers, and especially of the various species of marmot squirrels, there it is found in abundance; and in not a few instances small colonies are observed living apart from their ordinary associates, in holes apparently dug by themselves. They constitute a notable exception to the general rule of arboricole habits in this family, being specially fitted by their conformation for the subterranean mode of life for which they are designed, and are furthermore exceptional in their gregarious disposition, here carried to the extreme.

Having been noticed by the earlier writers in special connection with the singular settlements of the prairie-dog (*Cynomys ludovicianus*), and the life relations of the two creatures being really intimate in very many localities, an almost inseparable association of ideas has been brought about, which is only partly true; and it was a long time before the whole truth in the case became apparent. When competent observers, familiar with the animals, disagree, as they have, respecting the kind and degree of relation between the bird and the mammals, we need not be surprised at conflict of opinion in the books of naturalists who never saw either of them alive. The case is further complicated by the introduction of the rattlesnakes; and no little pure bosh is in type respecting the harmonious and confidential relations, imagined to subsist between the trio, which, like the "happy family" of Barnum, lead Utopian existences. According to the dense bathos of such nursery tales, in this underground Elysium the snakes give their rattles to the puppies to play with, the old dogs cuddle the Owlets, and farm out their own litters to the grave and careful birds; when an Owl and a dog come home, paw-in-wing, they are often mistaken by their respective progeny, the little dogs nosing the Owls in search of the maternal font, and the old dogs left to wonder why the baby Owls will not nurse. It is a pity to spoil a good story for the sake of a few facts, but as the case stands, it would be well for the Society for the Prevention of Cruelty to Animals to take it up. First, as to the reptiles, it may be observed that they are like other rattlesnakes, dangerous, venomous creatures; they have no business in the burrows, and are after no good when they do enter. They wriggle into the holes, partly because there is no other place for them to crawl into on the bare, flat plain, and partly in search of Owls' eggs, Owlets, and puppies, to eat. Next, the Owls themselves are simply attracted to the villages of prairie-dogs as the most convenient places for shelter and nidification, where they find eligible ready-made burrows, and are spared the trouble of digging for themselves. Community of interest makes them gregarious to an extent unusual among rapacious birds; while the exigencies of life on the plains cast their lot with the rodents. That the Owls live at ease in the settlements, and on familiar terms with their four-footed neighbors, is an undoubted fact; but that they inhabit the same burrows, or have any intimate domestic relations, is quite another thing. It is no proof that the quadruped and the birds live together, that they are often seen to scuttle at each other's heels into the same hole when alarmed; for in such a case the two simply seek the nearest shelter, independently of each other. The probability is, that young dogs often furnish a meal to the Owls, and that, in return, the latter are often robbed of their eggs; while certainly the young of both, and the Owls' eggs, are eaten by the snakes. In the larger settlements there are thousands upon thousands of burrows, many occupied by the dogs, but more, perhaps, vacant. These latter are the homes of the Owls. Moreover, the ground below is honey-combed with communicating passages, leading in every direction. If the underground plan could be mapped, it would resemble the city of Boston, with its tortuous and devious streets. The dogs are continually busy in fair weather in repairing and extending their establishments; the main entrances may be compared to the stump of a hollow tree, the interior of which communicates with many hollow branches that moreover intersect, these passages finally ending in little pockets, the real home of the animals. It is quite possible that the respective retreats of a dog and an Owl may have but one vestibule, but even this does not imply that they nest together. It is strong evidence in point, that usually there are the fewest Owls in the towns most densely populated by the dogs, and conversely. Scarcity of food, of water, or some obscure cause, often makes the dogs emigrate from one locality to another; it is in such "deserted villages" that the Owls are usually seen in the greatest numbers. I have never seen them so numerous as in places where there are plenty of holes, but where scarcely a stray dog remained.

I never undertook to unearth the nest of a Burrowing Owl, but others have been more zealous in the pursuit of knowledge under difficulties. Dr. Cooper says that he once dug two fresh eggs out of a burrow, which he followed down for three feet, and then traced five feet horizontally, at the end of which he found an enlarged chamber, where the eggs were deposited on a few feathers. In his interesting note in the American Naturalist, Dr. C. S. Canfield gives a more explicit account of the nesting: "I once took pains to dig out a nest of the Athene cunicularia. I found that the burrow was about four feet long, and the nest was only about two feet from the surface of the ground. The nest was made in a cavity of the ground, of about a foot in diameter, well filled with dry, soft horse-dung, bits of an old blanket, and fur of a coyote (Canis latrans) that I had killed a few days before. One of the parent birds was on the nest, and I captured it. It had no intention of leaving the nest, even when entirely uncovered with the shovel and exposed to the open air. It fought bravely with beak and claws. I found seven young ones, perhaps eight or ten days old, well covered with down, but without any feathers. There are very few birds that carry more rubbish into the nest than the Athene; and even the Vultures are not much more filthy. I am satisfied that the A. cunicularia lays a larger number of eggs than is attributed to it. I have frequently seen, late in the season, six, seven, or eight young birds standing around the mouth of a burrow, isolated from others in such a manner that I could not suppose that they belonged to two or more families."

The notes of the Burrowing Owl are peculiar. The birds do not "hoot," nor is there anything lugubrious or foreboding in their cry. Sometime they chuckle, chatter, and squeal in an odd way, as if they had caught a habit of barking from the "dogs" they live with, and were trying to imitate the sound. But their natural cry is curiously similar to that of the Rain Crow, or Cuckoo of America—so much so, that more than one observer has been deceived. They scream hoarsely when wounded and caught, though this is but seldom, since, if any life remains, they scramble quickly into a hole and are not easy to recover. The flight is perfectly noiseless, like that of other Owls, owing to the peculiar downy texture of the plumage. By day they seldom fly far from the entrance of their burrow, and rarely, if ever, mount in the air. I never saw one on wing more than a few moments at a time, just long enough for it to pass from one hillock to another, as it does by skimming low over the surface of the ground in a rapid, easy, and rather graceful manner. They live chiefly upon insects, especially grasshoppers; they also feed upon lizards, as I once determined by dissection, and there is no doubt that young prairie-dogs furnish them many a meal. As commonly observed, perched on one of the innumerable little eminences that mark a dog-town, amid their curious surroundings, they present a spectacle not easily forgotten. Their figure is peculiar, with their long legs and short tail; the element of the grotesque is never wanting; it is hard to say whether they look most ludicrous as they stand stiffly erect and motionless, or when they suddenly turn tail to duck into the hole, or when engaged in their various antics. Bolt upright, on what may be imagined their rostrum, they gaze about with a bland and self-satisfied, but earnest air, as if about to address an audience upon a subject of great pith and moment. They suddenly bow low, with profound gravity, and rising as abruptly, they begin to twitch their face and roll their eyes about in the most mysterious manner, gesticulating wildly, every now and then bending forward till the breast almost touches the ground, to propound the argument with more telling effect. Then they face about to address the rear, that all may alike feel the force of their logic; they draw themselves up to their fullest height, outwardly calm and self-contained, pausing in the discourse to note its effect upon the audience, and collect their wits for the next rhetorical flourish. And no distant likeness between these frothy orators and others is found in the celerity with which they subside and seek their holes on the slightest intimation of danger.

FRANK M. CHAPMAN

XVI

FRANK M. CHAPMAN

*A*MONG New World naturalists who devote themselves entirely to ornithology, Dr. Chapman would
be considered, I think, easily the most distinguished
of all the older men. Expert in the field and the museum
alike, systematist, life historian and behaviorist, ecologist and
sensitive appreciator of the beauty of bird life, he and his
writings have influenced young American ornithologists more
than any other living man and his work.

Frank Michler Chapman was born in Englewood, New
Jersey, in 1864. His mother was musically gifted, and to this
he attributes his receptivity toward the vocal charms and
speech of birds. His environment was then a country one, and
from childhood he enjoyed and followed the birds of orchard
and the sweet, cool temperate forest, of meadow and village
street. Such an environment was the perfect nurse for him.
To this he added the talents of a keen young sportsman. And
sportsmanship is undoubtedly one of the doorways by which
many naturalists have found their way to science. For a future
systematist and anatomist, a bird in the hand is indeed sometimes indispensable. So the boy shot and trapped and bird-
nested with the best of country lads, and stocked his mind
with a wealth of field knowledge.

While still very young he went to work in a New York
bank, not relinquishing his undirected and untrained interest
in birds but unable to imagine how he could use it save as a
diversion upon his rare holidays. The work at the bank was
very exacting, and Dr. Chapman still thanks it because it
taught him promptness and thoroughness, business manage-

ment, precision and responsibility with money affairs, qualities of which naturalists are sometimes lamentably unpossessed.

In the meantime Dr. Chapman had begun volunteer work in recording bird migrations and the use of valuable or endangered species of birds on New York millinery. In these fields, though almost without personal friends among the ornithologists, he attracted attention as by far the best amateur reporter. Then one day in the window of a Dodd, Mead bookshop, he tells us, he saw a copy of Elliott Coues' *Key to North American Birds*. He went in and purchased it, and, as any future student would have done (and no dabbling or mentally indolent amateur could have) he began to master it, technicalities and all. For the mark of a real scientist is that a new and difficult thing is a challenge he will not refuse. To a love of birds and a fowler's knowledge of their ways, he had now added pure or theoretical science. One thing more was needed to make him an ornithologist.

He tells in his *Autobiography* how this was attained, not as the result of an outward event, but as an inward and instant revelation or call:

"I had gone to the Union Trust Company, to collect a draft. While waiting, I saw a man whom I did not know but whom I recognized as a messenger of the First National Bank. . . . He was at least ten years older than I. . . . He, too, was waiting, but while he waited he wrote on a pad he held in his hand, and it seemed to me that what he wrote had no connection with the First National Bank. Rather did he look like a priest who, while acting as a bank messenger, was living the life of a student. Perhaps there was sufficient resemblance in our relation to our vocations to make him and his evident remoteness from his surroundings appeal strongly to my attention and imagination; and as I looked at him there suddenly sprang into my mind with the force of a revelation a determination to devote my life to the study of birds."

After thus changing his soul's identity on the road to Damascus, Dr. Chapman resigned from the bank and his next steps were also very instructive in the way to find the true short road to scientific eminence. He did not seek a position for a position's sake but, in the field and as a volunteer around the American Museum of Natural History, he began to make himself invaluable. Then the congenial employment sought *him* out, and at the age of twenty-four, with no university training in science, he had become associate curator of birds and mammals in a leading museum of the western world.

The rest of his museum career is too well known on both sides of the Atlantic to need mention here. Dr. Chapman is the creator of the new style in the museum exhibition of birds, and his influence in this line has spread all over the world, and directly and indirectly educated countless thousands. Among his many popular books which have given the first impulse to hosts of young ornithologists, his *Handbook of Birds of the Eastern United States* is still preëminent, going through many new editions. His public career has brought him the medal of the Roosevelt Memorial Association, the Burroughs Memorial medal, and the medals of the Linnaean Society of New York and the National Academy of Sciences. Enviable are his rich friendships, for he has known such diverse naturalists as Burroughs and Roosevelt, Grey and Hudson, Fuertes and Coues, Brewster and Merriam.

But in nothing does one envy him so much as in his wide experience of bird life, in every part of temperate North America and above all in the tropics—Mexico and the West Indies, Florida and the Bahamas, northern South America and, notably in his present studies, on Barro Colorado Island in the Canal Zone. He has enjoyed rapid trips covering wide areas, and long residence in a limited area. His fundamental attitude toward the study of bird life is significant. He says, "I had also a growing belief, which in time became almost a religion, in the re-creational and spiritual value of close contact with nature, and birds, I was convinced, are nature's most eloquent expressions."

From his delightful book *Camps and Cruises of an Ornithologist* (1908) I have selected his account of a visit to the nesting sites of the American flamingo, that bird incredible even when you see one. I say, "when you see one." Unless you are Dr. Chapman, or one of two negroes who frequent certain inaccessible "swashes" of Andros Island, you have not seen one, it is pretty safe to say—not in the wild. For this bird who looks like, and is, something out of another era in the earth's history, is now exceedingly rare as a nesting species. Its range in theory extends from southern Florida to Brazil and the Galapagos. Its actual occurrence in those regions is very scattered and irregular. In the Bahamas, where it finds abundance of a small spiral mollusc (*Cerithium*) and where the land is all sea, and the sea is all mud, the American flamingo still finds life possible.

THE FLAMINGO

*A*LL day we had been following broad, shallow creeks, which, meeting other creeks, widened at intervals into lagoons, while, on every side, the country spread away into the low, flat swash, neither land nor water and wholly worthless for everything—except Flamingos. When for the second time I asked Peter, "But where are the birds?" he replied, "Dere dey are, sir," and pointed across the swash to a thin pink line, distant at least a mile, but showing plainly against the green of the mangroves. Flamingos, surely; but were they nesting? We lost no time in speculation but started at once to investigate. Ten minutes wading through the mud and shallow water, brought us so near the now much enlarged pink streak that with a glass, the birds could be seen unmistakably seated on their conical nests, and with an utterly indescribable feeling of exultation, we advanced rapidly to view at short range this wonder of wonders in bird-life.

At a distance of about three hundred yards, the wind being from us, toward the birds, we first heard their honking notes of alarm, which increased to a wave of deep sound. Soon the birds began to rise, standing on their nests, facing the wind and waving their black, vermillion-lined wings. As we came a little nearer, in stately fashion the birds began to move; uniformly, like a great body of troops, they stepped slowly forward, pinions waving and trumpets sounding, and then, when we were still one hundred and fifty yards away, the leaders sprang into the air. File after file of the winged host followed. The very earth seemed to erupt birds, as flaming masses streamed heavenward. It was an appalling sight. One of the boatmen said, it looked "like hell," and the description is apt enough to be set down without impropriety.

The birds were now all in the air. At the time, I should have said that there were at least four thousand of them, but a subsequent census of nests showed that this number should be halved. This was a tense moment. Knowing, through many disappointed experiences, how excessively shy Flamingos are, I feared that even the lately aroused parental instinct might not be sufficient to hold them to their homes and that, after all, I should be denied the fruits of victory,—the privilege of studying these birds on their nesting ground. Imagine, then, a relief I cannot describe, when the birds, after flying only a short distance to windward, turned abruptly and with set wings sailed over us, a rushing, fiery cloud, to alight in a lagoon bordering the western edge of the rookery.

Soon we were among the apparently innumerable, close-set mud nests each with its single white egg, while two held newly hatched Flamingos! Not only were these the first young Flamingos ever seen in the nest by a naturalist, but their presence was an assurance that this rookery was not composed of the birds whose homes had been flooded by the storm of May 17, but another colony and one which had not suffered a similar catastrophe. I should not therefore have to wait at least three weeks for the eggs to hatch, but had arrived at the most favorable period it would have been possible to select.

While we were standing, half dazed by the whole ex-perience, the army of birds which had gathered in the lagoon rose, and with harsh honkings bore down on us. The action was startling. The birds in close array came toward us with-out a waver, and for a few moments one might well have believed they were about to attack; but with a mighty roar of wings and clanging of horns, they passed overhead, turned, and on set wings again shot back to the lagoon.

On every one of the hundreds of occasions when, in fancy, I had entered a city of Flamingos, I had devised some plan for a place of concealment from which the birds might be observed and photographed. But the sight of the birds over the swash, as we landed, had banished from my mind every thought but the desire to know whether they were nesting; the blind was forgotten, and fearing now to keep them too long from their homes, I erected around a small bush, some thirty feet from the border of the rookery, a shield of branches behind which the blind might be placed the following day.

We now returned to the boats, seeing, with immense satisfaction, the Flamingos go back to their nests when we were but half across the swash. The claim had been located; it promised nuggets at every step, and our next move was to prepare to work it.

The prospects of the morrow were fatal to sleep, and at an early hour preparations were made for the second invasion of the rookery. As with blind and cameras we now approached, the birds left their nests with the same orderly sequence of movement shown the preceding afternoon, gathering in a densely massed flock in the lagoon. The blind was quickly set in place arranged for it, and hung with mangrove branches and palmetto leaves. I entered it and Mrs. Chapman at once started for camp.

This was a moment of supreme interest. Would the birds return to their nests, the nearest of which were about thirty feet from me, or would the blind arouse their suspicions? Twice they rose in a body and swept over the rookery, each time alighting again in the lagoon. It was a reconnoissance in force, with evidently satisfactory results. No signs of danger were detected in the rookery, and, in the absence of ability to count, the retreat of one figure across the swash was as reassuring as the approach of two figures had been alarming.

Without further delay, the birds returned to their homes. They came on *foot*, a great red cohort, marching steadily toward me. I felt like a spy in an enemy's camp. Might not at least one pair of the nearly four thousand eyes detect something unnatural in the newly grown bush almost within their city gates? No sign of alarm, however, was shown; without confusion, and as if trained to the evolution, the birds advanced with stately tread to their nests. There was a bowing of a forest of slender necks as each bird lightly touched its egg or nest with its bill; then, all talking loudly, they stood up on their nests; the black wings were waved for a moment, and bird after bird dropped forward upon its egg. After a vigorous, wriggling motion, designed evidently to bring the egg into close contact with the skin, the body was still, but the long necks and head were for a time in constant motion, preening, picking material at the base of the nest, dabbling in a near-by puddle, or perhaps drinking from it. Occasionally a bird sparred with one of the three or four neighbors which were within reach, when, bill grasping bill, there ensued a brief and harmless test of strength.

In some instances a bird was seen adding to a nest in which an egg had already been deposited. Standing on the nest, it would drag up mud from the base with its bill, which was then used to press the fresh material into place. The feet were also of service in treading down the soft, marly clay.

The nests of this side of the rookery were below the average in size. Few of them reached a height of eight inches, while nests in the older part of this city of huts measured thirteen inches in height, with a diameter of fourteen inches at the top and twenty-two at the bottom. The depression forming the nest proper was never more than an inch in depth, and was without lining of any kind.

After watching a nesting colony of Flamingos in the Bahamas for "nearly an hour", at a distance of one hundred and fifty yards, Sir Henry Blake stated that the females sat upon the nests while the males stood up together, evidently near by. My dissections, however, showed that both sexes incubate, while continued observation from the tent revealed the presence of only one bird of the pair in the rookery at the same time. The bird on the nest was relieved late in the afternoon and early in the morning. The one, therefore, which incubated during the day, fed at night, and his or her place was taken by another which had been feeding during the day. Or as Peter put it: "I do t'ink sir, dat when de lady Fillymingo leave de nest, den de gen'leman Fillymingo take her place, sir; yes, sir."

Morning and evening, then, there was much activity in the rookery. Single birds, or files of as many as fifty, were almost constantly arriving and departing, coming from and radiating to every point of the compass.

Flamingos in flight resemble no other bird known to me. With legs and neck fully outstretched, and the comparatively small wings set half-way between bill and toes, they look as if they might fly backward or forward with equal ease. They progress more rapidly than a Heron, and, when hurried, fly with a singular serpentine motion of the neck and body, as if they were crawling in the air.

As noon approached, the birds disposed themselves for sleep. The long necks were arranged in sundry coils and curves, the heads tucked snugly beneath the feathers of the back, and, for the first time, there was silence in the red city. Suddenly—one could never tell whence it came—the honking alarm-note was given. Instantly, and with remarkable effect, the snake-like necks shot up all over the glowing bed of color before me, transforming it into a writhing mass of flaming serpents; then, as the alarm-note continued and was taken up by a thousand throats, the birds, like a vast congregation, with dignified precision of movement, gravely arose, pressing their bills into the nests to assist themselves.

Under circumstances of this kind the birds rarely left their nests, and it was difficult to determine the cause of their alarm. Often, doubtless, it was baseless, but at times it was due to a circling Turkey Vulture, the gaunt ogre of Flamingo-dom, which, in the absence of the parent birds, is said to eat not only eggs but nestlings. Possibly some slight sound from my tent, where, with ill-controlled excitement, I was making photograph after photograph, may have occasioned the deep-voiced, warning *huh-huh-huh*.

I had so often fruitlessly stalked these wary birds across the swash, that I was tempted to step out from my blind and address a word of triumph to the assembled multitude; but so sudden an alarm might not only have caused the destruction of many eggs, but might have resulted in the birds deserting their homes. Consequently, several hours after entering the blind, Mrs. Chapman, by arrangement, returned; the birds retreated to the lagoon, and I left my hiding place without their being the wiser.

Encouraged by this surprisingly successful attempt to study these wary birds at close range, I determined to enter the very heart of the city. Consequently, when, at our approach the following morning, the birds left their nests, the blind was hurriedly moved, from its position at the border of the rookery to a point near its center, where a buttonwood bush afforded it some concealment.

Nests were now within arm's reach; the blind itself covered an abandoned one. It seemed wholly beyond the bounds of probability that the birds would take their places so near me; but, as before, the departure of my assistant was the signal to advance. The great red army with clanging of horns, again approached, reached, and this time surrounded me. I was engulfed in color and clarionings. The wildest imagination could not have conceived of so thrilling an experience. Seated on the deserted nest, I myself seemed to have become a Flamingo.

The blind, strange to say, aroused no suspicion. Without

hesitation and with evident recognition of their home, the splendid creatures reoccupied their nests. For a time I feared detection. It was impossible to look from the blind in any direction without seeming to meet the glance of a dozen yellow-eyed birds at my threshold. Fortunately, the uproar of their united voices was so great that the various sounds made in the manipulation of my two cameras were barely audible even to my ears. With the wind in the right quarter, this honking chorus could be plainly heard at our camp. The adults uttered three distinct calls, all goose-like in character. The usual note of the young bird is a whistling crow.

The birds of this portion of the rookery had evidently begun to nest at an earlier date than those in the section before visited. Many of the nests contained an egg from which the chick was emerging, and in others were young evidently several days old; while birds which had left the nest were running about with their parents.

On leaving the shell, and before the plumage was dry, some chicks had sufficient strength to respond to their evidently instinctive sense of fear. At my approach they crawled to the edge of the nest and dropped over to the ground or water below, though beyond this they could progress but little. Chicks a day old jumped nimbly from the nest and ran or swam rapidly away. On subsequent days, it became necessary to enter my blind with caution, to avoid frightening the young in the near-by nests. At the best, some would leave their homes and scurry away, but they returned to the place of their birth apparently in response to a call uttered by the parent as it stood on or near the deserted nest. The little chick reached the top of the nest unaided by the parent bird, using its bill, feet, and wings in the effort. The thumb and index finger are both provided with a somewhat recurved nail, which in this connection may be functional. The parents evidently recognized their own offspring, and when a youngster lost his way, his nape was promptly pinched by every old bird within whose reach he came, a method which was effective in keeping him on the move until he found his own home.

The young stay in the nest until they are three or four days old. During this time they are brooded by the parents, one or the other of which is always in attendance. With a bill as large as their nestling's body, it was of special interest to observe how the latter would be fed. What, in effect, is regurgitated clam broth, is taken drop by drop from the tip of the parent's bill. At times the bird, standing above its chick, leans over and feeds it, or while brooding, a snowy head is pushed out from a vermilion wing, and with a swan-like movement the neck is gracefully curved as the food is administered.

This is the young bird's first meal. His next attempts at eating are of special interest. It will be observed that the bill in a newly hatched Flamingo bears small resemblance to the singular, decurved organ of the adult. In the chick the bill is short and straight, with no hint of future curvature; and at this stage of its existence the bird feeds in a manner wholly unlike that employed by the old birds. It *picks up* its food. The second meal, then, consists of bits of the egg-shell whence the chick has lately emerged. This bone-forming matter evidently now takes the place of the *Cerithium* shells which the parents seem to find essential to their well-being.

When the bird is about three weeks old, the bill first shows signs of convexity, and the bird now feeds after the singular manner of the adult, standing on its head, as it were, the maxilla, or upper half of the bill, being nearly parallel with the ground. Contrary to the rule among birds the lower portion of the bill is immovable, but the upper portion, moving rapidly, forces little jets of water from each side of the base of the bill, washing out the sand and the mud through the strainers with which the sides of the bill are beset, and leaving the shells on which the bird subsists. Or, as Peter expressed it: "It seems to me, sir, when de Fillymingo feed dat de upper lip do all de wuk, sir, when he chomp, chomp, chomp, and grabble in de mud."

Young Flamingos, taken from the rookery for further study, subsequently gave an apparently instinctive exhibit of a characteristic habit of the adult bird when feeding. As I have said, the old birds live on a small spiral shell and its contents. This food is always obtained under water which may reach to the bird's body. When the shells are apparently embedded in the marl, the feeding bird loosens them by a treading motion. It is the Flamingos' one undignified action. Birds thus occupied seem to be engaged in some ridiculous kind of jig, which they dance with the head and neck submerged.

The evidently excessive rainfall had flooded even the comparatively high ground on which their rookery was placed. Some nests were submerged, (my own particular nest had already crumbled before the unaccustomed usage to which it had been subjected), and all were surrounded by water. The necessity of erecting a structure of some height was thus plainly demonstrated.

This second catastrophe to a nesting colony emphasized the adverse climatic conditions with which Flamingos have to contend during the nesting season. Laying but one egg, it is probable that under favorable circumstances they can barely hold their own, and it is therefore to be deplored that man should be numbered among their enemies.

To my regret, our search for Flamingos so widely advertised the location of the rookery among the negroes of the island, that more than a dozen expeditions were planned to visit it for young birds.

Fresh meat is rarer than pink pearls in the outer Bahama

islands. Young Flamingos are excellent eating, and are, consequently, much sought after. As a result of this persecution on the nesting-ground, they are steadily diminishing in numbers.

At this time neither they, nor any other Bahaman bird was protected by law, and I take no small pleasure in saying that when this matter was brought to the attention of the proper authorities, an adequate bill was prepared and passed at the next session of the colonial legislature.

SIR EDWARD GREY

XVII

SIR EDWARD GREY

*I*F EVER Nature proved the solace of the man of state and great affairs, it was so in the case of Edward Viscount Grey of Fallodon. Born to responsibilities of statesmanship, as so many English aristocrats are, rather than drawn to it by inclination, the young graduate of Winchester and Balliol College, Oxford, was twenty-three when he entered Parliament in 1885 as Liberal member for Berwick-on-Tweed. He was the type of the English gentleman of the late Victorian and Edwardian school, a lover of the country, an amateur champion of the tennis court, and an inveterate fisherman. *The Encyclopædia Britannica* of 1911 describes his politics as "languid." Heckled by women suffrage agitators, his reply was customarily a courteous evasion. By never deeply committing himself, he had for years few enemies, or few, rather, who could say precisely where he opposed them.

If Europe had not been headed for catastrophe, Grey would have been remembered by history as an ornament of the imperialistic cabinet of Mr. Asquith, who by reticence and firmness came gradually to dominate the councils of Europe. As Foreign Secretary he consummated the Triple Entente between Great Britain, France, and Russia, and against Austria and Germany he took an unrelenting stand in 1908 over the annexation of Bosnia and Herzegovina and in 1911 in the quarrel between France and Germany over the Moroccan affair. In 1912, as director behind the scenes of the Balkan Wars, Grey was recognized by the astute as the strong, and also the silent, man of Europe.

But the whirlwind of the first World War was upon him.

When he besought Austria to give Serbia time for consideration of the ultimatum of 1914, and Germany to withhold mobilization, the countries he had outmanoeuvred at the council table had not forgiven him. His failure was complete; some have placed a crushing load of blame for the whole disaster upon him—the Germans because of his "duplicity," the western Allies because he did not, from the first, make it clear that England would fight if France were attacked. To me, a layman in matters of state, it would seem that the situation was not in his hands, hence the responsibility can scarcely rest upon his head.

In 1916 his failing eyesight drove Grey to resignation, and to seek the solace of Fallodon. He emerged only to represent his country as temporary ambassador to Washington where he negotiated in 1919 toward the impending peace settlement.

Up to this time Grey was the author only of *Fly Fishing*, a slender issue of 1899. But from the retreat of Fallodon, his estate in Northumberland, came forth in the sunset gleams of his life *Fallodon Papers*, which is brightened by many ornithological passages, and last, *The Charm of Birds* (1927) from which one selection is here made. Among bird lovers all over the English-speaking world this graceful volume has been making its way; today it is in a fair way to become a classic, not, of course, of natural history, for its author made no pretensions in that direction, but a classic of the literature of ornithophily.

Failing sight is a crushing blow for a passionate bird watcher. But it had in Grey's case the effect of sharpening all his other faculties. Since now he could not well observe the birds in the bush, the lord of Fallodon learned to bring them to his hand. It is a power that every one of us longs to possess. Our author makes the taming of wild birds sound quite easy, and just possibly it is easier with European birds than the shy *Aves* of the New World. But probably more than reasonable method explains Grey's success in this Franciscan art; it is, it seems to me, a knack, practically a gift. Whatever name it should have, it was subtly developed in the man who had in vain held out the hand of peace to fellow humans.

The man, and his generation, his class and his customs, are unconsciously revealed in the passage where he refers to the necessity of covering up one's evening clothes, if observing birds after the dinner hour. To the trans-Atlantic reader this is provocation for a tender smile. Perhaps even to British ornithologists, if of professional stamp, this would today mark Grey for a gentle amateur. In that class Grey would have placed himself, no doubt. But he brings himself thereby warmly and humanly nearer to thousands of us—the peer and statesman in formal evening attire entering the twilit woods to seek refuge in the free commonalty of birds.

ON TAMING BIRDS

THIS is an age of curiosity. There is a desire to know about the private life of people who are much before the public; and birds, as well as men and women, are the subject of more curious and particular observation than they have ever endured before.

My own experience has been mainly with robins. Several of these were tamed at different times, not with any intention of scientific observation, but solely for the pleasure of being on terms of intimacy with birds in a free and natural state. None of these robins were quite close to the house: none of them became house-birds, nor were they induced to lead an artificial life. They were visited once every day, each in its own territory, and offered meal-worms; but except for this supplement to their natural food, there was nothing to disturb or distort their natural habits.

The first robin had a small white feather on the right wing by which it was easy to identify him. His territory included both sides of one end of a pond. He would sit on my fingers and eat meal-worms out of a little box held open on my hand. In the nesting season he was feeding young birds: about the middle of July he disappeared and was not seen again till well on in August, when he presented himself once more and came on the hand as usual, and reoccupied precisely the same territory. Here he remained tame, but alone, till the spring, when a female was admitted to the territory. She would make a small note and he would feed her with meal-worms, just as if she were a young bird. If I appeared and held out the box when he was not near, the female would sit in a bush uttering the little notes till he came and fed her. She never offered to help herself.

Eventually the east side of the pond was annexed by another robin, and White Feather was restricted entirely to the west side. Here he was visited and fed. He had now become very tame, and after satisfying his appetite would sometimes sit on the hand so long that it was necessary to give him a gentle hint to go. On the last day of the year, he came to me at the usual spot; after that I never saw him again, and his place was taken by another robin. I searched in the hope that White Feather might only have been driven farther west; but there was no sign, and I fear that there had been combat to the death.

There is a white seat by another pond, where it is the habit of some one to sit about midday to feed such waterfowl as care to come out of the water for bread. On the right of this seat and close to it is a clump of dogwood. Here in February a robin and his mate were tamed. The male bird would sit on the hand and eat several meal-worms; the female would only perch for a moment, snatch a single meal-worm at a time and fly off with it. As spring advanced the female ceased to feed herself, but sat in the dogwood, uttering the plaintive note, and was fed attentively by the male. In time the female ceased coming to the seat, and the male would pack his beak with meal-worms, fly with them over the water to some bushes a hundred yards away, and return time after time to get more. The nest was evidently in the distant bushes, but I made no search for it, lest by finding I should betray it to some enemy.

Besides the white-seat robin I had three others that were hand-tame in the winter of 1925-26. Their territories adjoined and apparently met in a large spiraea bush. Two, and sometimes all three, birds came to this bush together, and whenever this was so, feeding was impossible; each bird as it perched on my hand was knocked off by another before it could eat. The incessant combats were wearisome, almost dis-

gusting, and I had to manoeuvre to get each bird fed peace-
fully in its own territory. One of these birds I judged to be
a female, for it would snatch meal-worms from the box and
not sit on my hand and eat quietly as the other two birds did.
By March one of the males was settled in a territory that
adjoined the east end of a greenhouse. He was a particularly
delightful bird and very tame. His singing place was high up
in a sycamore tree. I would hold out the box; the singing
would stop; there would be a short pause of silence, and then
he would fly straight down to my hand and sit there, till
satisfied; when he would again fly up to his sycamore perch
and sing. If he saw me in the greenhouse he would come to
me through the open ventilator at the top. Once after eating
a few meal-worms he sang while on my hand: a full and
proper song, loud and sustained, very ear-piercing at such close
quarters. "White Feather" often sang a few notes before he
left the hand, but this bird is the only one that has ever
treated my hand as a real singing perch.

Of the other two robins, the one that "snatched" was, as
I had supposed, a female; they paired; their two territories,
which were next to each other, were amalgamated: as in old
days a king would marry the queen or heiress to the throne
of a neighbouring country and combine the two kingdoms in
one realm.

Any male robin can be tamed; such at least is my experience. The bird is first attracted by crumbs of bread thrown
on the ground; then a meal-worm is thrown to it; then a box
—such as one of the small metal boxes in which chemists sell
lozenges—is placed open on the ground with meal-worms in
it. When the bird has become used to this, the next step is
to kneel down and place the back of one hand flat upon the
ground with the box open on the upturned palm, and the
fingers projecting beyond the box. This is the most difficult
stage, but robins will risk their lives for meal-worms, and the

bird will soon face the fingers and stand on them. The final stage, that of getting the bird to come on to the hand when raised above the ground, is easy. The whole process may be a matter of only two or three days in hard weather, when birds are hungry; and when once it has been accomplished the robin does not lose its tameness: confidence has been established and does not diminish when weather becomes mild and food plentiful.

A robin's method of feeding is to pick up a meal-worm crosswise in its beak and hold it thus for a second or two; then suddenly—there is no meal-worm: the act of swallowing is so quick that it is hardly perceptible. The first meal-worms are taken one after the other with little delay; but after these the bird has long pauses and stands pensively on the hand. In cold weather it is disagreeable to keep the bare hand extended so long, but one does not like to disturb the bird. The last meal-worm is generally taken to a bush or to the ground to be eaten, and this is a sign that the bird is satisfied. I find that four tame robins are as many as are convenient; to visit each and feed it in its own territory once a day is a sufficient demand upon leisure. If natural food is very plentiful a robin may be satisfied with four meal-worms, but the usual number is about nine; the most that I ever knew to be taken by one bird at one standing was twenty-two. Each meal-worm is eaten whole and alive. After several have been swallowed the sensations in the crop may account for the long pauses the bird makes and its thoughtful aspect.

One note used by robins is a very small, high sound, a note such as we might imagine to be made if a tiny bow were drawn across a single fine hair stretched on a tiny violin. This note expresses annoyance at the approach of another robin to the territory. It is a very inward note and seems to express the emotion of the bird that makes it, rather than to be a warning or a challenge. This note is often made when the bird is on the hunt.

Another note is a short warble, a smaller sound than the full song; it is very sweet in tone, but is in fact a warning or a challenge to a robin in neighbouring territory, and is either in answer to or is answered by the robin to which it is addressed. This warble is frequently given when standing on the hand, and the intention and reason of it are always apparent.

A fight between two robins is a serious affair. One cold January day "White Feather" came into the territory of another tame robin, when it was on my hand. A furious combat ensued at my feet, and when it was over there were pitiful-looking little dark feathers left strewn upon the snow. So many were they that had I found them without having seen how they came there, I should certainly have thought that some bird had been killed on the spot.

With leisure in an uninterrupted country life much more might be done in taming wild birds. Indeed, I have known of one garden, though I never had the good fortune to see it, where the owner by patience and regular habits succeeded in keeping many wild birds of several varieties on terms of intimacy with him, more remarkable than any described here.

More birds are to be seen, free and tame, in London than on any country estate. In London black-headed gulls, that are entirely wild birds, come in numbers in autumn and winter, and will feed, or at any rate snatch food from the hand. Several varieties of interesting waterfowl, especially pochards and tufted ducks, may be seen close to us, and yet free; and the sparrows and wood-pigeons positively invite attention. Now and then one comes across some one who is taking full advantage of the opportunities offered by the tameness of London birds. I met a man in Regent's Park one day who was feeding sparrows on his hand. I stood beside him; a wood-pigeon was walking about a few yards away. "Can you get that wood-pigeon to come on to your hand?" "Oh, yes," he said, and turning towards the bird held out his hand with a gesture, deliberate but smooth and quiet. The pigeon flew up, and fed with its pink feet planted on his hand. We had some conversation in which he gave me some information about grey and black squirrels, and made some interesting comments of his own upon them. When we parted I left with the inward assurance that here was some one who never lacked interest in his leisure, and who had one satisfaction that no one can have in the country—that of being completely trusted by a free wood-pigeon.

Any unusual gesture or movement affronts or frightens tame birds, but otherwise they seem to recognise people by clothes more than by anything else. The robins, it is true, are indifferent to clothes; they will come to the meal-worm box, whatever the garb of the person who offers it. But the water-fowl are perceptibly less tame if I wear dark clothes, though my whistle and gestures are familiar to them. In the long days of summer time the sunset feed is not till after dinner, and it is desirable when visiting them to conceal evening clothes (if one has dressed for dinner) with a light-coloured over-coat.

After the disappearance of the pair of robins in May 1926 six months passed without any sign of these or any tame robin. In November a new robin beyond the further pond began to show signs of intelligence. Its territory was out of sight of the greenhouse and distant about 300 yards.

On 22nd November I started with the box of meal-worms in my pocket to continue the education of this bird, which was not yet hand-tame. I had just left the greenhouse, when a robin presented itself obtrusively and expectantly in the spiraea bush. The box was offered to it; the bird came at once on to my hand, stood there for some time eating meal-worms and occasionally warbling a challenge to another robin a little way off. It was very pleasant to feel once more, after an interval of six months, the confident clasp of the slender feet upon my fingers.

HENRY DAVID THOREAU

XVIII

HENRY DAVID THOREAU

THERE had been a fresh fall of snow upon snow, when first I saw Walden woods and Walden pond, and it was the snow that drew us out. Five of us, at Harvard, went on the electric line to Belmont, and then began to slog the snowy road to Concord. It was a few moments after the early winter sunset when one who knew the road well sang out, "That's Walden pond." By the edge of the pond we stood a bit, asking each other whether the pines and the water and rocks had made the man or whether he had not, rather, made them what they are, famous around the world, loved by people who will never see them. We inquired into the nature of Transcendentalism. Someone decided that Transcendentalism had died, and the rest began to stray from the pond back to the road.

But I lingered a moment, and it seemed to me that the man rose up, on the farther shore, and revealed himself. For the pines and the granite, the ice and the lichens, the green winter sunset and the cold tingling air, the lake and the silence are some of the clearest printing in the book of Nature. I had been reading it all my life, in different places, and had come to love it even more than I loved my sciences, or the arts. And this particular verse and chapter, Thoreau had loved. I looked at it a long minute, and beheld the man.

I saw a man who was taller in the soul than others as an aspen is taller than the grey birch. I heard a man who knew more than he said, who expected you to understand him when he did not speak, and to love him when he was harsh. I knew a man who could run a straight surveyor's line, and thought that way. A wintry and granite man, but granite that could laugh, and winter like pure snow driven upon the old. A religious man too but, most originally, a deist who sought communion and identity with the works of God, and heard the bellowing inside the walls of a church with horror. A man who prayed standing.

It is my belief that Thoreau would have been the first to say that you could have read him by Walden pond in winter. If he had wanted the spotlight, if he had wanted only to preach, if he had loved words, and ink, and authorship, he would have written more books. As it is, he wrote chiefly in his diary and chiefly for himself. The *Journals* from which these extracts are taken saw publication only after his death. Thoreau never intended them for publication as they now stand. They were but his source books from which the materials were to be quarried for mature and polished end-products. What those books would have been like, we may judge from *Walden, or Life in the Woods*, a classic that is perfect. It was the first book of its kind in the world; there will never be another like it; it is utterly original, and it is inexhaustible.

Henry David Thoreau was born in 1817 very near to Concord. His mother was Cynthia Dunbar, and from her he inherited the gift of self-expression, vivacity and the love of the outdoors. His father was a quiet, "small" merchant with a turn for doing things with his hands. Henry Thoreau had a typical New England boyhood of the times. He hunted and fished, roamed the fields, and acquired a wide wood-wisdom. He attended Harvard, where his passion was the library, and the Greek poets and philosophers. His essays were remarked by his teachers for their strength and purity.

At the age of twenty-one Thoreau seems already to have begun his true career, which was what he called "sauntering," though it was a very busy kind. He lived at home with his family, without apparently any inner need for having one of his own. On several occasions he dwelt with the Emersons, and mingled a little in the Brook Farm experiment of communistic life according to the principles of Fourier.

The association with Emerson was crucial in his life, for through Emerson and his friends, Thoreau reached Oriental philosophy, Carlyle, the English Lake poets, and Goethe. The idea of owning no property he may have owed in part to Fourier. He New-Englandized this, as he did everything else, combining it with the pioneer tradition of self-reliance. He undoubtedly owed something to Bronson Alcott, who was in close touch with Goethe's "Romantic Natural Philosophy" (which is a chapter in the history of *Natural History*).

But equally important, I think, was his inclination toward the society of people who never sat at Emerson's feet, typical "Yankees" as the word is used in New England. These were farmers, hunters, fur-trappers, fishermen, loafers and whittlers with a fund of independence, little speech and all of that racy, native wit and a serene parochialism. They were protestants, in religion, or, if godless, in modes of life. They found their world good, and wide enough. Thoreau was born one of them; at Walden he lived rather like them. One can hardly say he enjoyed their society for they did not form a society. They were shy of each other and still more of strangers. So reserve and withdrawal were the keystones of Thoreau's character and of his particular type of communion with Nature. He was a truant who had read his Anacreon.

It was in 1845 that Thoreau built his hut on land belonging to Emerson, with an axe borrowed from Alcott. In the midst of the bluestocking gabble of Concord, Mr. Thoreau had chosen to go off and live by himself! Concord was agog. Everyone beat a path to his door, although he was the last man in the world who would have made a mousetrap. Absolute strangers snooped while he was out watching fox or nuthatch, and wrote articles about his unwashed pans and unmade bed. By quitting the world, he got himself bruited about in it. And here by the pond he lived the greatest moments of his life. What they were, how rapturously experienced, how he found himself completely, Walden has told for all time.

As he walked into the village one day he was arrested for non-payment of his poll tax. This was due to no negligence on his part, but to his intention of refusing every support to a government that expended its moneys for the capture and return of negro slaves. A relative paid his fine, but he never returned to the hut by the pond.

In early middle life Thoreau was stricken with tuberculosis, went to Minnesota (of all places for a cure) and when he saw he could not recover, returned home to die. He left the major portion of his work unfinished—something like a million words in his diaries.

I think it will not be questioned that Thoreau was the noblest stylist who ever devoted himself to Nature. I will not say, however, that the unfinished Journals bear this out completely, since they were only sketches for some final picture. But, for purposes of a bird book, they are still the best source. To judge from Walden and works he himself completed, Thoreau would have reduced all passages concerning birds to about a twelfth of the space they occupied in the Journals, nor is it conceivable that he would ever have published a book solely about the birds of Concord, though just such a book has been delightfully assembled under the title, Notes on New England Birds, edited by Francis Allen. Birds served Thoreau in Walden as a text or a vehicle. In the Journals he recorded them partly for their own sakes. That makes the Journals precious to us.

Thoreau early gave up the gun, and was long in acquiring a lens for bird study. In the interim, like any countryman, he relied on what he could see with the naked eye. When he did buy a glass, it was a telescope. This was an ideal instrument for watching waterfowl on the pond; it is quite impractical for birds of wood and field, and Thoreau is less successful with them. Though his manuals were Wilson and Nuttall, he never attained completely accurate field identification of birds. Thus, in his quoted passages on the thrush it is evident that he has confused the wood thrush and the hermit thrush, and never even distinguished the olive-backed. His ear for bird notes remained untrained. He has almost nothing to say of one of the commonest and most exquisite of singers, the whitethroat sparrow, and when he did hear it, sets the notes down sometimes to the myrtle warbler. A gull to Thoreau was a gull; a hawk was a hawk. Yet in matters botanical he was a nice systematist.

All this is a way of saying that Thoreau relied a little too much on self-reliance, and had a bit too much poetic scorn for science. There were then in Boston naturalists who could have assisted him to a deeper understanding, but he employed them only occasionally.

Yet Thoreau's mistakes are pardonable and negligible. He was by intention a meticulously truthful reporter, which is more than can be said of a host of those who are Nature writers rather than naturalists. A man who could spend hours over finding the one right word, pruning out adjectives, and turning perfect paragraphs, naturally carried over his discipline to Nature. He might have observed birds more knowingly, but nobody could have described them in his continent language, or so linked them to our inmost thoughts.

LOON

1845-47 (no exact date). The loon comes in the fall to sail and bathe in the pond, making the woods ring with its wild laughter in the early morning, at rumor of whose arrival all Concord sportsmen are on the alert, in gigs, on foot, two by two, three by three, with patent rifles, patches, conical balls, spy-glass or open hole over the barrel. They seem already to hear the loon laugh; come rustling through the woods like October leaves, these on this side, those on that, for the poor loon cannot be omnipresent; if he dive here, must come up somewhere. The October wind rises, rustling the leaves, ruffling the pond water, so that no loon can be seen rippling the surface. Our sportsmen scour, sweep the pond with spy-glass in vain, making the woods ring with rude[?] charges of powder, for the loon went off in that morning rain with one loud, long, hearty laugh, and our sportsmen must beat a retreat to town and stable and daily routine, shop work, unfinished jobs again.

Or in the gray dawn the sleeper hears the long ducking gun explode over toward Goose Pond, and, hastening to the door, sees the remnant of a flock, black duck or teal, go whistling by with outstretched neck, with broken ranks, but in ranger order. And the silent hunter emerges into the carriage road with ruffled feathers at his belt, from the dark pond-side where he has lain in his bower since the stars went out.

And for a week you hear the circling clamor, clangor, of some solitary goose through the fog, seeking its mate, peopling the woods with a larger life than they can hold.

For hours in fall days you shall watch the ducks cunningly tack and veer and hold the middle of the pond, far from the sportsmen on the shore,—tricks they have learned and practiced in far Canada lakes or in Louisiana bayous.

The waves rise and dash, taking sides with all water-fowl.

Oct. 8, 1852. P.M.—Walden. As I was paddling along the north shore, after having looked in vain over the pond for a loon, suddenly a loon, sailing toward the middle, a few rods in front, set up his wild laugh and betrayed himself. I pursued with a paddle and he dived, but when he came up I was nearer than before. He dived again, but I miscalculated the direction he would take, and we were fifty rods apart when he came up, and again he laughed long and loud. He managed very cunningly, and I could not get within half a dozen rods of him. Sometimes he would come up unexpectedly on the opposite side of me, as if he had passed directly under the boat. So long-winded was he, so unweariable, that he would immediately plunge again, and then no wit could divine where in the deep pond, beneath the smooth surface, he might be speeding his way like a fish. He had time and ability to visit the bottom of the pond in its deepest part. It was as well for me to rest on my oars and await his reappearing as to endeavor to calculate where he would come up. When I was straining my eyes over the surface, I would suddenly be startled by his unearthly laugh behind me. It was commonly a demoniac laughter, yet somewhat like a water-bird, but occasionally, when he had balked me most successfully and come up a long way off, he uttered a long-drawn unearthly howl, probably more like a wolf than any other bird. This was his looning. As when a beast puts his muzzle to the ground and deliberately howls; perhaps the wildest sound I ever heard, making the woods ring; and I concluded that he laughed in derision of my efforts, confident of his own resources. Though the sky was overcast, the pond was so smooth that I could see where he broke the surface if I did not hear him. His white breast, the stillness of the air, the smoothness of the water, were all against him. At length, having come up fifty rods off, he uttered one of those prolonged unearthly howls, as if calling on the god of loons to aid him, and immediately there came a wind from the east and rippled the surface, and filled the whole air with misty rain. I was impressed as if it were the prayer of the loon and his god was angry with me. How surprised must be the fishes to see this ungainly visitant from another sphere speeding his way amid their schools!

HERRING GULL

April 15, 1852. They come annually a-fishing here like royal
hunters, to remind us of the sea and that our town, after all,
lies but further up a creek of the universal sea, above the
head of the tide. So ready is a deluge to overwhelm our lands,
as the gulls to circle hither in the spring freshets. To see a
gull beating high over our meadowy flood in chill and windy
March is akin to seeing a mackerel schooner on the coast.
It is the nearest approach to sailing vessels in our scenery. I
never saw one at Walden. Oh, how it salts our fresh, our
sweet-watered Fair Haven all at once to see this sharp-beaked,
greedy sea-bird beating over it!

CANADA GOOSE

March 26, 1846. A flock of geese has just got in late, now in the dark flying low over the pond. They came on, indulging at last like weary travellers in complaint and consolation, or like some creaking evening mail late lumbering in with regular anserine clangor. I stood at my door and could hear their wings when they suddenly spied my light and, ceasing their noise, wheeled to the east and apparently settled in the pond.

April 19, 1852. That last flock of geese yesterday is still in my eye. After hearing their clangor, looking southwest, we saw them just appearing over a dark pine wood, in an irregular waved line, one abreast of the other, as it were breasting the air and pushing it before them. They carry weight, such a weight of metal in the air. These stormy days they do not love to fly; they alight in some retired marsh or river. From their lofty pathway they can easily spy out the most extensive and retired swamp. How many there must be, that one or more flocks are seen to go over almost every farm in New England in the spring!

March 26, 1853. Saw about 10 A.M. a gaggle of geese, forty-three in number, in a very perfect harrow flying northeasterly. One side of the harrow was a little longer than the other. They appeared to be four or five feet apart. At first I heard faintly, as I stood by Minott's gate, borne to me from the southwest through the confused sounds of the village, the indistinct honking of geese.

March 20, 1855. Trying the other day to imitate the honking of geese, I found myself flapping my sides with my elbows, as with wings, and uttering something like the syllables *mow-ack* with a nasal twang and twist in my head; and I produced

their note so perfectly in the opinion of the hearers that I
thought I might possibly draw a flock down.

Dec. 13, 1855. Sanborn * tells me that he was waked up
a few nights ago in Boston, about midnight, by the sound of
a flock of geese passing over the city, probably about the same
night I heard them here. They go honking over cities where
the arts flourish, waking the inhabitants; over State-houses
and capitols, where legislatures sit; over harbors where fleets
lie at anchor; mistaking the city, perhaps, for a swamp or
the edge of a lake, about settling in it, not suspecting that
greater geese than they have settled there.

Nov. 8, 1857. A warm, cloudy, rain-threatening morning. I
saw through my window some children looking up and pointing their tiny bows into the heavens, and I knew at once that
the geese were in the air. The children, instinctively aware of
its importance, rushed into the house to tell their parents.
These travellers are revealed to you by the upward-turned
gaze of men. And though these undulating lines are melting
into the southwestern sky, the sound comes clear and distinct to you as the clank of a chain in a neighboring smithy.
So they migrate, not flitting from hedge to hedge, but from
latitude to latitude, from State to State, steering boldly out
into the ocean of the air.

March 31, 1858. Just after sundown I see a large flock of
geese in a perfect harrow cleaving their way toward the north-
east, with Napoleonic tactics splitting the forces of winter.

* Mr. F. B. Sanborn of Concord, who was Thoreau's biographer.

HEN-HAWK

June 8, 1853. As I stood by this pond, I heard a hawk
scream, and, looking up, saw a pretty large one circling not
far off and incessantly screaming, as I at first supposed to
scare and so discover its prey, but its screaming was so incessant and it circled from time to time so near me, as I
moved southward, that I began to think it had a nest near
by and was angry at my intrusion into its domains. As I was
looking up at it, thinking it the only living creature within
view, I was singularly startled to behold, as my eye by chance
penetrated deeper into the blue,—the abyss of blue above,
which I had taken for a solitude,—its mate silently soaring
at an immense height and seemingly indifferent to me. We
are surprised to discover that there can be an eye on us on
that side, and so little suspected,—that the heavens are full of
eyes, though they look so blue and spotless. When I drew
nearer to the tall trees where I suspected the nest to be, the
female descended again, swept by screaming still nearer to
me just over the tree-tops, and finally, while I was looking
for the orchis in the swamp, alighted on a white pine twenty
or thirty rods off. (The great fringed orchis just open.) At
length I detected the nest about eighty feet from the ground,
in a very large white pine by the edge of the swamp. It was
about three feet in diameter, of dry sticks, and a young hawk,
apparently as big as its mother, stood on the edge of the nest
looking down at me, and only moving its head when I moved.

June 9, 1853. I have come with a spy-glass to look at the
hawks. They have detected me and are already screaming
over my head more than half a mile from the nest. I find no
difficulty in looking at the young hawk (there appears to be
one only, standing on the edge of the nest), resting the glass

in the crotch of a young oak. I can see every wink and the color of its iris. It watches me more steadily than I it, now looking straight down at me with both eyes and outstretched neck, now turning its head and looking with one eye. How its eye and its whole head express anger! Its anger is more in its eye than in its beak.

June 13, 1853. 9 A.M.—To Orchis Swamp.

Find that there are two young hawks; one has left the nest and is perched on a small maple seven or eight rods distant. Pratt, when I told him of this nest, said he would like to carry one of his rifles down there. But I told him that I should be sorry to have them killed. I would rather save one of these hawks than have a hundred hens and chickens. It was worth more to see them soar, especially now that they are so rare in the landscape. It is easy to buy eggs, but not to buy hen-hawks. My neighbors would not hesitate to shoot the last pair of hen-hawks in the town to save a few of their chickens! But such economy is narrow and grovelling. I would rather never taste chickens' meat nor hens' eggs than never to see a hawk sailing through the upper air again.

THRUSH

July 27, 1840. The wood thrush is a more modern philosopher than Plato and Aristotle. They are now a dogma, but he preaches the doctrine of this hour.

May 31, 1850. There is a sweet wild world which lies along the strain of the wood thrush—the rich intervales which border the stream of its song—more thoroughly genial to my nature than any other.

June 22, 1851. I hear around me, but never in sight, the many wood thrushes whetting their steel-like notes. Such keen singers! It takes a fiery heat, many dry pine leaves added to the furnace of the sun, to temper their strains! Always they are either rising or falling to a new strain. After what a moderate pause they deliver themselves again! saying ever a new thing, avoiding repetition, methinks answering one another. While most other birds take their siesta, the wood thrush discharges his song. It is delivered like a bolas, or a piece of jingling steel.

April 30, 1852. I hear a wood thrush here, with a fine metallic ring to his note. This sound most adequately expresses the immortal beauty and wildness of the woods. I go in search of him. He sounds no nearer. On a low bough of a small maple near the brook in the swamp, he sits with ruffled feathers, singing more low or with less power, as it were ventriloquizing; for though I am scarcely more than a rod off, he seems further off than ever.

July 5, 1852. Some birds are poets and sing all summer. They are the true singers. Any man can write verses during the love season. I am reminded of this while we rest in the shade on the Major Heywood road and listen to a wood thrush, now just before sunset. We are most interested in

those birds who sing for the love of the music and not of
their mates; who meditate their strains, and amuse themselves
with singing; the birds, the strains, of deeper sentiment; not
bobolinks, that lose their plumage, their bright colors, and
their song so early. The robin, the red-eye, the veery, the wood
thrush, etc., etc.

The wood thrush's is no opera music; it is not so much
the composition as the strain, the tone,—cool bars of melody
from the atmosphere of everlasting morning or evening. It
is the quality of the song, not the sequence. In the peawai's *
note there is some sultriness, but in the thrush's, though
heard at noon, there is the liquid coolness of things that are
just drawn from the bottom of springs. The thrush alone de-
clares the immortal wealth and vigor that is in the forest.
Here is a bird in whose strain the story is told, though Nature
waited for the science of aesthetics to discover it to man.
Whenever a man hears it, he is young, and Nature is in her
spring. Wherever he hears it, it is a new world and a free
country, and the gates of heaven are not shut against him.
Most other birds sing from the level of my ordinary cheerful
hours—a carol; but this bird never fails to speak to me out
of an ether purer than that I breathe, of immortal beauty
and vigor. He deepens the significance of all things seen in
the light of his strain. He sings to make men take higher and
truer views of things. He sings to amend their institutions;
to relieve the slave on the plantation and the prisoner in his
dungeon, the slave in the house of luxury and the prisoner
of his own low thoughts.

July 27, 1852. How cool and assuaging the thrush's note
after the fever of the day! I doubt if they have anything so
richly wild in Europe. So long a civilization must have banished it. It will only be heard in America, perchance, while

* The wood pewee.

our star is in the ascendant. I should be very much surprised if I were to hear in the strain of the nightingale such unexplored wildness and fertility, reaching to sundown, inciting to emigration. Such a bird must itself have emigrated long ago. Why, then, was I born in America? I might ask.

June 22, 1853. As I come over the hill, I hear the wood thrush singing his evening lay. This is the only bird whose note affects me like music, affects the flow and tenor of my thought, my fancy and imagination. It lifts and exhilarates me. It is inspiring. It is a medicative draught to my soul. It is an elixir to my eyes and a fountain of youth to all my senses. It changes all hours to an eternal morning. It banishes all trivialness. It reinstates me in my dominion, makes me the lord of creation, is chief musician of my court. This minstrel sings in a time, a heroic age, with which no event in the village can be contemporary. How can they be contemporary when only the latter is *temporary* at all? How can the infinite and eternal be contemporary with the finite and temporal? So there is something in the music of the cow-bell, something sweeter and more nutritious, than in the milk which the farmers drink. This thrush's song is a *ranz des vaches* to me. I long for wildness, a nature which I cannot put my foot through, woods where the wood thrush forever sings, where the hours are early morning ones, and there is dew on the grass, and the day is forever unproved, where I might have a fertile unknown for a soil about me. I would go after the cows, I would watch the flocks of Admetus there forever, only for my board and clothes. A New Hampshire everlasting and unfallen.

All that was ripest and fairest in the wilderness and the wild man is preserved and transmitted to us in the strain of the wood thrush. It is the mediator between barbarism and civilization. It is unrepentant as Greece.

April 27, 1854. The wood thrush afar,—so superior a strain to that of other birds. I was doubting if it would affect me as of yore, but it did measurably. I did not believe there could be such differences. This is the gospel according to the wood thrush.

JOHN JAMES AUDUBON

XIX

JOHN JAMES AUDUBON

*T*HE best loved of all American ornithologists, Audubon raises up for himself in every generation new hosts of admirers who discover him with passion. Such is no less than a definition of immortality. Even Europeans, though they have never heard the name of another American ornithologist, know of Audubon. And that is world fame. About him has grown a body of legends (as most of them are affectionate, it is not necessary, except when writing serious biography, to set them aside). And this amounts to canonization.

So that I can scarcely "introduce" an immortal genius, above all not to the likely readers of these words. I am under the obligation not so much to repeat the facts of his life as to avoid repeating too many of the well-known ones, and to discuss rather the place of his life work in science and in art (for his astounding genius bridged the wide gap between these two).

John James Audubon, it is now definitely established, was born in Haiti in 1785, the son of Captain Jean Audubon of the French Royal Navy, by a woman named in the documents by what is possibly a pseudonym, "Mlle. Rabin." After the death of his mother, he was brought back to France, and reared at Nantes by his foster mother, the Captain's wife. As a boy, he had a passion for birds, and nothing, not his schooling, not his father's attempts to control his bent, not his business ventures, nor his responsibilities as a husband and father, nor the derision and criticism of the society in which he moved in wilderness America, nor the lack of training both in science and art, nor the hostility and spiteful intrigues of Alexander Wilson's supporters, ever altered this passion. Very early he began to draw birds, as well as to watch, collect, and mount them. For years he annually tore up his drawings. His only formal training was a few months in the *atelier* of David in Paris. But Audubon's was an unruly spirit; he would not learn anything in a formal or routine way, and presumably David was not interested in bird painting. Audubon's only scientific training in early youth seems to have been a few months' rambling in western France with the gifted ornithologist d'Orbigny.

For lack of anything better to do with him, Captain Audubon packed the twenty-year-old lad off to America. Audubon proceeded to his father's property "Mill Grove," near Philadelphia, and there, not many miles from Wilson's school, but entirely unknown to naturalists in the Quaker city, he made the bird-banding experiment which is mentioned in the present selection called "The Phoebe." Technically the experiment was a failure, though Audubon does not seem to have realized this, but he was on the right track, and his attempt was made at a time when the whole question of migration was hazy. Migration was not even a thoroughly accepted fact, as my selections from Gilbert White prove. Wilson was trying to establish a system of correspondents to work out bird migration. But nobody other than Audubon devised the simple expedient of "ringing" a bird. By luck or intuition he chose a species that actually does return to the same nest. All he lacked was a modern aluminum band for the bird's leg.

At this time, however, Audubon's chief interest in birds was that of a young gentleman of fortune and leisure—he wanted to shoot game. His sport led to his meeting with a neighbor, the Englishman Bakewell, and Bakewell introduced him to his fifteen-year-old daughter, Lucy, a heroine now so famous and loved that there is no need to stop and praise her or her part in making Audubon's career.

We have to reconstruct a vanished scene, to picture to ourselves the Middle West as it was when John and Lucy took their wedding journey down the Ohio to Kentucky. Probably never in historic times had a naturalist such unrivaled opportunities to study virgin wilderness in the temperate zone. Certainly those times will never be seen again. The vast Mississippi basin, between Appalachians and Rockies, was an Eden of birds. In the east it was magnificently timbered; in the west rolled unspoiled prairie or New World steppe. And up this flyway and back moved the feathered hosts of the continent—or two continents. For the North American avifauna consists of two elements, the permanent residents, oceanic birds, and winter visitants which belong to the great circumpolar life zone, and are hence close kin to European kinds, and secondly the tropical American species, belonging in part to families unknown in Europe; these last, of course, are summer visitants. And while, in aboriginal America, they spread out everywhere, there were never such numbers at any time as passed over Kentucky, Louisiana, and Mississippi in the days when Audubon hunted, drew, and adventured there.

Among all these birds none made so deep an impression on every European as the passenger pigeons, of which we shall soon hear Audubon speak. Wilson's account of them is almost, but not quite, as stirring as Audubon's. They have become, for the American, a symbol of a vanished virginal beauty, an abundance that can never return. They mean to him what the bison meant, or the unbroken prairie, and what the redwoods still mean. They are gone now, the passengers. Though still often reported, they are never seen by a single competent ornithologist. The last went thirty years ago. Their destruction must in part be blamed, and heavily blamed, not so much on sportsmen as on commercial bird catchers and the persons of wealth and presumable intelligence who bought them in the markets up to the last. But perhaps, like the bison, they were doomed anyway. For they depended on the mast of the great beech forests of the Middle West, and the rich soil under these forests was needed for agriculture, to feed a growing nation.

The trumpeter swan, which is the subject of the second of these selections, is the largest of all North American wild fowl. It probably breeds nowhere now in the United States, except perhaps in the wilder portions of Montana and Wyoming. Even in Canada the Indians capture it in summer when its primaries have molted and it is unable to fly. Once its trumpetings were heard over the breadth of a continent, as it forged its powerful way from the tropics to the arctic. So Audubon heard it, as he tells, while encamped on the "Tawapatee Bottom" where ice had driven his merchant's bark from the Mississippi.

For a merchant he had become, and never was a man less suited to trade. One disheartening failure after another broke his spirit and tried his brave wife's. It was only when failure was complete, final, that they both realized that what had seemed like his truancy from responsibilities—his long excursions in the forest, his bird drawings, his overmastering passion—simply pointed to his proper destiny. So while Lucy gallantly undertook the support of the children, John set out to see the world of birds, and to paint them. He supported himself by painting portraits, teaching drawing, dancing, fencing, and French. And this is the period of his ebullient creation, the formative epoch of his genius. In this time he learned to draw birds as they live—not as, stuffed, they are wired to a perch. He drew them eating, fighting, soaring, dying, mating, hunting lice under their wings. He drew them amid their native scenes, surrounded by the food they prefer; he drew them in the most complex perspectives, catching them perpetually in action. His birds seem to leap off the page with a cry!

As this is the manner we require of any good bird painting today, it is necessary to remember that it is Audubon's own invention, his great contribution to scientific illustration. In his times the method had never been heard of. It roused positive rage among the academic, and still annoys some temperaments. There may be better drawings in existence today—but only because Audubon showed the way. And there are exactly none with Audubon's strange and original genius. When we pass from the work of one of his polished modern successors to Audubon's own, with all his faults and failures, it is like the change one senses in going back of Virgil to Homer. You have come to the father of them all.

It was the international ornithologist Charles Lucien Bonaparte who advised Audubon to take his work to Europe both in order to secure the necessary subscriptions to so monumental an undertaking, and to find engravers and colorists worthy to reproduce it. Audubon landed in England in 1826, proceeded to Edinburgh, found it cold to him, but successively made a conquest of Jameson the professor of zoölogy at the University, Sir William Jardine, editor of The Naturalist's Library, "Christopher North," the dreaded critic of Blackwood's, and Sir Walter Scott. Before he reached London he had made a lasting friend of P. J. Selby, author of British Birds, and Thomas Bewick the artist.

London was colder than Scotland. Yet he soon enlisted the help of Sir Thomas Lawrence the portraitist, and William Swainson and N. A. Vigors, the authors of the fantastic but then fashionable "quinary system" of bird classification. In Robert Havell, Audubon found the perfect engraver. Havell did much for Audubon, smoothing asperities, filling in tedious detail, laboring for perfection. The publication of The

Birds of America made Havell's fortune, and justly so.

The *Birds of America* began to appear in 1827, on double elephant folio sheets, copper plated and hand colored, the edition limited to one thousand copies and each set to cost one thousand dollars. Audubon, so often a business failure, paid Havell cash for this work, labored with Havell on every detail, found (heaven knows how) the necessary subscribers, collected the money (usually) and, in short, for eleven years successfully conducted a titanic publishing venture. Cuvier called it "the noblest monument that art has ever raised to Nature," and it was not overpraise.

No text accompanied the plates. Only later, Audubon conceived the idea of issuing a series of life histories. These began to appear under the title *Ornithological Biography* in 1831 and went on to 1839, issuing from Edinburgh. In later, quarto editions of *The Birds of America* the text and pictures are assembled, which is excellent for the biographies, but the pictorial work is most unsatisfactory. The scientific descriptions were written by William MacGillivray the young Scottish ornithologist, and he made the dissections and measurements for them. It is the biographical part, the field notes and life histories, that is Audubon's own, and in the following selections only these have been quoted. Occasionally inaccurate, due chiefly to the author's faulty memory, the biographies still stand today as priceless eye-witness accounts of bird life in our heroic age.

Now all these scientific associations gradually had their effect on Audubon. In the latter part of his life he became less an artist, but a far better scientist. He knew now what to look for, what to collect, and how to keep field notes. To make his work complete he repeatedly ransacked far corners of America—tropical Florida, the Texas coast, and the Labrador. He described new species, became increasingly precise; but never again could he be young, and never again would the wilderness be!

Audubon is noted, too, for his *Quadrupeds of America,* for which good John Bachman of Charleston supplied the dissections and scientific analyses, while the pictures were largely executed by Audubon's sons, though he would direct and take a hand. The biographical details, again, were largely the master's.

In the sunset of his life, beside the Hudson with his faithful Lucy, he enjoyed every honor he could ever have desired. He was the friend of younger naturalists; in particular Spencer F. Baird, the great zoölogist, was his protégé. The end came slowly, with wandering of the mind. Yet he never lost his imposing and beautiful appearance, but would sit, when he could no longer recognize his friends, with a westward-looking eye, like an old falcon who thinks only of the birds it has pursued, and does not even see what is not far away.

THE PHOEBE *

CONNECTED with the biography of this bird are so many incidents relative to my own, that could I with propriety deviate from my proposed method, the present number would contain less of the habits of birds than of those of the youthful days of an American woodsman. While young, I had a plantation that lay on the sloping declivities of the Perkiomen Creek. I was extremely fond of rambling along its rocky banks, for it would have been difficult to do so either without meeting with a sweet flower, spreading open its beauties to the sun, or observing the watchful King-fisher perched on some projecting stone over the clear water of the stream. Nay, now and then, the Fish Hawk itself, followed by a White-headed Eagle, would make his appearance, and by his graceful aerial motions, raise my thoughts far above them into the heavens, silently leading me to the admiration of the sublime Creator of all. These impressive, and always delightful, reveries often accompanied my steps to the entrance of a small cave scooped out of the solid rock by the hand of nature. It was, I then thought, quite large enough for my study. My paper and pencils, with now and then a volume of EDGEWORTH's natural and fascinating Tales or LAFONTAINE's Fables, afforded me ample pleasures. It was in that place, kind reader, that I first saw with advantage the force of parental affection in birds. There it was that I studied the habits of the Pewee; and there I was taught most forcibly, that to destroy the nest of a bird, or to deprive it of its eggs or young, is an act of great cruelty.

* Called by Audubon "The Pewee Flycatcher," but the name pewee is now invariably used for a different species. Audubon nowhere uses the name phoebe, but he can mean no other bird. [Ed.]

348

I had observed the nest of this plain-coloured Flycatcher fastened, as it were, to the rock immediately over the arched entrance of this calm retreat. I had peeped into it: although empty, it was yet clean, as if the absent owner intended to revisit it with the return of spring. The buds were already much swelled, and some of the trees were ornamented with blossoms, yet the ground was still partially covered with snow, and the air retained the piercing chill of winter. I chanced one morning early to go to my retreat. The sun's glowing rays gave a rich colouring to every object around. As I entered the cave, a rustling sound over my head attracted my attention, and on turning, I saw two birds fly off, and alight on a tree close by:—the Pewees had arrived! I felt delighted, and fearing that my sudden appearance might disturb the gentle pair, I walked off; not, however, without frequently looking at them. I concluded that they must have just come, for they seemed fatigued:—their plaintive note was not heard, their crests were not erected, and the vibration of the tail, so very conspicuous in this species, appeared to be wanting in power. Insects were yet few, and the return of the birds looked to me as prompted more by their affection to the place, than by any other motive. No sooner had I gone a few steps than the Pewees, with one accord, glided down from their perches and entered the cave. I did not return to it any more that day, and as I saw none about it, or in the neighbourhood, I supposed that they must have spent the day within it. I concluded also that these birds must have reached this haven, either during the night, or at the very dawn of that morn. Hundreds of observations have since proved to me that this species always migrates by night.

I went early next morning to the cave, yet not early enough to surprise them in it. Long before I reached the spot, my ears were agreeably saluted by their well-known note, and I saw them darting about through the air, giving chase to some insects close over the water. They were full of gaiety, frequently flew into and out of the cave, and while alighted on a favourite tree near it, seemed engaged in the most interesting converse. The light fluttering or tremulous motions of their wings, the jetting of their tail, the erection of their crest, and the neatness of their attitudes, all indicated that they were no longer fatigued, but on the contrary refreshed and happy. On my going into the cave, the male flew violently towards the entrance, snapped his bill sharply and repeatedly, accompanying this action with a tremulous rolling note, the import of which I soon guessed. Presently he flew into the cave and out of it again, with a swiftness scarcely credible: it was like the passing of a shadow.

Several days in succession I went to the spot, and saw with pleasure that as my visits increased in frequency, the birds became more familiarized to me, and, before a week had elapsed, the Pewees and myself were quite on terms of intimacy. It was now the 10th of April; the spring was forward that season, no more snow was to be seen, Redwings and Grakles were to be found here and there. The Pewees, I observed, began working at their old nest. Desirous of judging for myself, and anxious to enjoy the company of this friendly pair, I determined to spend the greater part of each day in the cave. My presence no longer alarmed either of them. They brought a few fresh materials, lined the nest anew, and rendered it warm by adding a few large soft feathers of the common goose, which they found strewn along the edge of the water in the creek. There was a remarkable and curious twittering in their note while both sat on the edge of the nest at those meetings, and which is never heard on any other occasion. It was the soft, tender expression, I thought, of the pleasure they both appeared to anticipate of the future. Their mutual caresses, simple as they might have seemed to another, and the delicate manner used by the male to please his mate, rivetted my eyes on these birds, and excited sensations which I can never forget.

The female one day spent the greater part of the time in her nest; she frequently changed her position; her mate exhibited much uneasiness, he would alight by her sometimes, sit by her side for a moment, and suddenly flying out, would return with an insect, which she took from his bill with apparent gratification. About three o'clock in the afternoon, I saw the uneasiness of the female increase; the male showed an unusual appearance of despondence, when, of a sudden, the female rose on her feet, looked sidewise under her, and flying out, followed by her attentive consort, left the cave, rose high in the air, performing evolutions more curious to me than any I had seen before. They flew about over the water, the female leading her mate, as it were, through her own meanderings. Leaving the Pewees to their avocations, I peeped into their nest, and saw there their first egg, so white and so transparent—for I believe, reader, that eggs soon loose this peculiar transparency after being laid—that to me the sight was more pleasant than if I had met with a diamond of the same size. The knowledge that in an enclosure so frail, life already existed, and that ere many weeks would elapse, a weak, delicate, and helpless creature, but perfect in all its parts, would burst the shell, and immediately call for the most tender care and attention of its anxious parents, filled my mind with as much wonder as when, looking towards the heavens, I searched, alas! in vain, for the true import of all that I saw.

In six days, six eggs were deposited; but I observed that as they increased in number, the bird remained a shorter time in the nest. The last she deposited in a few minutes after alighting. Perhaps, thought I, this is a law of nature, intended for keeping the eggs fresh to the last. About an hour after laying the last egg, the female Pewee returned, settled in her nest, and after arranging the eggs, as I thought, several times under her body, expanded her wings a little, and fairly commenced the arduous task of incubation.

Day after day passed by. I gave strict orders that no one should go near the cave, much less enter it, or indeed destroy any bird's nest on the plantation. Whenever I visited the Pewees, one or other of them was on the nest, while its mate was either searching for food, or perched in the vicinity, filling the air with its loudest notes. I not unfrequently reached out my hand near the sitting bird; and so gentle had they both become, or rather so well acquainted were we, that neither moved on such occasions, even when my hand was quite close to it. Now and then the female would shrink back into the nest, but the male frequently snapped at my fingers, and once left the nest as if in great anger, flew round the cave a few times, emitting his querulous whining notes, and alighted again to resume his labours.

At this very time, a Pewee's nest was attached to one of the rafters of my mill, and there was another under a shed in the cattle-yard. Each pair, any one would have felt assured, had laid out the limits of its own domain, and it was seldom that one trespassed on the grounds of its neighbour. The Pewee of the cave generally fed or spent its time so far above the mill on the creek, that he of the mill never came in contact with it. The Pewee of the cattle-yard confined himself to the orchard, and never disturbed the rest. Yet I sometimes could hear distinctly the notes of the three at the same moment. I had at that period an idea that the whole of these birds were descended from the same stock. If not correct in this supposition, I had ample proof afterwards that the brood of young Pewees, raised in the cave, returned the following spring, and established themselves farther up on the creek, and among the outhouses in the neighbourhood.

On some other occasion, I will give you such instances of

the return of birds, accompanied by their progeny, to the place of their nativity, that perhaps you will become convinced, as I am at this moment, that to this propensity every country owes the augmentation of new species, whether of birds or of quadrupeds, attracted by the many benefits met with, as countries become more open and better cultivated: but now I will, with your leave, return to the Pewees of the cave.

On the thirteenth day, the little ones were hatched. One egg was unproductive, and the female, on the second day after the birth of her brood, very deliberately pushed it out of the nest. On examining this egg, I found it containing the embryo of a bird partly dried up, with its vertebræ quite fast to the shell, which had probably occasioned its death. Never have I since so closely witnessed the attention of birds to their young. Their entrance with insects was so frequently repeated, that I thought I saw the little ones grow as I gazed upon them. The old birds no longer looked upon me as an enemy, and would often come in close by me, as if I had been a post. I now took upon me to handle the young frequently; nay, several times I took the whole family out, and blew off the exuviæ of the feathers from the nest. I attached light threads to their legs: these they invariably removed, either with their bills, or with the assistance of their parents. I renewed them, however, until I found the little fellows habituated to them; and at last, when they were about to leave the nest, I fixed a light silver thread to the leg of each, loose enough not to hurt the part, but so fastened that no exertions of theirs could remove it.

Sixteen days had passed, when the brood took to wing; and the old birds, dividing the time with caution, began to arrange the nest anew. A second set of eggs were laid, and in the beginning of August a new brood made its appearance.

The young birds took much to the woods, as if feeling

themselves more secure there than in the open fields; but before they departed, they all appeared strong, and minded not making long sorties into the open air, over the whole creek, and the fields around it. On the 8th of October, not a Pewee could I find on the plantation: my little companions had all set off on their travels. For weeks afterwards, however, I saw Pewees arriving from the north, and lingering a short time, as if to rest, when they also moved southward.

At the season when the Pewee returns to Pennsylvania, I had the satisfaction to observe those of the cave in and about it. There again, in the very same nest, two broods were raised. I found several Pewees' nests at some distance up the creek, particularly under a bridge, and several others in the adjoining meadows, attached to the inner part of sheds erected for the protection of hay and grain. Having caught several of these birds on the nest, I had the pleasure of finding that two of them had the little ring on the leg.

I was now obliged to go to France, where I remained two years. On my return, which happened early in August, I had the satisfaction of finding three young Pewees in the nest of the cave; but it was not the nest which I had left in it. The old one had been torn off from the roof, and the one which I found there was placed above where it stood. I observed at once that one of the parent birds was as shy as possible, while the other allowed me to approach within a few yards. This was the male bird, and I felt confident that the old female had paid the debt of nature. Having inquired of the miller's son, I found that he had killed the old Pewee and four young ones, to make bait for the purpose of catching fish. Then the male Pewee had brought another female to the cave! As long as the plantation of Mill Grove belonged to me, there continued to be a Pewee's nest in my favourite retreat; but after I had sold it, the cave was destroyed, as were nearly all the beautiful rocks along the shores of the creek, to build a new dam across the Perkiomen.

This species is so peculiarly fond of attaching its nest to rocky caves, that, were it called the Rock Flycatcher, it would be appropriately named. Indeed I seldom have passed near such a place, particularly during the breeding season, without seeing the Pewee, or hearing its notes. I recollect that while travelling in Virginia with a friend, he desired that I would go somewhat out of our intended route, to visit the renowned Rock Bridge of that State. My companion, who had passed over this natural bridge before, proposed a wager that he could lead me across it before I should be aware of its existence. It was early in April; and, from the descriptions of this place which I had read, I felt confident that the Pewee Flycatcher must be about it. I accepted the proposal of my friend and trotted on, intent on proving to myself that, by constantly attending to one subject, a person must sooner or later become acquainted with it. I listened to the notes of the different birds, which at intervals came to my ear, and at last had the satisfaction to distinguish those of the Pewee. I stopped my horse, to judge of the distance at which the bird might be, and a moment after told my friend that the bridge was short of a hundred yards from us, although it was impossible for us to see the spot itself. The surprise of my companion was great. "How do you know this?" he asked, "for," continued he, "you are correct."—"Simply," answered I, "because I hear the notes of the Pewee, and know that a cave, or a deep rocky creek, is at hand." We moved on; the Pewees rose from under the bridge in numbers; I pointed to the spot and won the wager.

This rule of observation I have almost always found to work, as arithmeticians say, both ways. Thus the nature of the woods or place in which the observer may be, whether high or low, moist or dry, sloping north or south, with whatever kind of vegetation, tall trees of particular species, or low shrubs, will generally disclose the nature of their inhabitants.

The flight of the Pewee Flycatcher is performed by a fluttering light motion, frequently interrupted by sailings. It is slow when the bird is proceeding to some distance, rather rapid when in pursuit of prey. It often mounts perpendicularly from its perch after an insect, and returns to some dry twig, from which it can see around to a considerable distance. It then swallows the insect whole, unless it happens to be large. It will at times pursue an insect to a considerable distance, and seldom without success. It alights with great firmness, immediately erects itself in the manner of Hawks, glances all around, shakes its wings with a tremulous motion, and vibrates its tail upwards as if by a spring. Its tufty crest is generally erected, and its whole appearance is neat, if not elegant. The Pewee has its particular stands, from which it seldom rambles far. The top of a fence stake near the road is often selected by it, from which it sweeps off in all directions, returning at intervals, and thus remaining the greater part of the morning and evening. The corner of the roof of the barn suits it equally well, and if the weather requires it, it may be seen perched on the highest dead twig of a tall tree. During the heat of the day it reposes in the shade of the woods. In the autumn it will choose the stalk of the mullein for its stand, and sometimes the projecting angle of a rock jutting over a stream. It now and then alights on the ground for an instant, but this happens principally during winter, or while engaged during spring in collecting the materials of which its nest is composed, in our Southern States, where many spend their time at this season.

I have found this species abundant in the Floridas in winter, in full song, and as lively as ever, also in Louisiana and the Carolinas, particularly in the cotton fields. None, however, to my knowledge, breed south of Charleston in South Carolina, and very few in the lower parts of that State. They leave Louisiana in February, and return to it in October. Occasionally during winter they feed on berries of different kinds, and are quite expert at discovering the insects impaled on thorns by the Loggerhead Shrike, and which they devour with avidity. I met with a few of these birds on the Magdeleine Islands, on the coast of Labrador, and in Newfoundland.

The nest of this species bears some resemblance to that of the Barn Swallow, the outside consisting of mud, with which are firmly impacted grasses or mosses of various kinds deposited in regular strata. It is lined with delicate fibrous roots, or shreds of vine bark, wool, horse-hair, and sometimes a few feathers. The greatest diameter across the open mouth is from five to six inches, and the depth from four to five. Both birds work alternately, bringing pellets of mud or damp earth, mixed with moss, the latter of which is mostly disposed on the outer parts, and in some instances the whole exterior looks as if entirely formed of it. The fabric is firmly attached to a rock, or a wall, the rafter of a house, &c. In the barrens of Kentucky I have found the nests fixed to the side of those curious places called sink-holes, and as much as twenty feet below the surface of the ground. I have observed that when the Pewees return in spring, they strengthen their tenement by adding to the external parts attached to the rock, as if to prevent it from falling, which after all it sometimes does when several years old. Instances of their taking possession of the nest of the Republican Swallow (*Hirundo fulva*) have been observed in the State of Maine. The eggs are from four to six, rather elongated, pure white, generally with a few reddish spots near the larger end.

In Virginia, and probably as far as New York, they not unfrequently raise two broods, sometimes three, in a season.

THE TRUMPETER SWAN

*J*N a note contained in the Journals of Lewis and Clark, written in the course of the expedition of these daring travellers across the Rocky Mountains, it is stated that "the Swans are of two kinds, the large and small. The large Swan is the same with the one common in the Atlantic States. The small differs from the large only in size and note; it is about one fourth less, and its note is entirely different. These birds were first found below the great narrows of the Columbia, near the Chilluckittequaw nation. They are very abundant in this neighbourhood, and remained with the party all winter, and in number they exceed those of the large species in the proportion of five to one." These observations are partly correct and partly erroneous. In fact, the smaller species of the two, which is the *C. Americanus* of Sharpless, is the only one abundant in the middle districts of our Atlantic coast, while the larger Swan, the subject of this article, is rarely if ever seen to the eastward of the mouths of the Mississippi.

The Trumpeter Swans make their appearance on the lower portions of the waters of the Ohio about the end of October. They throw themselves at once into the larger ponds or lakes at no great distance from the river, giving a marked preference to those which are closely surrounded by dense and tall cane-brakes, and there remain until the water is closed by ice, when they are forced to proceed southward. During mild winters I have seen Swans of this species in the ponds about Henderson until the beginning of March, but only a few individuals, which may have staid there to recover from their wounds. When the cold became intense, most of those which visited the Ohio would remove to the Mississippi, and proceed down that stream as the severity of the weather increased, or return if it diminished; for it has appeared to me, that neither very intense cold nor great heat suit them so well as a medium temperature. I have traced the winter migrations of this species as far southward as Texas, where it is abundant at times, and where I saw a pair of young ones in captivity, and quite domesticated, that had been procured in the winter of 1836. They were about two years old, and pure white, although of much smaller size than even the younger one represented in the plate before you, having perhaps been stinted in food, or having suffered from their wounds, as both had been shot. The sound of their well-known notes reminded me of the days of my youth, when I was half-yearly in the company of birds of this species.

At New Orleans, where I made the drawing of the young bird here given, the Trumpeters are frequently exposed for sale in the markets, being procured on the ponds of the interior, and on the great lakes leading to the waters of the Gulf of Mexico. This species is unknown to my friend, the Rev. JOHN BACHMAN, who, during a residence of twenty years in South Carolina, never saw or heard of one there; whereas in hard winters the *Cygnus Americanus* is not uncommon, although it does not often proceed farther southward than that State. The waters of the Arkansas and its tributaries are annually supplied with Trumpeter Swans, and the largest individual which I have examined was shot on a lake near the junction of that river with the Mississippi. It measured nearly ten feet in alar extent, and weighed above thirty-eight pounds. The quills, which I used in drawing the feet and claws of many small birds, were so hard, and yet so elastic, that the best steel-pen of the present day might have blushed, if it could, to be compared with them.

Whilst encamped in the Tawapatee Bottom, when on a fur-trading voyage, our keel-boat was hauled close under the eastern shore of the Mississippi, and our valuables, for I then had a partner in trade, were all disembarked. The party consisted of twelve or fourteen French Canadians, all of whom were pretty good hunters; and as game was in those days extremely abundant, the supply of deer, bear, racoons, and opossums, far exceeded our demands. Wild Turkeys, Grouse, and Pigeons, might have been seen hanging all around; and the ice-bound lakes afforded an ample supply of excellent fish, which was procured by striking a strong blow with an axe on the ice immediately above the confined animal, and afterwards extricating it by cutting a hole with the same instrument. The great stream was itself so firmly frozen that we were daily in the habit of crossing it from shore to shore. No sooner did the gloom of night become discernible through the grey twilight, than the loud-sounding notes of hundreds of Trumpeters would burst on the ear; and as I gazed over the ice-bound river, flocks after flocks would be seen coming from afar and in various directions, and alighting about the middle of the stream opposite to our encampment. After pluming themselves awhile they would quietly drop their bodies on the ice, and through the dim light I yet could observe the graceful curve of their necks, as they gently turned them backward, to allow their heads to repose upon the softest and warmest of pillows. Just a dot of black as it were could be observed on the snowy mass, and that dot was about half an inch of the base of the upper mandible, thus exposed, as I think, to enable the bird to breathe with ease. Not a single individual could I ever observe among them to act as a sentinel, and I have since doubted whether their acute sense of hearing was not sufficient to enable them to detect the approach of their enemies. The day quite closed by darkness, no more could be seen until the next dawn; but as often as the howlings of the numerous wolves that prowled through the surrounding woods were heard, the clanging

cries of the Swans would fill the air. If the morning proved
fair, the flocks would rise on their feet, trim their plumage,
and as they started with wings extended, as if racing in rivalry,
the pattering of their feet would come on the ear like the
noise of great muffled drums, accompanied by the loud and
clear sounds of their voice. On running fifty yards or so to
windward, they would all be on wing. If the weather was
thick, drizzly, and cold, or if there were indications of a fall
of snow, they would remain on the ice, walking, standing, or
lying down, until symptoms of better weather became apparent, when they would all start off. One morning of this latter
kind, our men formed a plot against the Swans, and having
separated into two parties, one above, the other below them
on the ice, they walked slowly, on a signal being given from
the camp, toward the unsuspecting birds. Until the boatmen
had arrived within a hundred and fifty yards of them, the
Swans remained as they were, having become, as it would
appear, acquainted with us, in consequence of our frequently
crossing the ice; but then they all rose on their feet, stretched
their necks, shook their heads, and manifested strong symptoms of apprehension. The gunners meanwhile advanced, and
one of the guns going off by accident, the Swans were thrown
into confusion, and scampering off in various directions took
to wing, some flying up, some down the stream, others making
directly toward the shores. The muskets now blazed, and
about a dozen were felled, some crippled, others quite dead.
That evening they alighted about a mile above the camp, and
we never went after them again. I have been at the killing
of several of these Swans, and I can assure you that unless
you have a good gun well loaded with large buck-shot, you
may shoot at them without much effect, for they are strong
and tough birds.

To form a perfect conception of the beauty and elegance
of these Swans, you must observe them when they are not

aware of your proximity, and as they glide over the waters of some secluded inland pond. On such occasions, the neck, which at other times is held stiffly upright, moves in graceful curves, now bent forward, now inclined backwards over the body. Now with an extended scooping movement the head becomes immersed for a moment, and with a sudden effort a flood of water is thrown over the back and wings, when it is seen rolling off in sparkling globules, like so many large pearls. The bird then shakes its wings, beats the water, and as if giddy with delight shoots away, gliding over and beneath the surface of the liquid element with surprising agility and grace. Imagine, reader, that a flock of fifty Swans are thus sporting before you, as they have more than once been in my sight, and you will feel, as I have felt, more happy and void of care than I can describe.

When swimming unmolested the Swan shews the body buoyed up; but when apprehensive of danger, it sinks considerably lower. If resting and basking in the sunshine, it draws one foot expanded curiously towards the back, and in that posture remains often for half an hour at a time. When making off swiftly, the tarsal joint, or knee as it is called, is seen about an inch above the water, which now in wavelets passes over the lower part of the neck and along the sides of the body, as it undulates on the planks of a vessel gliding with a gentle breeze. Unless during the courting season, or while passing by its mate, I never saw a Swan with the wings raised and expanded, as it is alleged they do, to profit by the breeze that may blow to assist their progress; and yet I have pursued some in canoes to a considerable distance, and that without overtaking them, or even obliging them to take to wing. You, reader, as well as all the world, have seen Swans labouring away on foot, and therefore I will not trouble you with a description of their mode of walking, especially as it is not much to be admired.

The flight of the Trumpeter Swan is firm, at times greatly elevated and sustained. It passes through the air by regular beats, in the same manner as Geese, the neck stretched to its full length, as are the feet, which project beyond the tail. When passing low, I have frequently thought that I heard a rustling sound from the motion of the feathers of their wings. If bound to a distant place, they form themselves in angular lines, and probably the leader of the flock is one of the oldest of the males; but of this I am not at all sure, as I have seen at the head of a line a grey bird, which must have been a young one of that year.

This Swan feeds principally by partially immersing the body and extending the neck under water, in the manner of freshwater Ducks and some species of Geese, when the feet are often seen working in the air, as if to aid in preserving balance. Often however it resorts to the land, and then picks at the herbage, not sidewise, as Geese do, but more in the manner of Ducks and poultry. Its food consists of roots of different vegetables, leaves, seeds, various aquatic insects, land snails, small reptiles and quadrupeds. The flesh of a cygnet is pretty good eating, but that of an old bird is dry and tough.

I kept a male alive upwards of two years, while I was residing at Henderson in Kentucky. It had been slightly wounded in the tip of the wing, and was caught after a long pursuit in a pond from which it could not escape. Its size, weight, and strength rendered the task of carrying it nearly two miles by no means easy; but as I knew that it would please my wife and my then very young children, I persevered. Cutting off the tip of the wounded wing, I turned it loose in the garden. Although at first extremely shy, it gradually became accustomed to the servants, who fed it abundantly, and at length proved so gentle as to come to my wife's call, to receive bread from her hand. "Trumpeter," as we named our bird, in accordance with the general practice of those

who were in the habit of shooting this species, now assumed
a character which until then had been unexpected, and laying
aside his timidity became so bold at times as to give chase to
my favourite Wild Turkey Cock, my dogs, children, and servants. Whenever the gates of our yard happened to be
opened, he would at once make for the Ohio, and it was not
without difficulty that he was driven home again. On one
occasion, he was absent a whole night, and I thought he
had fairly left us; but intimation came of his having travelled
to a pond not far distant. Accompanied by my miller and six
or seven of my servants, I betook myself to the pond, and
there saw our Swan swimming buoyantly about as if in de-
fiance of us all. It was not without a great deal of trouble
that we at length succeeded in driving it ashore. Pet birds,
good reader, no matter of what species they are, seldom pass
their lives in accordance with the wishes of their possessors;
in the course of a dark and rainy night, one of the servants
having left the gate open, Trumpeter made his escape, and
was never again heard of.

THE PASSENGER PIGEON

CHE Passenger Pigeon, or, as it is usually named in America, the Wild Pigeon, moves with extreme rapidity, propelling itself by quickly repeated flaps of the wings, which it brings more or less near to the body, according to the degree of velocity which is required. Like the Domestic Pigeon, it often flies, during the love season, in a circling manner, supporting itself with both wings angularly elevated, in which position it keeps them until it is about to alight. Now and then, during these circular flights, the tips of the primary quills of each wing are made to strike against each other, producing a smart rap, which may be heard at a distance of thirty or forty yards. Before alighting, the Wild Pigeon, like the Carolina Parrot and a few other species of birds, breaks the force of its flight by repeated flappings, as if apprehensive of receiving injury from coming too suddenly into contact with the branch or the spot of ground on which it intends to settle.

I have commenced my description of this species with the above account of its flight, because the most important facts connected with its habits relate to its migrations. These are entirely owing to the necessity of procuring food, and are not performed with the view of escaping the severity of a northern latitude, or of seeking a southern one for the purpose of breeding. They consequently do not take place at any fixed period or season of the year. Indeed, it sometimes happens that a continuance of a sufficient supply of food in one district will keep these birds absent from another for years. I know, at least, to a certainty, that in Kentucky they remained for several years constantly, and were nowhere else to be found. They all suddenly disappeared one season when the mast was exhausted, and did not return for a long period. Similar facts have been observed in other States.

Their great power of flight enables them to survey and pass over an astonishing extent of country in a very short time. This is proved by facts well known. Thus, Pigeons have been killed in the neighbourhood of New York, with their crops full of rice, which they must have collected in the fields of Georgia and Carolina, these districts being the nearest in which they could possibly have procured a supply of that kind of food. As their power of digestion is so great that they will decompose food entirely in twelve hours, they must in this case have travelled between three and four hundred miles in six hours, which shews their speed to be at an average of about one mile in a minute. A velocity such as this would enable one of these birds, were it so inclined, to visit the European continent in less than three days.

This great power of flight is seconded by as great a power of vision, which enables them, as they travel at that swift rate, to inspect the country below, discover their food with facility, and thus attain the object for which their journey has been undertaken. This I have also proved to be the case, by having observed them, when passing over a sterile part of the country, or one scantily furnished with food suited to them, keep high in the air, flying with an extended front, so as to enable them to survey hundreds of acres at once. On the contrary, when the land is richly covered with food, or the trees abundantly hung with mast, they fly low, in order to discover the part most plentifully supplied.

Their body is of an elongated oval form, steered by a long well-plumed tail, and propelled by well-set wings, the muscles of which are very large and powerful for the size of the bird. When an individual is seen gliding through the woods and close to the observer, it passes like a thought, and on trying to see it again, the eye searches in vain; the bird is gone.

The multitudes of Wild Pigeons in our woods are astonishing. Indeed, after having viewed them so often, and under so many circumstances, I even now feel inclined to pause, and assure myself that what I am going to relate is fact. Yet I have seen it all, and that too in the company of persons who, like myself, were struck with amazement.

In the autumn of 1813, I left my house at Henderson, on the banks of the Ohio, on my way to Louisville. In passing over the Barrens a few miles beyond Hardensburgh, I observed the Pigeons flying from north-east to south-west, in greater numbers than I thought I had ever seen them before, and feeling an inclination to count the flocks that might pass within the reach of my eye in one hour, I dismounted, seated myself on an eminence, and began to mark with my pencil, making a dot for every flock that passed. In a short time finding the task which I had undertaken impracticable, as the birds poured in in countless multitudes, I rose, and counting the dots then put down, found that 163 had been made in twenty-one minutes. I travelled on, and still met more the farther I proceeded. The air was literally filled with Pigeons; the light of noon-day was obscured as by an eclipse; the dung fell in spots, not unlike melting flakes of snow; and the continued buzz of wings had a tendency to lull my senses to repose.

Whilst waiting for dinner at Young's inn at the confluence of Salt river with the Ohio, I saw, at my leisure, immense legions still going by, with a front reaching far beyond the Ohio on the west, and the beech-wood forests directly on the east of me. Not a single bird alighted; for not a nut or acorn was that year to be seen in the neighbourhood. They consequently flew so high, that different trials to reach them with a capital rifle proved ineffectual; nor did the reports disturb them in the least. I cannot describe to you the extreme beauty of their aerial evolutions, when a Hawk chanced to press upon the rear of a flock. At once, like a torrent, and with a noise like thunder, they rushed into a compact mass, pressing upon each other towards the centre. In these almost solid masses, they darted forward in undulating and angular lines, descended and swept close over the earth with inconceivable velocity, mounted perpendicularly so as to resemble a vast column, and, when high, were seen wheeling and twisting within their continued lines, which then resembled the coils of a gigantic serpent.

Before sunset I reached Louisville, distant from Hardensburgh fifty-five miles. The Pigeons were still passing in undiminished numbers, and continued to do so for three days in succession. The people were all in arms. The banks of the Ohio were crowded with men and boys, incessantly shooting at the pilgrims, which there flew lower as they passed the river. Multitudes were thus destroyed. For a week or more, the population fed on no other flesh than that of Pigeons, and talked of nothing but Pigeons.

It is extremely interesting to see flock after flock performing exactly the same evolutions which had been traced as it were in the air by a preceding flock. Thus, should a Hawk have charged on a group at a certain spot, the angles, curves, and undulations that have been described by the birds, in their efforts to escape from the dreaded talons of the plunderer, are undeviatingly followed by the next group that comes up. Should the bystander happen to witness one of these affrays, and, struck with the rapidity and elegance of the motions exhibited, feel desirous of seeing them repeated, his wishes will be gratified if he only remain in the place until the next group comes up.

As soon as the Pigeons discover a sufficiency of food to entice them to alight, they fly around in circles, reviewing the country below. During their evolutions, on such occasions, the dense mass which they form exhibits a beautiful appear-

ance, as it changes its direction, now displaying a glistening
sheet of azure, when the backs of the birds come simultaneously into view, and anon, suddenly presenting a mass of
rich deep purple. They then pass lower, over the woods, and
for a moment are lost among the foliage, but again emerge,
and are seen gliding aloft. They now alight, but the next
moment, as if suddenly alarmed, they take to wing, producing
by the flappings of their wing a noise like the roar of distant
thunder, and sweep through the forests to see if danger is
near. Hunger, however, soon brings them to the ground.
When alighted, they are seen industriously throwing up the
withered leaves in quest of the fallen mast. The rear ranks
are continually rising, passing over the main-body, and
alighted in front, in such rapid succession, that the whole
flock seems still on wing. The quantity of ground thus swept
is astonishing, and so completely has it been cleared, that the
gleaner who might follow in their rear would find his labour
completely lost. Whilst feeding, their avidity is at times so
great that in attempting to swallow a large acorn or nut,
they are seen gasping for a long while, as if in the agonies of
suffocation.

On such occasions, when the woods are filled with these
Pigeons, they are killed in immense numbers, although no
apparent diminution ensues. About the middle of the day,
after their repast is finished, they settle on the trees, to enjoy
rest, and digest their food. On the ground they walk with
ease, as well as on the branches, frequently jerking their
beautiful tail, and moving the neck backwards and forwards
in the most graceful manner. As the sun begins to sink beneath the horizon, they depart en masse for the roosting-
place, which not unfrequently is hundreds of miles distant,
as has been ascertained by persons who have kept an account
of their arrivals and departures.

Let us now, kind reader, inspect their place of nightly

rendezvous. One of these curious roosting-places, on the banks of the Green river in Kentucky, I repeatedly visited. It was, as is always the case, in a portion of the forest where the trees were of great magnitude, and where there was little underwood. I rode through it upwards of forty miles, and, crossing it in different parts, found its average breadth to be rather more than three miles. My first view of it was about a fortnight subsequent to the period when they had made choice of it, and I arrived there nearly two hours before sunset. Few Pigeons were then to be seen, but a great number of persons, with horses and wagons, guns and ammunition, had already established encampments on the borders. Two farmers from the vicinity of Russelsville, distant more than a hundred miles, had driven upwards of three hundred hogs to be fattened on the pigeons which were to be slaughtered. Here and there, the people employed in plucking and salting what had already been procured, were seen sitting in the midst of large piles of these birds. The dung lay several inches deep, covering the whole extent of the roosting-place. Many trees two feet in diameter, I observed, were broken off at no great distance from the ground; and the branches of many of the largest and tallest had given way, as if the forest had been swept by a tornado. Every thing proved to me that the number of birds resorting to this part of the forest must be immense beyond conception. As the period of their arrival approached, their foes anxiously prepared to receive them. Some were furnished with iron-pots containing sulphur, others with torches of pine-knots, many with poles, and the rest with guns. The sun was lost to our view, yet not a Pigeon had arrived. Every thing was ready, and all eyes were gazing on the clear sky, which appeared in glimpses amidst the tall trees. Suddenly there burst forth a general cry of "Here they come!" The noise which they made, though yet distant, reminded me of a hard gale at sea, passing through the rigging of a close-reefed vessel. As the birds arrived and passed over me, I felt a current of air that surprised me. Thousands were soon knocked down by the pole-men. The birds continued to pour in. The fires were lighted, and a magnificent, as well as wonderful and almost terrifying, sight presented itself. The Pigeons, arriving by thousands, alighted everywhere, one above another, until solid masses were formed on the branches all round. Here and there the perches gave way under the weight with a crash, and, falling to the ground, destroyed hundreds of the birds beneath, forcing down the dense groups with which every stick was loaded. It was a scene of uproar and confusion. I found it quite useless to speak, or even to shout to those persons who were nearest to me. Even the reports of the guns were seldom heard, and I was made aware of the firing only by seeing the shooters reloading.

No one dared venture within the line of devastation. The hogs had been penned up in due time, the picking up of the dead and wounded being left for the next morning's employment. The Pigeons were constantly coming, and it was past midnight before I perceived a decrease in the number of those that arrived. The uproar continued the whole night; and as I was anxious to know to what distance the sound reached, I sent off a man, accustomed to perambulate the forest, who, returning two hours afterwards, informed me he had heard it distinctly when three miles distant from the spot. Towards the approach of day, the noise in some measure subsided: long before objects were distinguishable, the Pigeons began to move off in a direction quite different from that in which they had arrived the evening before, and at sunrise all that were able to fly had disappeared. The howlings of the wolves now reached our ears, and the foxes, lynxes, cougars, bears, racoons, opossums and pole-cats were seen sneaking off, whilst eagles and hawks of different species, accompanied by a crowd of vultures, came to supplant them, and enjoy their share of the spoil.

It was then that the authors of all this devastation began their entry amongst the dead, and dying, and the mangled. The Pigeons were picked up and piled in heaps, until each had as many as he could possibly dispose of, when the hogs were let loose to feed on the remainder.

Persons unacquainted with these birds might naturally conclude that such dreadful havoc would soon put an end to the species. But I have satisfied myself, by long observation, that nothing but the gradual diminution of our forests can accomplish their decrease, as they not unfrequently quadruple their numbers yearly, and always at least double it. In 1805 I saw schooners loaded in bulk with Pigeons caught up the Hudson river, coming in to the wharf at New York, when the birds sold for a cent a piece. I knew a man in Pennsylvania, who caught and killed upwards of 500 dozens in a clap-net in one day, sweeping sometimes twenty dozens or more at a single haul. In the month of March 1830, they were so abundant in the markets of New York, that piles of them met the eye in every direction. I have seen the Negroes at the United States' Salines or Saltworks of Shawanee Town, wearied with killing Pigeons, as they alighted to drink the water issuing from the leading pipes, for weeks at a time; and yet in 1826, in Louisiana, I saw congregated flocks of these birds as numerous as ever I had seen them before, during a residence of nearly thirty years in the United States.

The breeding of the Wild Pigeons, and the places chosen for that purpose, are points of great interest. The time is not much influenced by season, and the place selected is where food is most plentiful and most attainable, and always at a convenient distance from water. Forest-trees of great height are those in which the Pigeons form their nests. Thither the countless myriads resort, and prepare to fulfill one of the great laws of nature. At this period the note of the Pigeon is a soft coo-coo-coo-coo, much shorter than that of

the domestic species. The common notes resemble the mono-
syllables kee-kee-kee-kee, the first being the loudest, the others
gradually diminishing in power. The male assumes a pom-
pous demeanour, and follows the female, whether on the
ground or on the branches, with spread tail and drooping
wings, which it rubs against the part over which it is moving.
The body is elevated, the throat swells, the eyes sparkle. He
continues his notes, and now and then rises on the wing, and
flies a few yards to approach the fugitive and timorous female.
Like the domestic Pigeon and other species, they caress each
other by billing, in which action, the bill of the one is introduced transversely into that of the other, and both parties
alternately disgorge the contents of their crop by repeated
efforts. These preliminary affairs are soon settled, and the
Pigeons commence their nests in general peace and harmony.
They are composed of a few dry twigs, crossing each other,
and are supported by forks of the branches. On the same tree
from fifty to a hundred nests may frequently be seen:—I
might say a much greater number, were I not anxious, kind
reader, that however wonderful my account of the Wild
Pigeon is, you may not feel disposed to refer it to the marvellous. The eggs are two in number, of a broadly elliptical
form, and pure white. During incubation, the male supplies
the female with food. Indeed, the tenderness and affection
displayed by these birds towards their mates, are in the highest degree striking. It is a remarkable fact, that each brood
generally consists of a male and a female.

Here again, the tyrant of the creation, man, interferes,
disturbing the harmony of this peaceful scene. As the young
birds grow up, their enemies, armed with axes, reach the
spot, to seize and destroy all they can. The trees are felled,
and made to fall in such a way that the cutting of one causes
the overthrow of another, or shakes the neighbouring trees
so much, that the young Pigeons, or squabs, as they are named,
are violently hurried to the ground. In this manner also,

immense quantities are destroyed.

The young are fed by the parents in the manner described above; in other words, the old bird introduces its bill into the mouth of the young one in a transverse manner, or with the back of each mandible opposite the separations of the mandibles of the young bird, and disgorges the contents of its crop. As soon as the young birds are able to shift for themselves, they leave their parents, and continue separate until they attain maturity. By the end of six months they are capable of reproducing their species.

The flesh of the Wild Pigeon is of a dark colour, but affords tolerable eating. That of young birds from the nest is much esteemed. The skin is covered with small white filmy scales. The feathers fall off at the least touch, as has been remarked to be the case in the Carolina Turtle-dove. I have only to add, that this species, like others of the same genus, immerses its head up to the eyes while drinking.

In March 1830, I bought about 350 of these birds in the market of New York, at four cents a piece. Most of these I carried alive to England, and distributed them amongst several noblemen, presenting some at the same time to the Zoölogical Society.

INDEX

Donald Culross Peattie (1898–1964) was one of the most influential American nature writers of the twentieth century. Peattie was born in Chicago and grew up in the Smoky Mountains of North Carolina, a region that sparked his interest in the immense wonders of nature. He studied at the University of Chicago and Harvard University. After working for the U.S. Department of Agriculture, he decided to pursue a career as a writer. In 1925 he became a nature columnist for the *Washington Star* and went on to pen more than twenty fiction and nonfiction books over the next five decades. Widely acclaimed and popular in his day, Peattie's work has inspired a modern age of nature writing.